The Joy of QUILTING

Joan Hanson & Mary Hickey

That Patchwork Place®

Acknowledgments

Judy Pollard—who, over the years, has lent us unconditional support, encouragement, friendship, and countless quilts. This time she provided us with two truly wonderful samples: "Garland Star" and "It All Started with Ralph's Mother."

Tricia Lund—who not only allowed us to use her stunning quilts but also generously did many of the mathematical calculations and writing for each of her quilts. Tricia's quilts— "Shining Stars," "Good Neighbors," and "Nesting Birds"—contribute greatly to the variety of styles and color palettes in the book.

Connie Nordstrom—who sent her firstborn quilts, "Butterflies at the Crossroads" and "Green Gables," to distant unknown regions so that we could share her exceptional talent with you.

Frieda Martinis—who is one of the master quiltmakers in the Northwest and who generously lent her "Christmas Bear Paw" quilt.

Gayle Ducey—an exceptionally gracious and generous friend, gifted designer, and craftswoman, who shared her striking "Hearts and Gizzards" quilt with us.

Hazel Montague—who has a magic needle, gifted hands, and a kind and generous heart. Hazel never hesitated to hand quilt top after top and meet our tight deadlines.

Virginia Lauth—who is a gifted artist and who also pitched in and worked her quilting magic for us.

Amanda Miller—who broke all records for speed and goodness by graciously arranging to have twenty-two tops quilted to meet our dreadful deadlines.

Miriam Nathan-Roberts—who graciously granted us permission to use our simplified version of her well-known interwoven series of quilts.

Joan Colvin—who introduced us to the birds that enliven and animate the Nesting Birds design and inspired our Exampler quilts.

Marsha McCloskey—whose beautiful Meadow Lily pattern inspired our "Line Dancing Lilies" quilt.

Philip Hickey—who, rather than complaining about boring meals, planned and cooked the meals for us. Phil sat night after night checking and rechecking mathematical calculations, proofread and reread, and was, in general, kind, loving, supportive, and patient through the whole process, offering only encouragement and assistance.

Jim Hanson—who, rather than complaining about boring meals, ordered and ate so much pizza he now dreams in Italian and goes by the name Pepperoni Hanson. Jim sat night after night on homework duty, tolerated having a ghost wife for many months, and refrained from asking "Will this ever be over?"

Credits

Editor-in-Chief .... Barbara Weiland
Technical Editor ...... Ursula Reikes
Managing Editor .... Greg Sharp
Copy Editor .... Liz McGehee
Proofreaders .... Tina Cook
Leslie Phillips
Design Director .... Judy Petry
Text & Cover Designer ... Kay Green
Design Assistant .... Shean Bemis
Photographer .... Brent Kane
Illustrators .... André Samson
Laurel Strand
Illustration Assistant .. Lisa McKenney
Photo Stylist .... Susan I. Jones

Printed in Hong Kong
00 99 98   6 5 4 3
Library of Congress Cataloging-in-Publication Data
Hanson, Joan,
   Joy of quilting / Joan Hanson and Mary Hickey.
      p.   cm.
   ISBN 1–56477–070–2 :
   1. Quilting—Patterns. 2. Patchwork—Patterns. I. Hickey, Mary.
II. Title.
TT835.H3364 1995
746.46—dc20
                              94–22711
                                  CIP

MISSION STATEMENT

WE ARE DEDICATED TO PROVIDING QUALITY PRODUCTS THAT ENCOURAGE CREATIVITY AND PROMOTE SELF-ESTEEM IN OUR CUSTOMERS AND OUR EMPLOYEES.

WE STRIVE TO MAKE A DIFFERENCE IN THE LIVES WE TOUCH.

That Patchwork Place is an employee-owned, financially secure company.

The Joy of Quilting
©1995 by Joan Hanson
and Mary Hickey

That Patchwork Place, Inc.,
PO Box 118,
Bothell, WA 98041-0118
USA

Table of Contents

Dedication

For Mark and Derek Hanson and
Molly, Josh, and Maureen Hickey—
the most treasured joys in our lives.

Preface

We intended to write a serious textbook on quilting. We started out in a very dignified manner, making sedate traditional quilts and writing carefully constructed, proper English sentences in an instructional format. But then a bird landed on our sampler. We were a little surprised, but we adjusted. However, when an entire flock of birds arrived on one quilt, we knew it was going to be tough staying solemn. When we realized one of our quilts had ladybugs lunching, we persevered in our attempts to be restrained and proper. By some mysterious means, three more quilts took over some of the pages, one jiggling and jumping, another with chickens in the chimney, and a third adorned with—gizzards! It's hard to be grim when the lilies are line dancing and an incredibly cool rocket is blasting off for cosmic regions. Finally, our dignity crumbled and quilts were fun again.

This, then, is our message to you: quilting is fun. Quilters greatly enjoy making quilts, delight in looking at quilts, and relish talking about quilts. Of course, fabric shopping is a wonderful form of entertainment, and going to quilt conferences is almost more fun than should be allowed. If you know the basics and follow a few simple rules, quiltmaking will mean far more to you than the stitching of a bedcover. It will become one of the central joys of your life, a medium for you to create your own art form, a chance for you to preserve our culture and create heirlooms, and, best of all, a vehicle to form deep friendships with thousands of quilters in the world. So, pull out your fabrics, pick a project, plan a quilt, and play with your patches!

Introduction

We hope that you will think of *The Joy of Quilting* as a friend who wants to share the fun of quilting with you. We have tried to create a nonthreatening, step-by-step guide that will inspire you with confidence and furnish you with all the basic information for many types of gorgeous quilts. Be aware, though, that the pastime of cutting out little patches of wonderful fabrics and sewing them back together again is highly addictive.

We have organized the book around the shapes of the patches most commonly used in quilting rather than the number of patches in a block. Traditionally, quiltmakers drew around templates, cut out the shapes with a scissors, sewed them together, and finally pressed the seams. Since the advent of the rotary cutter, quilters find it far simpler and more accurate to sew and press strips of contrasting fabrics and cut shapes or units from the sewn strips. By sewing and pressing before cutting, there is far less opportunity to distort the cut units. Notice that we refer to the patches as "units" after they have been sewn and cut. Thus, if a square is composed of four triangles, we refer to it as a "quarter-square unit." As the units become more complex, the difficulty of the quilt increases slightly. Each chapter builds on the knowledge that you have mastered in previous chapters. If this is your introduction to quilting, take some time to read and follow the instructions in the beginning of each chapter before attempting some of the quilts with more difficult shapes and piecing techniques.

Notice that each quilt project has charts giving information for a variety of sizes, the amount of each fabric to purchase for each size, and the number and size of strips and units to cut. Take a few minutes to familiarize yourself with the charts. A chart is a capsule of valuable information. Place a small ruler or strip of paper next to the quilt size you intend to make. This will enable you to see quickly the measurements and numbers that concern you. A Template Cutting Chart is provided for each quilt for those quilters who prefer to cut their fabric using templates. **Do not use these charts if you are using rotary-cutting methods unless otherwise instructed.**

If you are new to quilting and anxious to jump in, head straight for the Exampler quilt on page 246. The Exampler provides you with the opportunity to learn to sew many different shapes, using a variety of techniques. Squares, rectangles, large and small triangles, odd-shaped pieces, and appliqué are all included in one quilt. As you make each unit for the quilt, refer to the chapter with the same name as the unit. For example, see "Mastering Quarter-Square Units" for detailed directions on making quarter-square units.

We want you to enjoy the creative process as much as we do. Be kind to yourself, allow yourself to make a few mistakes, and laugh at your goofs. Be aware that we have probably made the same blunders. Do send us pictures of the projects that you create! We will reply to all with a postcard.

Meet the Authors

Picture two women sitting in a sunny sewing room, designing, cutting, sewing, and pressing quilts. They chat companionably and laugh hilariously at stories about their families and friends and their many sewing goofs. They are confident, capable, and creative. Imagine these same two women sitting at a computer, playing it like a piano, one running the keyboard, the other operating the mouse and the function keys. They call up a variety of menus, select options in dialog boxes, create merges, and command the computer to do intricate graphics and complex math. They are computer literate, even computer affectionate, because computers are friendly to quilts.

Joan, who wrote *Calendar Quilts* and *Sensational Settings*, and Mary, the author of *Little by Little*, *Basket Garden*, *Angle Antics*, *Pioneer Storybook Quilts*, and one of the authors of *Quick & Easy Quiltmaking*, both travel and teach extensively. Both are experienced teachers who love to share their passion for quilting and creating with other quilters. However, both found writing books to be a solitary and isolating activity. The idea of writing *The Joy of Quilting* together appealed to these amiable companions. Joan and Mary set a firm goal when they started this project—they would not let undertaking the book harm their friendship, and they are pleased to say they are still the fondest of friends. They found that it was much more fun working on a book with a partner they could call and moan with than writing it alone.

Mary and Joan both enjoy their families, love the Washington coast, have a dreadful weakness for china, are passionate fabric shoppers, and like the same kinds of quilts. Neither Joan nor Mary ever dreamt what a staggering scope this project had until it was far too late to back out.

These two dear friends who have so much in common share one more characteristic: both of them are turrible speelers and mizerable tipests. Don't worry, though; they can hit the "Spell Checker" button with never a missed stroke. Joan and Mary both sincerely hope that you enjoy reading this book as much as they enjoyed writing it.

Gathering Tools, Supplies, and Fabrics

As with any job, having the right tools and work space is half the battle. On the following pages, you will find a list of tools and a set of tips on choosing fabrics and colors.

Tools and Supplies

Every quilter has tools she just wouldn't be without. Here are our essentials. These are for your guidance. Even if it takes you some time to accumulate all these items, you will find each one well worth the investment.

Fabric Scissors—A fine pair of scissors will become one of your treasured possessions. Good fabric scissors should not be used by other family members. Mark them for fabric and for your use only.

Small Scissors—Treat yourself to a good pair of small scissors. Use these for cutting threads, trimming seams, and cutting small appliqué shapes, as well as countless other tasks.

Seam Ripper—The seam ripper, also known as the reverse sewing tool, is indispensable. Since one is never enough, consider buying several and scattering them in spots that will be handy in your hour of need.

Paper Scissors—Use an inexpensive pair of large, sharp scissors to cut everything—paper, template plastic, cardboard—**except** fabric.

Pins—Steel pins with glass or plastic heads and a magnetic pin holder are handy for most pinning jobs. Very thin pins with regular heads are helpful when pinning points of matching. If the pins are extremely thin and you sew slowly, you can leave them in place while machine sewing. Many quilters like to have large, glass-headed pins for basting quilts. Safety pins are essential when basting quilts for machine quilting.

Transparent Plastic Drafting Ruler—2" x 18" marked with $\frac{1}{8}$" grid lines—Use this ruler for drafting templates and other pencil work, not for rotary cutting.

Sewing Machine—Sew with a machine that you are comfortable with, one that is your friend and doesn't fight you every step of the way. A good straight stitch is really all you need. Clean and oil your machine regularly; cotton lint accumulates quickly. If you have only a few bobbins for your machine, treat yourself to six or eight more. Wind two or three with a neutral color of thread so you don't have to stop in the middle of a project to wind bobbins.

Rotary Equipment

Rotary cutters have done for quilting what microwaves have done for cooking. A good set of rotary-cutting equipment allows you to cut far more rapidly and with greater accuracy than scissors.

Rotary Cutter—A rotary cutter consists of a sharp circular blade attached to a handle. It looks much like a pizza wheel and has a razor-sharp blade with a safety guard. Purchase a cutter with a 2" blade for quilting projects. Retract the safety guard only while cutting. Keep the guard in position at all other times. Look at the instructions on the back of the package to see the proper way to hold the brand you purchased.

Cutting Mat—A good cutting mat not only saves your tabletop but is essential for the life of the blade. One cut on a wood, plastic, or cardboard surface and the blade is history. Look for a cutting mat with a matte surface, not a slick or pebbly one. For general use, purchase one that is at least 18" x 24" and is marked with 1" grid lines. The 18" x 24" size enables you to cut folded cotton fabric, and the grid lines help you make straight cuts that are perpendicular to the fold. Always store your mat flat so that it doesn't warp. Mats are sensitive to heat and shouldn't be left in the sun, in a hot car, or under a hot cup of coffee.

Acrylic Cutting Rulers—Acrylic cutting rulers should be $\frac{1}{8}$" thick. The thickness of the ruler guides the rotary cutter and protects your fingers from the razor-sharp blade. They come in a variety of shapes and sizes and can be divided into two types: general cutting rulers and special technique cutting rulers. To start, you will need a 6" x 24" ruler marked in both directions every $\frac{1}{8}$". Use this ruler to cut strips of 42"-wide fabric folded in half. Strips are the backbone for most quilt pieces. You will also need a 15" x 15" square, for cutting large shapes and squaring up blocks; a 6" x 6" Bias Square® for smaller shapes; and a BiRangle™ for cutting rectangles and skinny triangles. Many other helpful rulers can be added to your collection as you gain quilting experience. You will become familiar with some of the specialty rulers as you learn various techniques presented in this book.

Pressing Equipment

Iron—Many quilters prefer a steam iron.

Ironing board or pressing pad—Place your ironing board several feet away from your sewing machine, so that you can avoid sitting and sewing in one position for so long that your back and shoulders stiffen.

Pressing Cloth—Pressing wool quilts requires a pressing cloth. Cut ½ yard of muslin for an ample-size cloth. Simply dampen the pressing cloth and lay it over the wool as you press the seams.

Work Space

If you don't already have a work space to call your own, rethink the spaces in your home and find a space where you can work and not have to clean up and put away every time you have a few minutes to sew. Use the space you have as efficiently as possible. Ideally, you will need an area for rotary cutting, a comfortable table for sewing, a board for pressing, a wall for designing, and several shelves and drawers for storing fabric, tools, and supplies. Spend some time and effort getting your space well organized, and you will be rewarded with many happy hours of creativity! Here are a few suggestions to help you set up a work space.

Lighting—Overhead, color-corrected fluorescent lighting is wonderful for choosing colors that go well together, as well as reducing shadows while you work. Good "task lighting" is also important; gooseneck clamp-

ons or free-standing lights are affordable and shine light right where you need it.

Work Table—Make your work table a comfortable height for standing while you cut and work. Most people like the cutting table about 36" high. Consider using a hollow-core door mounted on top of wire storage drawers for a good work table. You can make a padded pressing area at one end and place a large rotary-cutting mat on the rest of the door.

Use the wire drawers for fabric and tool storage.

Flannel Board—A large, wall-mounted flannel board allows you to stand back and "audition" the progress of your projects. One or two 4' x 8' sheets of insulation board (a soft pressed board that is easy to pin into), covered with pale gray or white flannel, is ideal. However, a flannel sheet or a piece of thin batting pinned to a wall will do nicely.

Selecting Colors and Fabrics

Choosing colors and fabrics for a quilt is one of the most exciting and challenging tasks facing quiltmakers. These color choices are probably the most important factors in determining the success of your quilt. The variety of colors and prints available is immense. What a joy when the colors dance and sparkle—or soothe and comfort! And what a disappointment when the colors are boring or dull!

Picture yourself, a normal quilter, piecing a few blocks in your only spare time—10:30 at night. You're all set to start sewing, except for that square in the right-hand corner of the block. The rose you chose in the store now looks like copper, and you can't start sewing until you have the proper shade of rose. The quilt shop is only about a mile and a half away, but it is closed. If you have a fabric stash (better known as a fabric library), you can open your bag or box of pinks and find a nice briar rose and be blissfully sewing in no time.

Consider developing a fabric library. It is rarely possible to make a whole quilt just from your fabric collection, but it is also difficult to make a quilt just from the fabrics available at any one time in the quilt shop. Value yourself as an artist creating heirlooms for your family, friends, and society. Give yourself enough respect to purchase fine cottons and plenty of them to make your quilts.

If you don't feel wealthy enough to purchase a piece of every fabric ever printed, choose a selection in colors you are always drawn to and cultivate friends and neighbors who also collect fabrics. Then follow the suggestions on the next few pages to help you get started on the process of choosing the fabrics for your quilts. No one idea will solve all your problems, but taken together, these tips may help you feel more confident in your choices.

As you read through these strategies, keep in mind the need for background fabrics. If every fabric in a quilt is spectacular, the viewer's eyes will become exhausted and confused. Remember to select a shy, demure fabric or a neutral fabric to act as a background so the colorful shapes can shine.

As you choose your fabrics, faithfully remember to give them two tests. First, be sure to place them next to each other. Be aware that colors have a sneaky way of adding and subtracting color to and from each other when they are side by side in a quilt. Second, stand back at least six feet and look at the fabric to see how the colors in a printed fabric mix together and "read" from a distance.

Color Schemes Based on a Theme Fabric

Try selecting one fabric that will inspire the color scheme for the rest of the quilt. Often, this one fabric will provide the key to the rest of the colors in the quilt. Look for a fabric that you cannot live without, one that has several colors. Study the "Cheerful Child" quilt on page 104 for an example of a quilt based on a theme fabric.

Once you have chosen this fabric, make yourself stand six feet away from it to see what colors it "reads." Resist the temptation to use a fabric because it has a few tiny dots of the perfect shade—or to reject it because it has a speck of the wrong color.

The mood or style of the theme fabric can give you clues about the types of fabrics that will work well with it. Ask yourself if it is romantic or flashy, Victorian or rustic, dainty or bold. Does it have an ethnic flair? Is it modern or old-fashioned?

The answers to these questions will help you choose a group of fabrics in colors and patterns that are in the design of your theme fabric. Vary the size and texture of the prints you select. Mix some larger prints with smaller ones and some linear or geometric ones with flowery ones.

Color Schemes Based on the Color Wheel

Monochromatic Color Schemes

Monochromatic quilts are made with tints and shades of one color. They are usually pretty, but can be a bit dull. To avoid making a boring quilt, try to have many tints and shades of your color and use a variety of prints to add depth to your design. Include a splash of a brilliant hue of your color to give your quilt life and interest. See the "Butterflies at the Crossroads" quilt on page 105 for an excellent example of a quilt incorporating a wide variety of tints and shades of rose.

Complementary Color Schemes

Colors that are opposites on the color wheel are complements of each other. Complementary colors intensify each other and yet harmonize in a pleasing way. Keep the following ideas in mind as you work with them.

Hot colors, like yellow and orange, quickly dominate a design and advance toward the eye. So, unless you want the warms to dominate, it is wise to reduce the amount of warm colors in relation to cool colors, or to use tints and shades of the warm colors to reduce their impact. Look at "The Incredibly Cool Cosmic Rocket Ship" quilt on page 167 for an example of a color scheme of yellows and blues in pleasing proportions. Don't be afraid to use warm colors; just be aware of their power and use it to your advantage.

Using a deep, dark shade of at least one color adds depth and dimension to your quilt. Consider including some neutral colors in a complementary color scheme. Neutrals give the viewer's eye a place to rest and allow the stronger colors to show their beauty.

Try to include a brilliant hue of one of your colors—just a bit—to add spark and interest. Notice the effect of the bright yellow plaid in the "Green Gables" quilt on page 107.

A color with warm tones in it, such as barn red, usually looks best with a complement that has warm tones, such as moss green, as demonstrated by the "Glowing Star" quilt on page 195. If you look at the "Line Dancing Lilies" quilt on page 134, you will notice that the same holds true for cool tones.

If you have chosen a color and cannot seem to find a complement for it, try to see its afterimage. Stare directly at the fabric for about 60 seconds. Then close your eyes and see what color appears in your "mind's eye." Usually, you see a tint of the perfect complementary color. Don't worry. Quilt shop owners have seen customers do many strange things when trying to choose colors.

Analogous Color Schemes

Colors that are next to each other on the color wheel are called analogous. They usually make lovely color schemes. The colors in the "Chickens in the Chimney" quilt on page 42 are all neighbors on the color wheel. If you are looking for a new way to work with your favorite colors, working in analogous colors may be a wonderful way to stretch your creative limbs. Remember to use some darks, a variety of tints and shades of your colors, and a bit of a brilliant hue.

Borrowed Color Schemes

Scrap or Multicolored Schemes

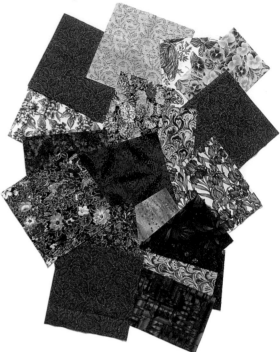

Natural objects are valuable sources for color inspiration. Study the colors in flowers, birds, animals, fish, seeds, leaves, trees, sea-shells, sunsets, and landscapes. Notice the proportions of the colors. If you have to, measure to see how much of each color there is in the object. Also, notice the color grada-tions in the natural objects.

Signs, logos, clothing, scarves, greeting cards, paintings, and, of course, other quilts are often good sources of color inspiration. Again, notice not only the colors but also how much of each color is used in the object. The logo on a city bus inspired the color combination in the "Chickens in the Chim-ney" quilt on page 42.

A single strong color used more than the rest of the colors will often give order and composition to a scrappy color scheme. Simi-larly, keeping one element constant, like the sky and chimney sections of the "Good Neigh-bors" quilt on page 214, will create some unity in the quilt. Another way to hold a multicolored quilt together is to use all clear, bright colors—or all grayed or beige colors.

Value, the lightness or darkness of a color, is important in a scrap quilt. At first, try making your blocks with the strongest value always in the same position in the block. Do the same with the mediums and lights. This will help the viewer make sense of the pattern even when the colors change from one block to another. For example, see the "Cheerful Child" quilt on page 104. The strongest color in most of the blocks appears in the four triangles in the middle of the blocks. If you have trouble seeing whether a print is light, medium, or dark, try squinting at the fabric or looking at it through a Ruby Beholder™ or a clear red plastic report cover. The red will subtract the color from the fabric, enabling you to see only the value.

Gradated Color Schemes

Color Recipe

A progression of one color from light to dark or from color to color can add tremendous luminosity to your quilts. The area where the two lightest colors meet each other appears to glow. Look at the "Glowing Star" quilt on page 195 for an example of the lovely effect of the gradation from color to color.

Notice the illusion of woven rows of color in the "Over, Under, Around, and Through" quilt on page 43. The over-and-under effect is achieved by having the darkest shade of one color intersect with the lightest tint of the other color. Look also at the pieced border of the "Nesting Birds" quilt on page 215. The progression of color from dark to light and from color to color draws your eye to the quilt and creates a lovely illusion of light and motion. If you are looking for a new way to work, or for a more artistic look to your quilts, working in color gradations may be quite satisfying for you.

After you have chosen a group of fabrics, assign a position for each color family in the block. Place a fabric from that color family in the same position in each block, but feel free to use different fabrics and prints in that position. By keeping the colors in the same positions but varying the prints and fabrics, you will add interest to the quilt without confusing the viewer. Be brave and vary the scale of your prints, use a variety of shades of each color, and do not hesitate to do the unexpected.

Prewashing Fabrics

All fabrics coming into your sewing studio must make a detour through the washing machine and dryer. Since you are working with 100% cotton fabrics, the fabrics should be preshrunk and the excess dye must be washed out. Prewashing will help you avoid any unwelcome surprises when you wash your gorgeous quilt. Wash darks and lights separately in warm water in your washing machine. Tumble dry in a warm dryer and iron before putting away.

Yardage requirements for the quilts in this book are based on 42" of usable fabric after preshrinking and cutting off selvages. If your fabric measures less than 42", you may need a bit more fabric. It's always wise to buy a little extra fabric anyway in case you make a wrong cut. You can always add any leftovers to your fabric library for future projects.

Colorfastness Test Tip
To test for colorfastness of dark fabrics (especially reds), cut small swatches of the dark fabrics and stitch them onto a larger swatch of your background fabric.

Wash the test swatches in warm water and tumble dry. This simple test will show you if the fabrics you are using will run in your finished quilt and give you the confidence to wash your quilt when needed.

Planning Blocks, Settings, and Borders

Although we have spared you the necessity of drawing the blocks in this book, knowing how to draft a block allows you to create your own original designs or change the size of existing blocks to suit your needs. This may prove to be very helpful if you ever want to design your own quilts.

The arrangement of the blocks in a quilt is called the setting. As you look through the quilts in this book, you will find examples of a variety of quilt settings. Planning a quilt setting is an exciting and challenging part of the quiltmaking process. Coming up with a setting design is like playing with Lego® blocks. You can juggle the pieces around and add a few extra pieces here and there until everything fits.

After you've assembled all your blocks in the perfect setting, the next step is to decide whether or not your quilt needs a border. You will notice that many of the quilts in this book are framed by a simple border, while a few have no borders at all. Whether made of plain strips of fabric or rows of piecing, thoughtfully planned borders can greatly enhance a quilt. The best way to decide whether or not your quilt will benefit by adding a border is to experiment with a few variations.

Browse through the ideas and techniques in this section of the book and look for inspirations that you can use in your own original way.

Understanding how blocks are created will help you determine the piecing sequence of blocks and give you the confidence to draft your own templates from a photo or a sketch. With a little patient practice, using simple and inexpensive tools, you can become a quilt designer. Who knows? You may become the Picasso of quilting.

Blocks are divided into sections called grids. Then, the grid sections are divided into squares, rectangles, triangles, or curves. As you look at a block, try to break it down into its grid pattern. The number of grid divisions in a block helps you to decide what sort of a block it is. Some of the most commonly used grids are: 9-patch, 16-patch, 25-patch, 36-patch, and 49-patch.

Drafting your own blocks is great fun. If you are fortunate enough to have a computer and a quilt-design program, patiently following a few of the lessons in the manual will enable you to draft and color both blocks and quilts and to create accurate templates with $1/4$" seam allowances! If you are not fond of electronic gadgets, simply get out some $1/4$" graph paper, a transparent ruler with $1/8$" grid lines, and a sharp pencil. Keep an eraser handy so you can play around with the lines until you find a pleasing design.

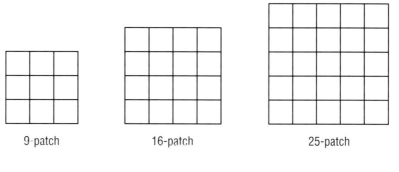

9-patch   16-patch   25-patch

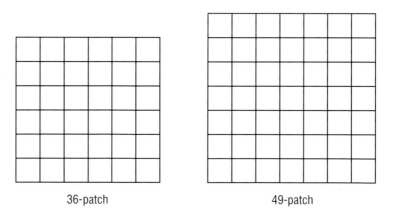

36-patch   49-patch

1. Start with a rough sketch divided into a grid. Add or take away lines until you are satisfied with your design.

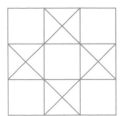

2. Give the grid unit (patch) a size, such as 1½", 2", 3", 4", etc. Multipy the number of patches times the grid size to determine the finished size of the block. In the example below, the finished size of the Variable Star block is 6" (3 patches x 2" = 6")

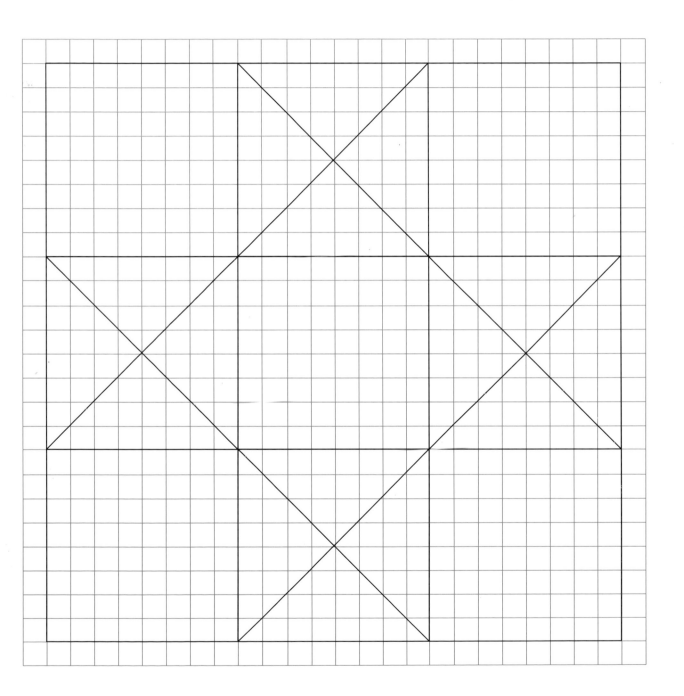

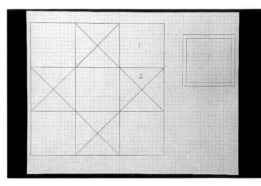

3. Use a sharp pencil and a drafting ruler to draw your block, full size, on ¼" graph paper. We drafted the Variable Star block on a 3" grid to make a 9" finished block. Redraw simple shapes next to your full-size block, then add the ¼"-wide seam allowances to make the templates for your block.

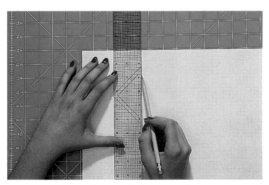

4. For triangles and diamonds, trace each shape from the block you drafted onto another piece of graph paper and use the ¼" line on your transparent drafting ruler to add the ¼" seam allowances. Align the ¼" line of the ruler on each line of the shape. Draw another line along the edge of the ruler to add the seam allowances. These lines will be your cutting lines.

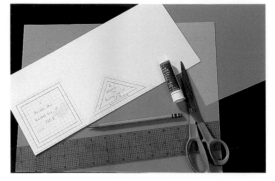

5. If you are going to use the templates for cutting the fabric shapes, use a glue stick to mount them on cardboard, template plastic, or X-ray film. You can also use the templates as a guide to determine strip sizes for your pieces and to check the accuracy of your pieces when rotary cutting.

6. Label each template with its number, the name of the block, the finished block size, an arrow to show the direction of the grain lines, and the number of pieces needed from each color fabric. When cutting odd-shaped triangles and parallelograms for symmetrical blocks, half of the pieces must be cut with the template right side up and half with the template right side down. Designate this by writing 1 + 1r on the template.

Setting Blocks

A number of design problems can be solved by the quilt setting you choose. For example, you can make a limited number of blocks cover a large area if you turn the blocks on point and add an alternate block. Study the "Chickens in the Chimney" quilt on page 42 to see how the addition of a simple alternate block adds both size and the illusion of space to the quilt. By adding a sashing frame to each block, you can create a unified quilt from a variety of different-size blocks as seen in "The Incredibly Cool Cosmic Rocket Ship" quilt on page 167. Look at the "Winter in the Woods" quilt on page 212 to see a clever setting for blocks that refused to multiply evenly into rows.

Common quilt settings can be divided into eight categories. Some block designs lend themselves to a particular setting, while others work well in more than one category. As you look at quilts that appeal to you, pay attention to each setting and keep the settings in mind for future projects.

Side by Side

One of the simplest settings is the side-by-side setting. Just line up your blocks and sew them together. Try this setting for blocks that create a secondary design when joined together.

Alternating Plain Blocks

This setting can stretch a few blocks into a larger quilt, calm down and show off an elaborate block, or connect blocks visually at the corners to give diagonal movement. Try the alternating block setting for designs that connect at the corners or complex pieced or appliqué blocks.

Alternating Pieced Blocks

Many interesting combinations result when two different pieced or appliqué blocks are combined. Usually one of the blocks is more complex than the other. Try to find blocks that have the same divisions (9-patch, 16-patch, 25-patch, etc.), so that some of the intersections line up and carry the eye across the quilt.

Simple Sashing

Simple sashing adds a unifying element to blocks that don't hold together on their own. It also produces a calming element to blocks that need a little space between them. Experiment with the width of the sashing. Narrow sashing lets the design jump easily from block to block, while wider sashing sets the blocks apart. Carefully consider the color of the sashing. Sashing that matches the background fabric in the blocks will cause the blocks to "float" on the surface of the quilt, while a contrasting sashing helps to define each block. Be aware that a contrasting sashing may also take over the quilt and dominate it.

Sashing and Cornerstones

Adding sashing and cornerstones can help connect the design diagonally and carry the eye across the quilt surface, or it can simply add more interest to a design. Use a design element that relates to the block in the sashing and cornerstones.

Framed Blocks

Adding frames to each of your blocks will standardize different-size blocks that would otherwise be difficult to join. Frames also give space to blocks that don't relate well to each other.

Stripped Sets

A setting in which blocks touch each other in one direction and have sashing in the other direction is called a "strippy set" or a "garland set." For horizontally set quilts, the sashing can run crosswise or lengthwise. When this idea is carried over to a diagonal setting, it produces a zigzag effect.

Medallion Sets

Medallions use one or more blocks to create a central focus. When you add borders, blocks, or a combination of pieced or appliquéd elements, the quilt becomes a unified whole. Often, the various elements switch from a diagonal setting to a horizontal setting, creating the illusion that one part is placed on top of another.

Whatever set you choose for your quilt, the general construction rules for sewing blocks still apply.
1. Sew exact $1/4"$ seams from edge to edge.
2. Look for the longest straight seams.
3. If possible, keep the straight of grain on the outside edges of the quilt sections.
4. Press for opposing seams. See page 35.
5. Generously pin the points of matching. See page 34.

Adding Borders

Well-designed borders echo the color, size, and shapes of the block pieces. The color of the outside border will bring out that same color in the quilt. For example, look at the border of the "Jiggle and Jump" quilt on page 168. Aqua, teal, magenta, and purple are used in almost equal amounts. Adding a magenta border intensifies the magenta in the blocks.

The size of the border strips or pieces is usually similar to the size of the pieces in the blocks and, if the borders are pieced, the shapes of the pieces should have some relationship to the shapes in the blocks.

Borders can also be used to enlarge a quilt to the desired size without making more blocks. Be careful, though, not to make the borders so wide that they outweigh the quilt design in visual importance.

Borders should be cut to fit the actual size of the center of the quilt top, not the outer edges, which are often different on opposite sides. It is important that the quilt end up "square" with 90° corners and with opposite sides equal to each other. First, cut border strips longer than you think you'll need. Later, trim them to fit the measurements of the quilt-top center.

Cutting Border Strips

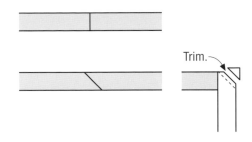

Yardage requirements for most borders are based on border strips cut across the width of the fabric. For quilts larger than 42", sew strips together with a straight or diagonal seam to obtain the correct length.

If you prefer unpieced borders, you will need to buy more fabric and cut the border strips from the lengthwise grain of the fabric. Because the lengthwise grain is more stable than the crosswise grain, the borders cut on the lengthwise grain will stretch less. In most instances you will have fabric left over to use in other projects.

Straight-Cut Borders

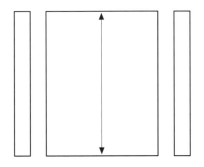

Measure center of
quilt, top to bottom.

1. Measure the length of the quilt at the center. Trim two of the border strips to that measurement. Sew these strips to the sides of the quilt, easing as necessary. Encouraging the quilt to fit the measured strips will help your finished quilt remain square with flat borders. This step is important, so resist the temptation to skip it. You may have to ease one side of a quilt and stretch the opposite side slightly to fit the same dimension.

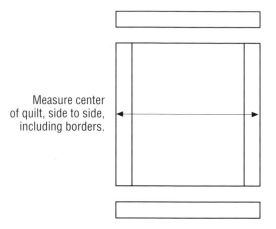

Measure center of quilt, side to side, including borders.

2. For the top and bottom borders, measure the width of the quilt at the center, including the side borders and seam allowances as shown. Cut the borders to that measurement and sew them to the top and bottom edges of the quilt, easing or stretching as necessary. If you plan to add more than one plain border with straight-cut corners, follow the same procedure for each border as outlined above, sewing the sides first and then the top and bottom.

Pieced Borders

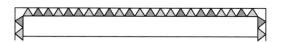

Attach pieced borders the same way as plain borders. Always measure the center of the quilt and sew the borders to the sides first, then to the top and bottom edges of the quilt. The length of the pieced strips will be governed by the size of the pieces; the length and width of the plain strips will have to be adjusted to enable the pieced strips to fit the quilt. (See the "Christmas Bear Paw" quilt on page 106.)

Mitered Borders

Quilts with three or four borders often look better with mitered corners. The "Women in the Men's Club" quilt on page 168 illustrates what stunning results can be achieved when mitering corners with an unusual fabric. The procedure for mitering corners is the same, whether you are adding a single border or multiple borders treated as a single unit.

1. Center your border strips on each other and sew them together, creating a striped fabric that will be treated as a single unit. Sewing the strips together makes it easier to match the fabrics on the corners and simplifies sewing the strips to the quilt top.

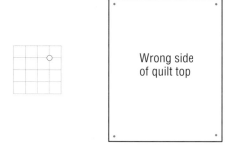

Wrong side of quilt top

2. Using graph paper mounted on X-ray film or template plastic, make a guide to pinpoint the $1/4$"-wide seam allowance on both sides of the corners. Using an awl or a $1/8$" hole punch, punch a hole in one corner of the reinforced graph paper, $1/4$" in from both sides. Use the guide to make a pencil mark on the wrong side of the quilt top on all four corners.

3. To measure the fit for mitered corners, you will need two sets of dimensions. First, determine the finished outside dimensions of the quilt, including the borders. Cut borders about 4" longer than this measurement for seam allowances and ease of matching.

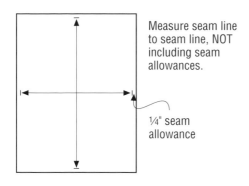

Measure seam line to seam line, NOT including seam allowances.

¼" seam allowance

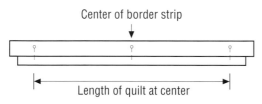

Center of border strip

Length of quilt at center

4. Next, measure the width and length of the quilt through the center, seam line to seam line, not including seam allowances. Use pins to mark the center and the seam lines on each set of border strips.

5. Center the border strip on one side of the quilt so that the strip extends an equal distance beyond each end of the top. Match the centers and the pins on the border to the corresponding pencil marks on the quilt top. Working on a large, flat surface if possible, generously pin the border to the quilt.

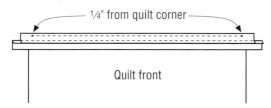

¼" from quilt corner

Quilt front

6. Sew the borders to the quilt top, using a ¼"-wide seam. Start and end ¼" in from the corners of the quilt top, backstitching at both ends. Add the other three strips in the same manner.

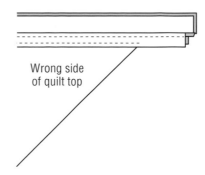

Wrong side of quilt top

7. Fold the quilt top diagonally from the corner, right sides together, and arrange the border strips on either side of the corner so that the long edges are aligned as shown.

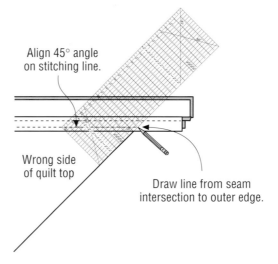

Align 45° angle on stitching line.

Wrong side of quilt top

Draw line from seam intersection to outer edge.

8. Using a ruler with a 45° angle printed on it, align the 45° angle on the stitching line. Draw a line on the wrong side of each strip from the intersection of the stitching lines to the outer edge.

9. Pin carefully, matching the drawn lines on both border strips, and sew on the line. Backstitch at both ends. Trim seams to ¼" and press open.

Cutting with Rotary Cutter and Scissors

Few collections look as lovely as a stack of fabrics arranged for a quilt. The colors and textures urge us to touch them, rearrange them, and add and subtract one or two. After a period of enjoying the fabrics, you must be brave and cut into them to begin the quilt in earnest. Quilters cut fabrics with either rotary-cutting equipment or templates and fabric scissors.

The introduction of rotary equipment to quiltmaking has revolutionized the process of cutting pieces for quilts. You can cut more thicknesses of fabric with far greater accuracy and speed using a rotary cutter. A variety of clever strip cutting-and-piecing techniques have been developed to go along with the use of rotary equipment. If you are new to rotary equipment, the time you spend mastering its use will be rewarded with many projects you never thought you had the time or patience to create. Refer to page 7 for further information on rotary equipment.

A Few Preliminary Tips

Whether you are a newcomer to rotary equipment or have been using it for some time, get into the habit of following a few precautions. The rotary blade is extremely sharp, and before you notice, you can unintentionally cut something important, like yourself. Make the following safety rules a habit whenever you use your rotary cutter.

• Always push the blade guard into place whenever you finish your cut. Keep the nut tight enough so that the guard won't slide back unintentionally.

• If you have small children, keep your cutter in a safe place when not in use.

• Get in the habit of always rolling the cutter away from you.

The following helpful hints may also make rotary cutting easier for you.

• If you stand with your body centered over your cutting line, you will find that your cutting becomes more accurate.

• If you have trouble with the ruler shifting as you cut, try cutting about 8" or 10" and then walking your hand forward on the ruler before cutting the next few inches. As soon as the cutter reaches the fabric next to your fingertips, stop and walk your hand forward again on the ruler.

• When your cutter starts to drag, try oiling the blade. Unscrew the nut on the back and lay out the pieces in order. Gently wipe the lint off the blade and guard with a scrap of fabric. Place a drop of sewing-machine oil on the side of the blade that touches the guard and reassemble the cutter. A drop of oil will often revive an ailing blade. If the blade starts to skip or becomes too dull to cut easily, replace the blade. Place the oiled side of the new blade toward the guard.

Rotary-Cutting Strips

The first step in accurate rotary cutting is to make a "clean-up" cut. Fold your fabric in half with the selvages together and press.

Reverse the directions if you are left-handed.

1. Place the fabric on your cutting mat with the selvages toward you and the fold even with a horizontal line at the top of the cutting mat. Place a 6" x 24" acrylic ruler so that the raw edges of both layers of fabric are covered and the lines of your ruler match up with the vertical grid on your mat. Rolling the cutter away from you, cut from the selvages to the fold.

2. As you make additional cuts, align the required measurement on the ruler with the cut edge of the fabric. Use the grid on your mat to double-check that you are making accurate cuts.

Once you have cut the strips, you can cut simple shapes like squares, rectangles, and triangles, using a cutting ruler or a template. For some projects, you will sew strips together and then cut the sewn strips and reassemble them into blocks.

1. To cut squares, cut strips in the required widths. Align the required measurement on the ruler with the left edge of the strip and cut a square. Continue cutting until you have the number of squares needed.

2. You can also cut odd-shaped pieces from strips using templates. Cut strips as wide as the widest portion of your template. Place the template on the fabric strip and position a cutting ruler over the template so that the edge of the ruler is exactly over one edge of the template. Carefully cut along the edge with the rotary cutter.

3. Reposition the ruler over another edge, and cut. Continue in this manner to cut all the sides of the shape.

4. Another way of cutting a shape is to make a template for the part that will be cut off. For example, to make a Snowball block, cut a square and use a cut-off template to remove the triangles on each corner. Place the cut-off template on the corner of the square you want to remove. Then position a cutting ruler along the edge you will be cutting; trim.

Squares and Rectangles

To determine the size of square or rectangle to cut, add $^1/_2$" ($^1/_4$" for each side) to the finished size of a square or rectangle for the seam allowance. For example, for a finished 3" square, you need to cut a $3^1/_2$" square (3" + $^1/_2$").

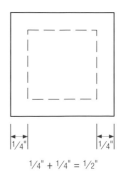

$^1/_4$" $^1/_4$"

$^1/_4$" + $^1/_4$" = $^1/_2$"

Triangles for Block Piecing

Half-square triangle

Quarter-square triangle

The straight of grain on triangles must be parallel to the edges of your block. This stabilizes the edge of your piece, preventing it from stretching out of shape.

Half-Square Triangles

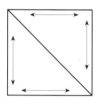

$1/4" + 5/8" = 7/8"$

Cut a square once diagonally to yield two half-square triangles. Use half-square triangles if you need the straight of grain to be on the short sides of the triangle. To determine the size square to cut, add $7/8"$ to the finished short side of the triangle. For example, to cut two triangles with a finished short side of 3", cut a square $3 7/8"$ ($3" + 7/8" = 3 7/8"$).

Quarter-Square Triangles

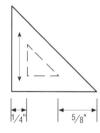

$5/8" + 5/8" = 1 1/4"$

Cut a square twice diagonally to yield four quarter-square triangles. Use quarter-square triangles if you need the straight of grain to be on the long side of the triangle. To determine the size of square to cut, add $1 1/4"$ to the finished long side of the triangle. For example, to cut four triangles with a finished long side of 3", cut a square $4 1/4"$ ($3" + 1 1/4" = 4 1/4"$).

Piecing Tip

When triangles are joined to squares and different-size triangles, a corner extends beyond the seam allowance. It is easier to match up the shapes if these tiny corners are trimmed off before stitching. Use the templates as a guide for trimming your pieces.

Corner and Side Fill-in Triangles for Diagonal Settings

When blocks are set diagonally, the corners and sides must be filled in with triangles. For the straight of grain to be parallel to the edges of the quilt, use half-square triangles for the corner triangles, and quarter-square triangles for the side triangles.

Corner Triangles

Corner triangles are made from a square cut once diagonally so that the straight grain is on the short sides of the triangle. This means that the long side of the triangle must be the same size as the block size in the quilt.

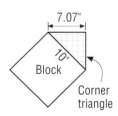

$10" \div 1.414 = 7.07 + .875 = 7.95"$ or $8"$

To calculate the size of square needed, divide the finished block size by 1.414 and add .875" ($7/8"$) for seam allowances. Round this up to the nearest $1/8"$. Cut the squares and then cut them once diagonally to yield half-square triangles for the corners.

Side Triangles

Side triangles are made from a square cut twice diagonally so that the straight of grain is on the long side of the triangle. This means that the short side of the triangle must be the same size as the block size in the quilt. To calculate the size of square needed, multiply the finished block size by 1.414 and add 1.25" ($1\frac{1}{4}$") for seam allowances, rounding up to the nearest $\frac{1}{8}$". Cut the squares and then cut them twice diagonally to yield quarter-square triangles for the sides.

Block 10"
Block 10"
Side triangle 14.14"
15½"

10" x 1.414 = 14.14" + 1.25 = 15.39" or 15½"

Sizes for Corner and Side Triangles

This chart gives you the measurements for corner and side triangles for the most commonly used quilt-block sizes.

Finished Block Size	Cut Size of Square for Corner Triangles	Cut Size of Square for Side Triangles
2"	$2\frac{3}{8}$"	$4\frac{1}{8}$"
3"	3"	$5\frac{1}{2}$"
4"	$3\frac{3}{4}$"	7"
5"	$4\frac{1}{2}$"	$8\frac{3}{8}$"
6"	$5\frac{1}{8}$"	$9\frac{3}{4}$"
7"	$5\frac{7}{8}$"	$11\frac{1}{4}$"
8"	$6\frac{5}{8}$"	$12\frac{5}{8}$"
9"	$7\frac{1}{4}$"	14"
10"	8"	$15\frac{1}{2}$"
12"	$9\frac{3}{8}$"	$18\frac{1}{4}$"
14"	$10\frac{7}{8}$"	$21\frac{1}{8}$"
16"	$12\frac{1}{4}$"	$23\frac{7}{8}$"
18"	$13\frac{5}{8}$"	$26\frac{3}{4}$"
20"	$15\frac{1}{8}$"	$29\frac{5}{8}$"
24"	$17\frac{7}{8}$"	$35\frac{1}{3}$"

TIP TIP TIP TIP TIP TIP TIP

Cutting Tip
Since it is easier to cut fabric smaller rather than make it grow bigger, cut squares for corner and side triangles $\frac{1}{2}$"–1" larger and trim them down once your top is pieced together.

Cutting Fabric Using Templates

Templates are provided on pages 254–71 if you prefer to cut the pieces for your quilts using templates. Refer to Lesson 11— Creating with Templates on pages 209–11 for directions on how to use the templates. A Template Cutting Chart is provided with each quilt indicating the templates to use and the number of pieces to cut from each fabric.

Caution: *If you follow the Template Cutting Chart to cut your fabrics,* **DO NOT** *cut fabrics using the Rotary-Cutting Chart unless otherwise instructed.*

Stitching Blocks and Matching Points

When a quilt design jumps out of a book and lands in your mind, there is nothing to do but whip up a set of blocks and sew a quilt. Whether you are a master quilter or a beginner, the one skill that will enable you to really enjoy quilting is the ability to sew perfect points and crisp corners.

In this lesson, we provide many tips on mastering the skills necessary to make beautiful quilts. This lesson will also unlock the mysterious world of chain piecing, aiming for the X, opposing seams, easing, unsewing, squaring blocks, and best of all, sword pins.

As you use the ideas to improve your accuracy, keep in mind that quilting is a form of recreation and an opportunity for expression. You will enjoy your quilt if it is accurately sewn, but don't let perfection become your only goal. Remember the Joys of Quilting—pattern and rhythm, color and light, creation and expression, friendship and sharing.

Establishing an Accurate Seam Guide

The most important key to your quiltmaking enjoyment and success lies in learning to sew perfect $1/4$"-wide seams. If your $1/4$" seam is a little off, say $1/16$", then a block that is eight squares wide will be $1/2$" off kilter on one side. If your quilt is eight blocks wide, then it will be 4" wider on one side than on the other. If you have ever tried to ease an extra 4" of collar into a neckband, you know this is like trying to squeeze a pillow into your purse. And since you want this to be fun and a loving expression of the art practiced by our foremothers, you must find a way to make sure your seams are exactly $1/4$" wide.

Most sewing machines have markings to indicate $1/4$". Don't trust them. Many sewing machines claim to have a presser foot that is $1/4$" wide. Don't believe it.

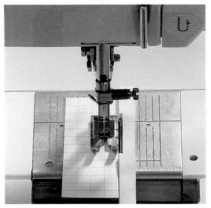

Find the $1/4$" seam line on your machine by placing a piece of $1/4$"-grid graph paper under your presser foot and lowering your needle through the first $1/4$" grid line from the right-hand edge of the paper. Place several layers of masking tape or foam shoe padding next to the edge of the graph paper.

Start your guide about 1" or 2" in front of the presser foot and extend it about 1" behind the presser foot.

This will give you a long ridge to guide your fabric along as you sew.

If you have a newer machine and the opening of the feed dogs extends beyond the $1/4$" line for your guide, you will need to cut out a notch before placing the guide. If you cover the feed dogs, you will have trouble feeding the fabric under the presser foot evenly.

While the graph paper is in position, check the distance from the needle to the right edge of the presser foot. If it is $1/4$", you can use the edge of your presser foot as an additional guide. Some machines have a left-to-right needle adjustment that allows the needle to be moved so that the right edge of the presser foot can be used as an accurate guide along with the tape.

A few minutes of experimenting and adjusting will save you great frustration later when you are assembling your quilt blocks.

Piecing Basics

Now that you have mastered the $1/4$" seam, you are ready to learn the tips and tricks that clever quilters have developed and shared over the years.

Set the stitch-length dial on your sewing machine to about 12 stitches per inch (written as 2.5 on many machines).

Backstitching

Since every seam in a quilt is crossed by another seam, you do not need to backstitch at the beginning of a seam. However, if you feel you must backstitch (for many of us, the habit is quite ingrained), go ahead and do so as long as it does not affect your accuracy. You should backstitch when adding the final border and when sewing set-in

seams, such as in the "Glowing Star" quilt on page 195 and the "Shining Stars" quilt on page 213.

Piecing Diagrams

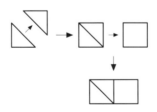

A piecing diagram shows you the steps to follow to join the pieces of your block. When quilters make a block, they sew small shapes to each other to make larger shapes. For example, when two right triangles are joined, they form a square. When two squares are joined, they form a rectangle.

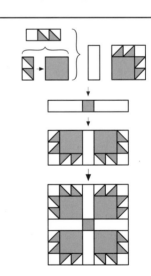

These larger shapes, in turn, are sewn together to create the block. By following the piecing diagram, you avoid the frustration of having to sew around corners and having to "set in" seams. In general, try to sew in an order that allows you to sew progressively longer straight lines.

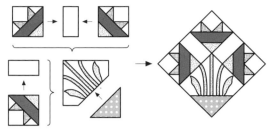

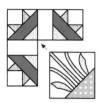

Right way

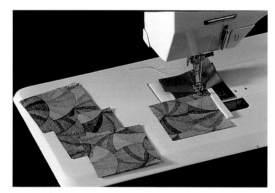

Wrong way

The illustrations above show the right and wrong ways to piece the block in "Line Dancing Lilies" and why it is important to follow the piecing diagrams.

Chain Piecing

Chain piecing, also known as sweat-shop sewing, is an efficient sewing system that saves time and thread.

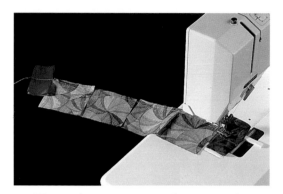

1. Place the pieces that are to be joined right sides together. Arrange them in a stack with the side to be sewn on the right.

2. A useful trick when chain piecing is to use a "chain leader." Keep a supply of four or five squares of scrap fabric (about 3" x 3") next to your sewing machine. Before you start your chain, fold one of the scrap squares in half and send it through your sewing machine to lead the other pieces through.

Feed the first pair of pieces as close as possible to the chain leader. This prevents the feed dogs from devouring the edge of your first pair of pieces, enables you to sew the first edge accurately, and permits your machine to sew without a thread jam.

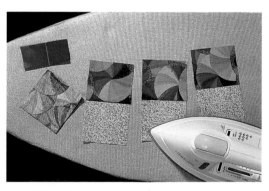

3. Try to be consistent when you chain-piece. Start with the same edge on each pair and the same color on top. This will help you avoid confusion. Stitch the first seam but do not lift the presser foot or cut the threads. Feed the next pair of pieces as close as possible to the previous pair. Sew all the seams you can at one time in this way. Before removing the "chain" from the sewing machine, send another folded scrap through the machine to enable you to sew the final edge of your chain without distorting it. Clip the little thread string that connects the chain of pieces to the chain follower. Leave the scrap in place on the machine to become the next chain leader.

4. Take the whole chain of pieces to the ironing board and snip the pairs apart as you press them. Chain piecing leaves very few hanging threads so you save time clipping threads.

Easing

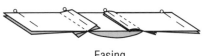

Easing

If a fabric piece is shorter than the one it is supposed to match, pin the places where the two pieces should match and place the pieces under your presser foot with the shorter one on top. The feed dogs, combined with a gentle tug on the fabrics, will help ease the two pieces together.

X Marks the Spot

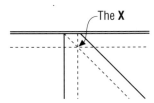

When pairs of triangles are sewn together, the stitching lines cross each other on the back, creating an X. As you sew triangle units to other units, sew with the triangle units on top and aim your stitching through the X to maintain the crisp points on your triangles.

Sword Pins

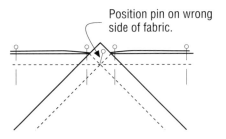

Sewing pairs of triangles together can be difficult, especially when the pieces that meet have two different angles as in the "Jiggle and Jump" quilt on page 168. Insert a pin through the back of the first triangle pair right at the tip of the triangle. Pull the two triangle pairs

apart far enough to see the tip of the second pair. Push the pin right through the tip of the second triangle and pull it tight to establish the proper point of matching. Leave the end of the pin loose like a sword. Place a pin on either side of the positioning pin, about $^1/_8$" away. Remove the sword pin at the last minute just before the needle can hit it. If these points don't match up properly, they will haunt you—or at least spoil the design.

Pinning Short Seams

"Less is better" is the general rule for pinning. When you sew small shapes together, there is no need to pin them **unless there are points to match.** One of the many features of 100% cotton is that the fabric has bonding tendencies. In other words, when two pieces of cotton are placed together, tiny little fibers reach out and grab hold of each other and prevent the fabrics from slipping and sliding as you sew. Even 42"-long strips will not slip. Lay the two strips together and gently smooth the two edges so that they are even. A quality sewing machine will walk the fabrics straight through the needle without puckering, shifting, or stretching them. However, if you feel unsure and would prefer sewing with pins, go ahead and pin.

Pinning Long Seams

Be sure to pin the long seams of a block where seams and points should match. Use sword pins to pin the points of matching. Once these important points are firmly pinned, pin the rest of the seam. Pull the sword pins out just before the needle hits them.

Unsewing

If you decide to remove a line of stitching, use your seam ripper (also known as the reverse sewing tool). Slip the long point of the ripper under one stitch and slide the point farther under the stitch until the sharp curve of the ripper cuts the thread. On straight-grain stitching, cut about every third or fourth stitch and pull the seam apart. However, on a bias seam, cut every stitch to avoid stretching the bias as you pull the seam open.

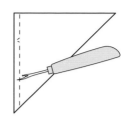

Pressing

To Steam or Not to Steam— A Burning Question

Precise piecing is a combination of accurate sewing and gentle pressing. Remember the difference between ironing and pressing. When ironing, you exert a downward pressure on the fabric with a hot iron. Quilters let the weight of the iron do the work and move the iron gently and quickly over the fabric. In other words, when pressing, don't press down.

Frequent light pressing enables you to see where the pieces should be matched. Some quilters use a dry iron, some prefer steam, some favor a shot of steam, and some like to use a damp press cloth on the blocks and large sections of the quilt. Experiment with your iron on cotton fabrics to find the method that best suits you. The important point to remember is to press frequently but lightly.

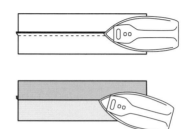

Press the seam on the wrong side first to get the seam folded down in the direction you want. Then turn the pieces over and press from the top to make sure the seam is pressed flat without a pleat along the seam line.

If you are using wool, press your seams open to reduce the bulk. To avoid burning your fingers, use a wooden Popsicle stick to hold the seam open as you press. Press from the back only with lots of steam. Any pressing done on the right side of the fabric must be done with a damp pressing cloth to avoid a shiny look to the fabric.

Pressing Seams to the Side

The traditional rule is to press seams to one side, toward the darker color whenever possible. Side-pressed seams add strength to the quilt, evenly distribute the bulk of the fabrics, and prevent the darker fabrics from showing through the lighter ones.

Pressing for Opposing Seams

Occasionally, the instructions in a quilt plan will tell you to press the seams in opposite directions or toward a particular shape or color to make it easier for you to match the points or corners. This creates what we call opposing seams.

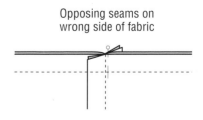

Opposing seams on wrong side of fabric

No matter how precisely you cut or how accurately you sew, the edges of your blocks may be a little off because of the stretch in the fabric. Trimming up the edges will make it easier to join your blocks together.

1. Use a 12" or 15" square acrylic ruler for squaring your blocks. Place the ruler on top of your block. Line up the block with the ruler grid lines that correspond to the unfinished dimensions of the block. For example, if your block should be $9\frac{1}{2}$" unfinished, line up the bottom and left edges of your block with the $9\frac{1}{2}$" grid lines.

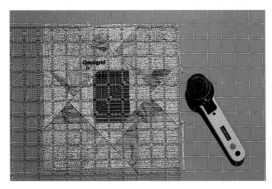

2. If your block is a little too large, it will extend beyond the top and right edges of the ruler. Center the block within the $9\frac{1}{2}$" grid lines so that the excess is evenly distributed all the way around. With your rotary cutter, trim the excess off the right and top edges of the block.

Before you trim, visualize where the $\frac{1}{4}$" seam line will be and consider what trimming will do to your block design, such as the points of stars. You might prefer to remake a few large blocks rather than cut into the design.

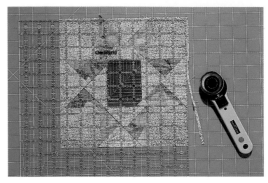

3. Lift the ruler and turn the block so the trimmed edges are now the left and bottom edges. Line up the $9\frac{1}{2}$" grid lines on these trimmed edges and trim any excess that extends beyond the right and top edges of the ruler.

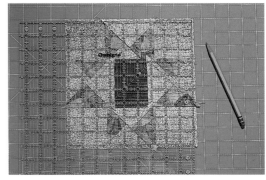

4. If your block is a bit too small, you may still be able to use it. A seam as narrow as $\frac{1}{8}$" will hold on most 100% cotton fabric, unless it is loosely woven. Use your large square ruler to mark the seam line so you will remember to take a narrow seam on these blocks. For example, if your block finishes to 9", center your block and, using 9" as a guide, mark the stitching line. Whatever is left over is the seam allowance.

Sewing Squares and Rectangles

Quilts made from rectangles and squares are some of the easiest to make, yet they have a humble charm all their own. Their simplicity makes them perfect for beginners. If you are making your first quilt, choose a design from this section and make it in a crib size. A small project will develop your rotary-cutting and machine-piecing skills and offer fast results.

As you look at the designs in this section, notice how often the same units are repeated. These units can be broken down into smaller pieces that can be cut into strips, sewn, cut into segments, and reassembled for quick and accurate blocks.

You can make multiple units more efficiently if you stitch strips into a long strip unit and then rotary-cut them into segments. This saves time and increases your accuracy in two ways. By cutting with a rotary cutter, you can cut many pieces at the same time and eliminate the use of templates. Also, by sewing the long strips together and then cutting the desired shape, you reduce the chance of losing accuracy when you sew or press because these steps have been done before you cut the desired shapes!

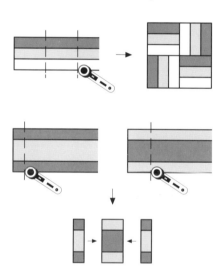

Strips of the same width are stitched together to make Ninepatch blocks, Rail Fence blocks, and checkerboards. Strips of several different widths are sewn together to create portions of the Chimney Stone blocks in the "Chickens in the Chimney" quilt on page 42 and the Y Block in the "Women in the Men's Club" quilt on page 168.

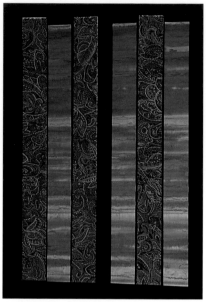

1. For a simple Ninepatch block, cut the number of strips given in the cutting chart for the quilt size you are making. Use your 6" x 24" ruler to make this long cut. Arrange the strips into 2 strip units.

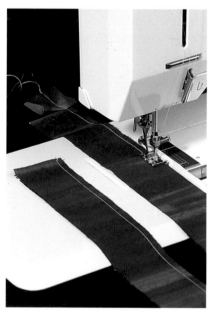

2. Stitch strips in each strip unit together using an exact ¼"-wide seam allowance.

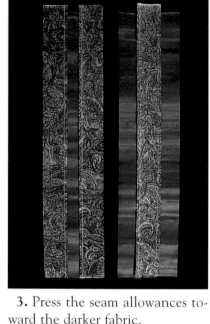

3. Press the seam allowances toward the darker fabric.

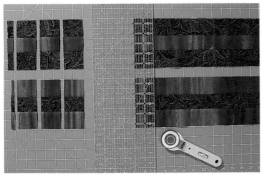

4. Trim the ends of the strip units and cut segments in the specified widths for the quilt you are making.

5. Arrange a stack of the first two segments that you plan to stitch, right sides together. Pin the points of matching and stack them so that the same segment is always on the top and the next segment is always on the bottom. For example, if in the first pair, you placed a dark-light-dark segment on the top and a light-dark-light segment on the bottom, arrange all the pairs that same way.

7. Place the third segment on each unit just sewn. Double-check to make sure you have the third segment on the correct side of the unit. Again, pin the points of matching and stack them next to your machine, then chain-piece the segments together.

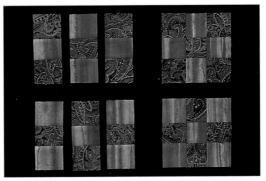

The Ninepatch block is just one of many blocks you can sew quickly and accurately using quick-cutting and -piecing methods.

You are now ready to move on to making quilts with squares and rectangles. Study the pictures, choose a project, and courageously cut your fabrics.

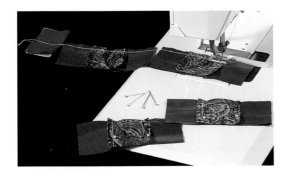

6. Start with a chain leader and chain-piece the segments together by feeding them under the presser foot one after the other using a 1/4"–wide seam allowance. See page 33. Press the new seam allowances toward the side with the most dark fabrics.

Ladybug's Luncheon

By Joan Hanson, 1993, Seattle, Washington, 66" x 86". A warm summer day, a picnic basket filled with tasty treats, and a few ants go hand in hand with this charming quilt. Quilted by Joan Hanson. Directions begin on page 45.

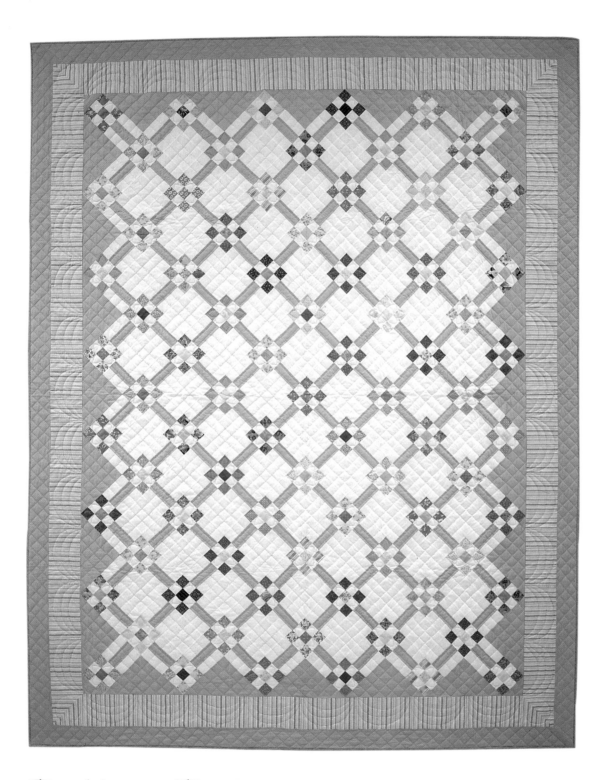

Breakfast in Bed

By Joan Hanson, 1993, Seattle, Washington, 88" x 113". Ninepatch blocks were lovingly made by members of the Needle & I Guild, Seattle, Washington. Quilted by Polly Schlabach. Directions begin on page 50.

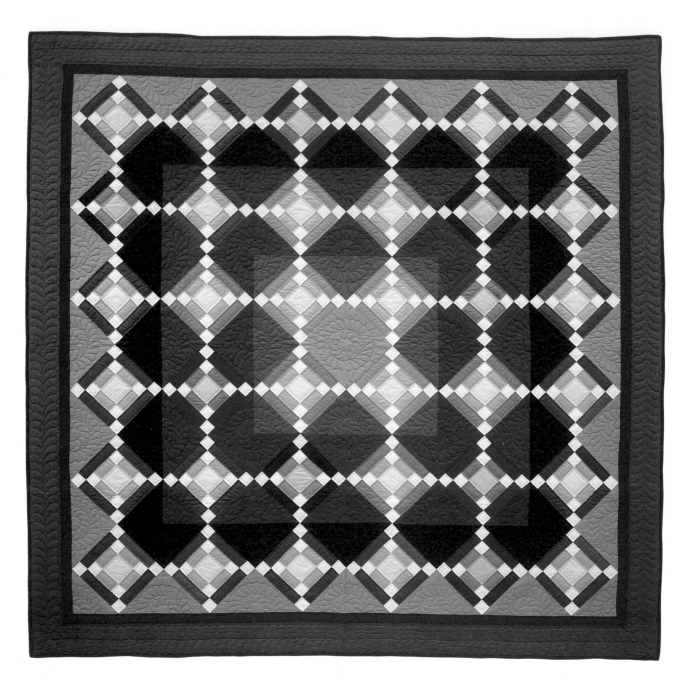

Chickens in the Chimney

By Mary Hickey, 1993, Seattle, Washington, 88$\frac{1}{2}$" x 88$\frac{1}{2}$". Bold colors set on subtle backgrounds create a quilt that looks both traditional and contemporary. Quilted by Sarah Hershberger. Directions begin on page 55.

Over, Under, Around, and Through

By Joan Hanson, 1993, Seattle, Washington, 53" x 63". When winter is on the wane, this quilt is hung to welcome spring. Quilted by Susan Hershberger. Directions begin on page 60.

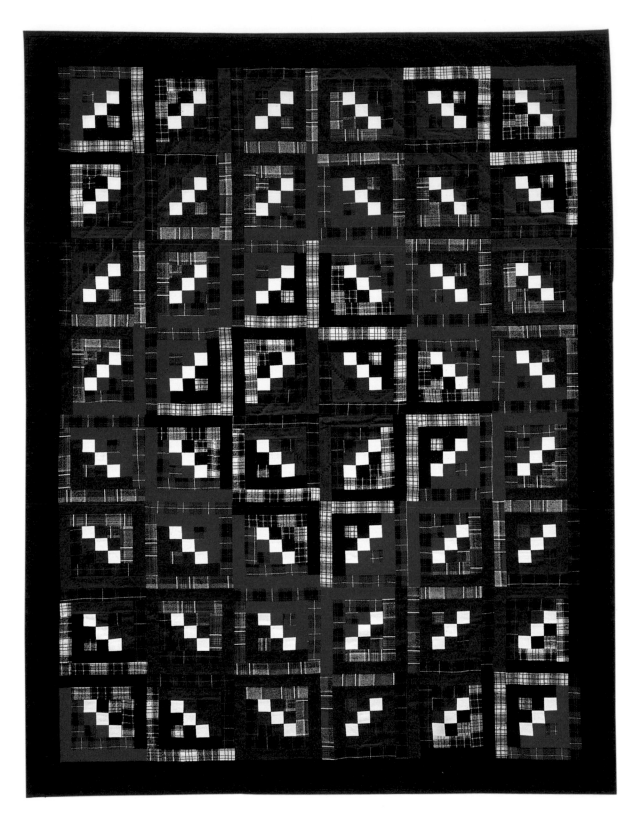

Winter in the Cabin

By Joan Hanson, 1993, Seattle, Washington, 73" x 94". On a cold winter night, when the fire burns low, this wool quilt with a cotton flannel backing keeps the little ones warm and snug. Quilted by Laura Raber. Directions begin on page 64.

Quilt Plan

King | Double/Queen | Twin | Crib

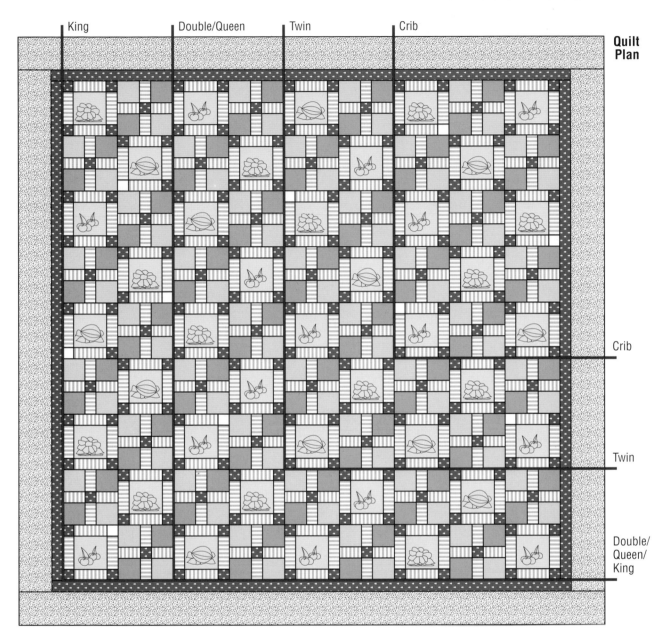

Crib

Twin

Double/Queen/King

Color photo on page 40.

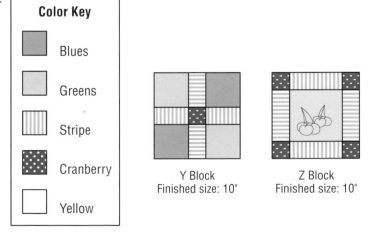

Color Key

- ▢ Blues
- ▢ Greens
- ▥ Stripe
- ▦ Cranberry
- ▢ Yellow

Y Block
Finished size: 10"

Z Block
Finished size: 10"

GETTING STARTED

A novelty print containing charming seed packets was the inspiration for this light-hearted quilt. Novelty prints are always tempting to collect, but it is often difficult to incorporate them into a quilt design. The large center square in this design is the perfect spot to showcase a favorite fabric.

Color Scheme: Scrappy blues, greens, reds, and coordinating prints. Notice how a few yellow squares were sprinkled in for accent.

Setting: Alternating Pieced Blocks. Two blocks that alternate with each other form eye-catching combinations where the blocks intersect, in this case, a stair-step effect around the seed packets.

Quilt Vital Statistics

Measurements given are for finished sizes.

	Crib	Twin	Dbl/Qn	King
Quilt Size	46" x 66"	66" x 86"	86" x 106"	106" x 106"
Block Layout	3 x 5	5 x 7	7 x 9	9 x 9
No. of Y Blocks	8	18	32	41
No. of Z Blocks	7	17	31	40
Inner Border Width	2"	2"	2"	2"
Outer Border Width	6"	6"	6"	6"

Materials: 44"-wide fabric

Purchase the required yardage for the quilt size you are making. Fabric requirements are in yards and are based on 42" of usable fabric width after preshrinking.

	Crib	Twin	Dbl/Qn	King
Asst. Med. Blues	1/2	3/4	1 1/8	1 5/8
Asst. Med. Greens	1/2	3/4	1 1/8	1 5/8
Stripe	1	1 7/8	2 7/8	3 1/2
Cranberry*	3/4	1 1/3	1 5/8	1 7/8
Yellow	1/8	1/8	1/8	1/8
Novelty Print**	1/2	2/3	1 1/4	1 1/2
Outer Border	1 1/3	1 5/8	2	2 1/8
Binding	1/2	2/3	3/4	7/8
Backing	4	5	7 1/2	9
Piecing for backing				

*Yardage includes fabric for inner border.

**If your novelty print needs to be cut out individually, purchase enough "repeats" to equal the number of Z blocks listed above.

Rotary-Cutting Chart

Cut all strips across the fabric width. Measurements include ¼"-wide seam allowances.

	Strip Size	Crib	Twin	Dbl/Qn	King
		No. of Strips			
Strip Unit 1					
Blues	4½" x 42"	2	4½*	8	10½*
Greens	4½" x 42"	2	4½*	8	10½*
Stripe	2½" x 42"	2	4½*	8	10½*
Strip Unit 2					
Cranberry	2½" x 42"	½*	1½*	2	3
Stripe	4½" x 42"	1	3	4	6
Strip Unit 3					
Stripe	2½" x 42"	3	6	11	14
Novelty	6½" x 42"	1½*	3	5½*	7
Strip Unit 4					
Stripe	6½" x 42"	1	2½*	4	5
Cranberry**	2½" x 42"	2	5	8	10

* ½ strip = 21"

**Cut one 2½"-wide strip of yellow to add interest.

Block Assembly

Y Blocks

1. Sew the 4½" strips of green and blue, and the 2½" stripe strip together as shown to make Strip Unit 1. To make ½ of a strip unit, cut the 42" strips in half to yield 2 strips 21" long, then sew 21"-long strips together to make the strip unit. Press seams toward the dark fabric. Cut the strip units into 4½"-wide segments.

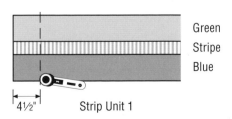

Green
Stripe
Blue

4½"   Strip Unit 1

	Crib	Twin	Dbl/Qn	King
No. of Strip Units to Make	2	4½	8	10½
No. of Segments to Cut	16	36	64	82

2. Sew a 4½" stripe strip to opposite sides of a 2½" cranberry strip as shown to make Strip Unit 2. Press seams toward the dark fabric. Cut the strip units into 2½"-wide segments.

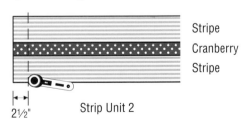

Stripe
Cranberry
Stripe

2½"   Strip Unit 2

	Crib	Twin	Dbl/Qn	King
No. of Strip Units to Make	½	1½	2	3
No. of Segments to Cut	8	18	32	41

3. Sew the segments together, positioning the green and blue squares in opposite corners. Press seams toward the dark fabric.

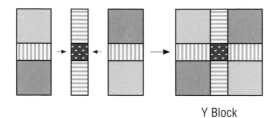

Y Block

Z Blocks

1. Sew a 2½" stripe strip to opposite sides of a 6½" novelty print strip as shown to make Strip Unit 3. Press seams toward the dark fabric. Cut the strip units into 6½"-wide segments.

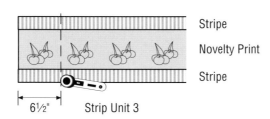

Stripe

Novelty Print

Stripe

6½"   Strip Unit 3

	Crib	Twin	Dbl/Qn	King
No. of Strip Units to Make	1½	3	5½	7
No. of Segments to Cut	7	17	31	40

TIP TIP TIP TIP TIP TIP TIP

Piecing Tip
If you are using a print that has a design centered in the large square, you can chain-piece the units by placing the strip face up on your machine and the novelty print square face down on top of the strip, one after another.

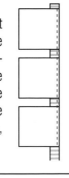

2. Sew a 2½" cranberry strip to opposite sides of a 6½" stripe strip as shown to make Strip Unit 4. Use a half strip of yellow instead of the cranberry for an accent if desired. Press seams toward the dark fabric. Cut the strip units into 2½"-wide segments.

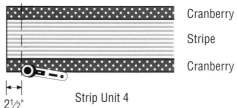

Cranberry

Stripe

Cranberry

2½"   Strip Unit 4

	Crib	Twin	Dbl/Qn	King
No. of Strip Units to Make	1	2½	4	5
No. of Segments to Cut	14	34	62	80

3. Sew the segments together to complete the block. Press seams toward the dark fabric.

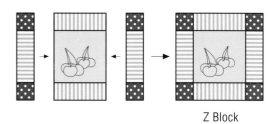

Z Block

Quilt Top Assembly and Finishing

1. Arrange the blocks, alternating the Y and Z blocks as shown in the quilt plan on page 45. Sew the blocks into horizontal rows. Press seams toward the Z blocks. Sew the rows together, making sure to match the seams between the blocks.

2. Cut the required number of inner border strips as shown below. Join strips as necessary to make borders long enough for your quilt. Measure, cut, and sew borders to the sides first, then to the top and bottom edges of the quilt top, following directions on pages 23–24 for straight-cut borders. Repeat with outer border.

3. Layer the quilt top with batting and backing; baste. Quilt as desired and bind the edges. Refer to the general directions for quilt finishing, beginning on page 238.

Quilting Suggestion

Border Cutting Chart

	Strip Size	Crib	Twin	Dbl/Qn	King
		No. of Strips			
Inner Border	2¹⁄₂" x 42"	6	8	10	11
Outer Border	6¹⁄₄" x 42"	6	8	10	11

Template Cutting Chart

Templates begin on page 254.

Templates for Y Block

Templates for Z Block

	Templates	Crib	Twin	Dbl/Qn	King
Y Blocks					
Blues	S-5	16	36	64	82
Greens	S-5	16	36	64	82
Stripe	R-8	32	72	128	164
Cranberry	S-2	8	18	32	41
Z Blocks					
Novelty	S-8	7	17	31	40
Stripe	R-9	28	68	124	160
Cranberry	S-2*	28	68	124	160

*Cut a few of Template S-2 from yellow to add some interest to the Z blocks.

Breakfast in Bed

Quilt Plan

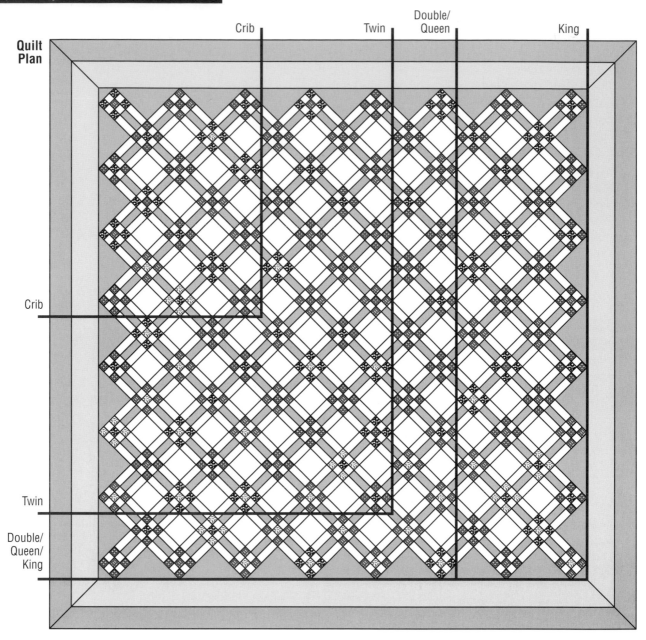

Crib

Twin

Double/Queen

King

Crib

Twin

Double/Queen/King

Color photo on page 41.

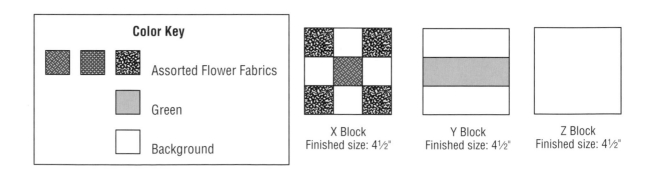

Color Key

Assorted Flower Fabrics

Green

Background

X Block
Finished size: 4½"

Y Block
Finished size: 4½"

Z Block
Finished size: 4½"

GETTING STARTED

Ninepatch blocks are an easy first block for beginning quilters. Scrappy spring flowers blooming all over this refreshing quilt give this beginner block a new look.

Color Scheme: Flower colors with green "stems." Soft green strips give a predominant color to this otherwise scrappy quilt.

Setting: Alternating Pieced Blocks, diagonally set. A diagonal setting and a combination of three blocks give a humble Ninepatch block a new twist.

TIP TIP TIP TIP TIP TIP TIP TIP

A fun way to get a good assortment of scrap Ninepatch blocks is to ask your quilter friends to make some blocks from their scraps.

Quilt Vital Statistics				
Measurements given are for finished sizes.				
	Crib	Twin	Dbl/Qn	King
Quilt Size	42" x 54"	75" x 101"	88" x 113"	113" x 113"
No. of X Blocks	18	59	83	113
No. of Y Blocks	24	96	140	196
No. of Z Blocks	7	38	58	84
Inner Border Width	5"	5"	5"	5"
Outer Border Width	—	4"	4"	4"

Materials: 44"-wide fabric				
Purchase the required yardage for the quilt size you are making. Fabric requirements are in yards and are based on 42" of usable fabric width after preshrinking.				
	Crib	Twin	Dbl/Qn	King
Background	$7/8$	3	$4^3/8$	$5^7/8$
Green	$1^1/8$	2	$2^3/8$	$3^1/8$
Asst. Flower Fabrics (Total)	$1/2$	1	$1^1/2$	2
Inner Border	$7/8$	$1^3/8$	$1^5/8$	$1^3/4$
Outer Border	—	$1^3/8$	$1^5/8$	$1^3/4$
Binding	$1/2$	$3/4$	$7/8$	1
Backing	$1^3/4$	$6^1/8$	8	10
Piecing for Backing	☐	▯▯	⊟	▯▯▯

Rotary-Cutting Chart

Cut all strips across the fabric width. Measurements include ¼"-wide seam allowances.

	Strip Size	Crib	Twin	Dbl/Qn	King
			No. of Strips		
X Blocks					
Background	2" x 42"	4	12	19	24
Asst. Flower Fabrics	2" x 42"	5	15	23	30
Y Blocks					
Background	2" x 42"	6	24	36	50
Green	2" x 42"	3	12	18	25
Z Blocks					
Background	5" x 42"	1	5	8	11
Crosscut into 5" squares		7	38	58	84
Side and Corner Triangles					
4⅛" green squares		2	2	2	2
14" green squares		3	5	6	7

Block Assembly

X Blocks

1. Sew 2" background strips and 2" assorted flower strips as shown to make Strip Units 1 and 2. Press seams toward the flower fabric. Cut strip units into 2"-wide segments.

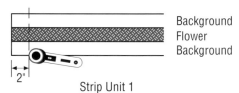

Background
Flower
Background

2"

Strip Unit 1

	Crib	Twin	Dbl/Qn	King
No. of Strip Units to Make	1	3	5	6
No. of Segments to Cut	18	59	83	113

Flower
Background
Flower

2"

Strip Unit 2

	Crib	Twin	Dbl/Qn	King
No. of Strip Units to Make	2	6	9	12
No. of Segments to Cut	36	118	166	226

2. Sew 1 segment from Strip Unit 1 between 2 matching segments from Strip Unit 2 to make X blocks. Press seams away from the center segment.

X Block

Y Blocks

Sew a 2" background strip to opposite sides of a 2" green strip. Press seams toward the green fabric. Cut strip units into 5"-wide segments to make Y blocks.

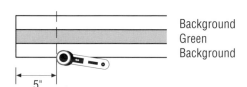

Background
Green
Background

5"

	Crib	Twin	Dbl/Qn	King
No. of Strip Units to Make	3	12	18	25
No. of Segments to Cut	24	96	140	196

Quilt Top Assembly and Finishing

1. Cut the 14" green squares twice diagonally for side triangles. Cut the $4^1/8$" green squares once diagonally for corner triangles.

2. Arrange the X, Y, and Z blocks, rotating them as necessary, following the quilt plan on page 50. Add the corner and side triangles.

3. Starting in the upper left corner, sew blocks together into diagonal rows. Sew 2 rows together and add the side triangles to each end. To join the 3 middle rows, sew the seam of the first 2 rows about 8" from one end as shown and add the side triangle; then sew the seam of the second and third rows about 8" from the other end and add the side triangle. Sew the remaining portion of the three middle rows together after the side triangles have been added. Sew remaining rows together; add corner triangles last to complete the quilt top. Press seams toward rows with X blocks.

4. Cut the required number of border strips as shown on page 54. Join strips as necessary to make borders long enough for your quilt. Measure, cut, and sew borders to the quilt top, following directions on pages 24–25 for mitered borders.

5. Layer the quilt top with batting and backing; baste. Quilt as desired and bind the edges. Refer to the general directions for quilt finishing, beginning on page 238.

Quilting Suggestion

Border Cutting Chart

	Strip Size	Crib	Twin	Dbl/Qn	King
		No. of Strips			
Inner Border	5½" x 42"	5	8	10	11
Outer Border	4¼" x 42"	—	9	11	12

Template Cutting Chart

Templates begin on page 254.

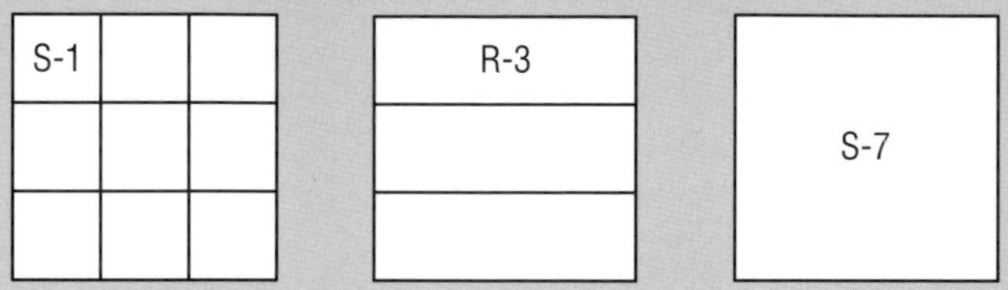

Template for X Block (S-1)

Template for Y Block (R-3)

Template for Z Block (S-7)

	Templates	Crib	Twin	Dbl/Qn	King
X Blocks					
Background	S-1	72	236	332	452
Asst. Flower Fabrics	S-1	90	295	415	565
Y Blocks					
Background	R-3	48	192	280	392
Green	R-3	24	96	140	196
Z Blocks					
Background	S-7	7	38	58	84
Corner Triangles Green	H-11	4	4	4	4
Side Triangles See Rotary-Cutting Chart on page 52 for cutting these triangles.					

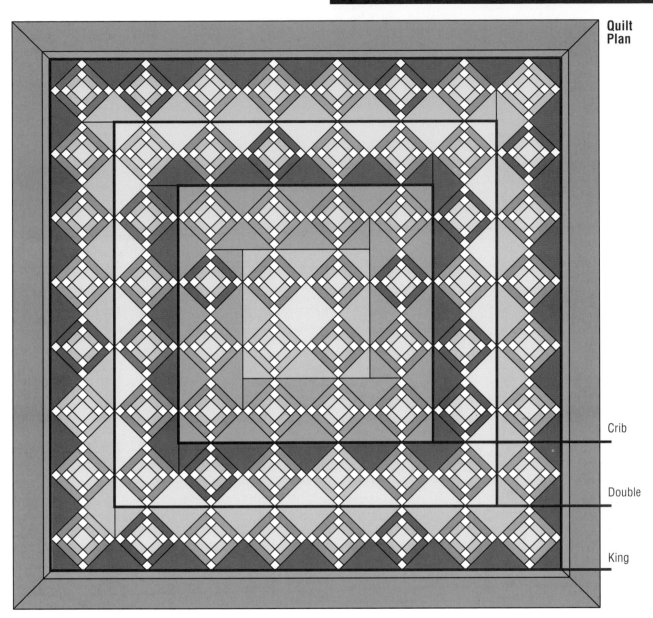

Quilt Plan

Crib

Double

King

Color photo on page 42.

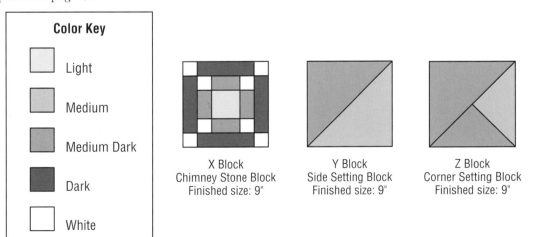

Color Key

Light

Medium

Medium Dark

Dark

White

X Block
Chimney Stone Block
Finished size: 9"

Y Block
Side Setting Block
Finished size: 9"

Z Block
Corner Setting Block
Finished size: 9"

A simple Chimney Stone block combines with two unassuming setting blocks to create this stunning quilt. Brilliant colors, dancing whites, and deep blues produce the subtle interplay of color, light, and shadow.

The small white squares link with the pale shades of color and form an unbroken chain across the surface of the quilt.

Color Scheme: Predominately green and turquoise with magenta and purple accents. You may want to keep these proportions in mind when you select your colors. Each block has three gradated shades of a single color and white.

Setting: Alternating Pieced Blocks, diagonally set . By gradually changing the shade of the large triangles in the setting blocks, the Chimney Stone blocks seem to float forward while the background recedes.

Quilt Vital Statistics

Measurements given are for finished sizes.

	Crib	Double	King
Quilt Size	60" x 60"	88$\frac{1}{2}$" x 88$\frac{1}{2}$"	117" x 117"
No. of X Blocks	16	36	64
No. of Y Blocks	4	16	36
No. of Z Blocks	4	8	12
Inner Border Width	1$\frac{1}{2}$"	1$\frac{1}{2}$"	1$\frac{1}{2}$"
Outer Border Width	3"	4$\frac{1}{2}$"	6"

Materials: 44"-wide fabric

Purchase the required yardage for the quilt size you are making. Fabric requirements are in yards and are based on 42" of usable fabric width after preshrinking.
Select a variety of light, medium, and dark fabrics for the Chimney Stone blocks, totaling the amounts given in the chart.

	Crib	Double	King
X Blocks			
Whites	$\frac{5}{8}$	1	1$\frac{3}{4}$
Lights	$\frac{3}{8}$	$\frac{5}{8}$	$\frac{3}{4}$
Mediums	$\frac{5}{8}$	1	1$\frac{1}{2}$
Darks	$\frac{7}{8}$	1$\frac{1}{2}$	2$\frac{2}{3}$
Y and Z Blocks			
Lt. Blue	$\frac{3}{8}$	1$\frac{5}{8}$	2$\frac{1}{8}$
Med. Blue	$\frac{3}{8}$	$\frac{3}{8}$	$\frac{3}{8}$
Med. Dark Blue	1$\frac{5}{8}$	1$\frac{3}{8}$	1$\frac{3}{8}$
Dark Blue	—	1$\frac{3}{8}$	2$\frac{5}{8}$
Inner Border	$\frac{1}{2}$	$\frac{5}{8}$	$\frac{3}{4}$
Outer Border	$\frac{7}{8}$	1$\frac{3}{8}$	2$\frac{1}{4}$

Materials (cont.)

	Crib	Double	King
Binding	$5/8$	$7/8$	1
Backing	$3^3/4$	8	$10^1/4$
Piecing for Backing	▯▯	▯▯▯	▯▯▯

Rotary-Cutting Chart

Cut all strips across the fabric width. Measurements include $1/4$"-wide seam allowances.

	Strip Size	Crib	Double	King
		No. of Strips		
X Blocks				
White Strips	2" x 42"	8	16	28
Light Strips	$3^1/2$" x 42"	2	4	6
Medium Strips	2" x 42"	4	8	12
	$3^1/2$" x 42"	2	4	7
Dark Strips	2" x 42"	6	12	22
	$6^1/2$" x 42"	2	4	7
Y and Z Blocks				
Light Blue	$9^7/8$" x $9^7/8$"	1	1	25
Medium Blue	$9^7/8$" x $9^7/8$"	2	2	2
	$10^1/4$" x $10^1/4$"	1	1	1
Medium Dark Blue	$9^7/8$" x $9^7/8$"	4	10	10
	$10^1/4$" x $10^1/4$"	1	2	2
Dark Blue	$9^7/8$" x $9^7/8$"	—	8	8
	$10^1/4$" x $10^1/4$"	—	1	1
Side Triangles				
Light Blue	14" x 14"	—	5	—
Medium Dark Blue	14" x 14"	3	—	—
Dark Blue	14" x 14"	—	—	7
Corner Triangles				
Light Blue	$7^1/4$" x $7^1/4$"	—	2	—
Medium Dark Blue	$7^1/4$" x $7^1/4$"	2	—	—
Dark Blue	$7^1/4$" x $7^1/4$"	—	—	2

Block Assembly

X Blocks

1. Sew a 2" medium strip to opposite sides of a $3^1/2$" light strip as shown. Press seams toward the medium strips. Cut the strip units into $3^1/2$"-wide segments.

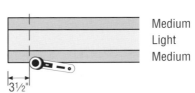

Medium
Light
Medium

$3^1/2$"

	Crib	Double	King
No. of Strip Units to Make	2	4	6
No. of Segments to Cut	16	36	64

2. Sew a 2" white strip to opposite sides of a 3½" medium strip as shown. Press seams toward the medium strip. Cut the strip units into 2"-wide segments.

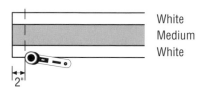

White
Medium
White

2"

	Crib	Double	King
No. of Strip Units to Make	2	4	7
No. of Segments to Cut	32	72	128

3. Sew a 2" white strip to opposite sides of a 6½" dark strip as shown. Press seams toward the dark strip. Cut the strip units into 2"-wide segments.

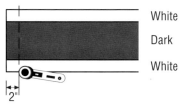

White
Dark
White

2"

	Crib	Double	King
No. of Strip Units to Make	2	4	7
No. of Segments to Cut	32	72	128

4. Cut the remaining 2" dark strips into 6½"-wide segments.

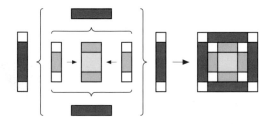

Dark

6½"

	Crib	Double	King
No. of Segments to Cut	32	72	128

5. Assemble the segments as shown in the piecing diagram to make the X Blocks (Chimney Stone blocks).

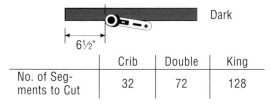

Y Blocks (Side Setting Blocks)

1. Cut the 9⅞" squares once diagonally to yield 2 half-square triangles.
2. Sew 2 different colored half-square triangles together to make the Y blocks. Refer to the quilt plan on page 55 to make the number of Y blocks in the color combinations required for the quilt size you are making.

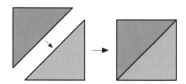

Z Blocks (Corner Setting Blocks)

1. Cut the 10¼" squares twice diagonally to yield 4 quarter-square triangles.
2. Sew 2 different colored quarter-square triangles together. Sew the unit to a half-square triangle. Refer to the quilt plan to make the number of Z blocks in the required color combinations.

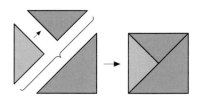

Quilt Top Assembly and Finishing

1. Cut the 14" squares twice diagonally for the side triangles. Cut the 7¼" squares once diagonally for the corner triangles.
2. Following the quilt plan on page 55, arrange the blocks, rotating Y and Z blocks as necessary. Add the side triangles and corner triangles.
3. Sew the blocks together into diagonal rows, adding a side triangle to the end of each row. Press the seams away from the X blocks. Join the rows to complete the quilt top, making sure to match the seams between blocks. Add corner triangles last.

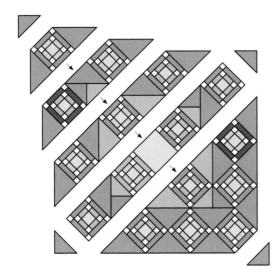

4. Cut the required number of border strips as shown below. Join strips as necessary to make borders long enough for your quilt. Measure, cut, and sew borders to the quilt top, following directions on pages 24–25 for mitered borders.

5. Layer the quilt top with batting and backing; baste. Quilt as desired and bind the edges. Refer to the general directions for quilt finishing, beginning on page 238.

Quilting Suggestion

Border Cutting Chart

		Crib	Double	King
	Strip Size	**No. of Strips**		
Inner Border	2" x 42"	6	8	11
Outer Border	3$\frac{1}{4}$" x 42"	7	—	—
	4$\frac{3}{4}$" x 42"	—	9	—
	6$\frac{1}{4}$" x 42"	—	—	12

Template Cutting Chart

Templates begin on page 254.

S-1	R-4	← S-1
	R-2 ▶	
	S-4	

Templates for
X Block

	Templates	Crib	Double	King
Whites	S-1	128	288	512
Lights	S-4	16	36	64
Mediums	R-2	64	144	256
Darks	R-4	64	144	256

Refer to the Rotary-Cutting Chart on page 57 to cut pieces for Y and Z blocks, and side and corner triangles.

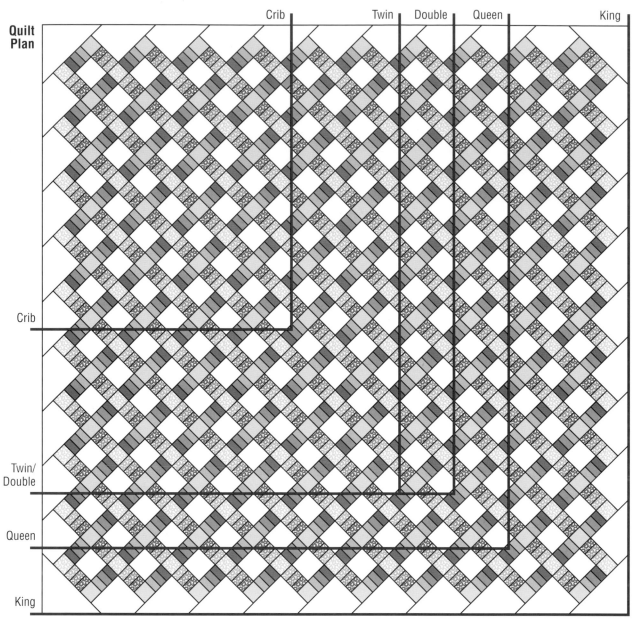

Quilt Plan

Crib | Twin | Double | Queen | King

Crib

Twin/ Double

Queen

King

Color photo on page 43.

Color Key

Light Green	Light Pink
Med. Light Green	Med. Light Pink
Med. Green	Med. Pink
Dark Green	Dark Pink
Background	

X Block
Finished size: 4½"

Y Block
Finished size:
3" x 4½"

Z Block
Finished size: 3"

GETTING STARTED

Creating the illusion of ribbons weaving over and under each other is easier than it looks. Miriam Nathan-Roberts of Berkeley, California, has designed a series of spectacular quilts made using packets of hand-dyed fabrics to achieve a woven look. This version has been simplified by using fewer fabrics, while still maintaining the three-dimensional feeling that is so intriguing.

Color Scheme: Complementary. A floral print was chosen as a theme fabric for the background. The fuchsia pink and sea foam green found in the print were selected for the woven ribbons.

Setting: Alternating Pieced Blocks, diagonally set. The diagonal setting adds grace and movement to the quilt without adding to its overall difficulty.

Quilt Vital Statistics

Measurements given are for finished sizes.

	Crib	Twin	Double	Queen	King
Quilt Size	53" x 63"	73" x 94"	84" x 94"	94" x 105"	115" x 115"
No. of X Blocks	32	83	99	128	181
No. of Y Blocks	80	192	224	288	400
No. of Z Blocks	49	110	127	161	220

Materials: 44"-wide fabric

Purchase the required yardage for the quilt size you are making. Fabric requirements are in yards and are based on 42" of usable fabric width after preshrinking.
Choose two colors for the woven ribbons in four shades from light to dark. This is a good project for hand-dyed fabrics.

	Crib	Twin	Double	Queen	King
Z Blocks					
Light Green	$1/2$	$2/3$	$3/4$	1	$1^1/8$
Light Pink	$1/2$	$2/3$	$3/4$	1	$1^1/8$
Y Blocks					
Medium Light Greens	$3/8$	$5/8$	$3/4$	1	$1^1/4$
Medium Green	$3/8$	$5/8$	$3/4$	1	$1^1/4$
Dark Green	$3/8$	$5/8$	$3/4$	1	$1^1/4$
Medium Light Pink	$3/8$	$5/8$	$3/4$	1	$1^1/4$
Medium Pink	$3/8$	$5/8$	$3/4$	1	$1^1/4$
Dark Pink	$3/8$	$5/8$	$3/4$	1	$1^1/4$
X Blocks					
Background	2	$3^1/3$	$4^1/8$	$4^3/8$	$6^1/4$
Binding	$5/8$	$3/4$	$7/8$	1	1
Backing	$3^3/8$	$5^3/4$	$5^3/4$	$8^3/8$	$10^1/4$
Piecing for Backing					

Rotary-Cutting Chart

Cut all strips across the fabric width. Measurements include 1/4"-wide seam allowances.

	Crib	Twin	Double	Queen	King
Lt. Green for Z Blocks					
3¹/₂" x 42" strips	3	5	6	8	10
Crosscut into 3¹/₂" squares	24	54	63	80	110
Lt. Pink for Z Blocks					
3¹/₂" x 42" strips	3	5	6	8	10
Crosscut into 3¹/₂" squares	25	56	64	81	110
3 Greens for Y Blocks					
2" x 42" strips	4 each	9 each	11 each	14 each	19 each
3 Pinks for Y Blocks					
2" x 42" strips	4 each	9 each	11 each	14 each	19 each
Background for X Blocks					
5" x 42" strips	4	11	13	16	23
Crosscut into 5" squares	32	83	99	128	181
Background for Corner and Side Triangles					
15" squares*	4	6	7	8	9
14" squares*	2	2	2	2	2

*When you cut the 14" and 15" squares for the side and corner triangles, you will have pieces left over from each strip. To conserve fabric, cut some of the 5" squares from the excess strips.

Block Assembly
Y Blocks

Sew the 2" medium light, medium, and dark strips of green together as shown. Press seam allowances toward the dark fabric. Cut the strip units into 3¹/₂"-wide segments. The segments should measure 3¹/₂" x 5". Repeat with 2" medium light, medium, and dark strips of pink.

Medium Light
Medium
Dark

3½"

From each color:

	Crib	Twin	Double	Queen	King
No. of Strip Units to Make	4	9	11	14	19
No. of Segments to Cut	40	96	112	144	200

Quilt Top Assembly
and Finishing

1. Arrange the 3¹/₂" squares (Z blocks), the 5" background squares (X blocks), and the pieced Y blocks, following the quilt plan on page 60 and the color photo on page 43. Sew the blocks together into diagonal rows. Do not add the side and corner triangles yet. Press the seams in opposite directions from row to row.

2. Cut the 15" background squares twice diagonally for the side triangles. Cut the 14" background squares once diagonally for the corner triangles. These triangles are oversized and will be trimmed later.

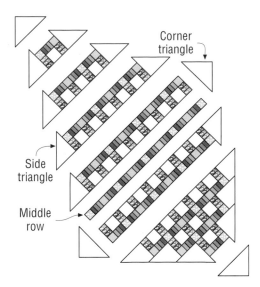

Corner triangle

Side triangle

Middle row

4. Use a long cutting ruler and rotary cutter to trim the edges of the quilt. Align the 2" mark on the ruler with the block points and trim the quilt edges to 2" from these points.

5. Layer the quilt top with batting and backing; baste. Quilt as desired and bind the edges. Refer to the general directions for quilt finishing, beginning on page 238.

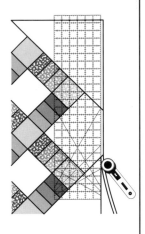

3. Starting from opposite corners, sew the rows together in pairs and add the over-sized side triangles to each end as shown above. Then sew the pairs of rows together to make 2 halves. Sew the middle row between the 2 halves. Press the long seams toward the Y blocks. Add the corner triangles last.

Quilting Suggestion

Template Cutting Chart

Templates begin on page 254.

S-7

Template for X Block

R-2

Template for Y Block

S-4

Template for Z Block

	Templates	Crib	Twin	Double	Queen	King
Light Green	S-4	24	54	63	80	110
Light Pink	S-4	25	56	64	81	110
Background	S-7	32	83	99	128	181
Med. Lt. Green	R-2	40	96	112	144	200
Medium Green	R-2	40	96	112	144	200
Dark Green	R-2	40	96	112	144	200
Med. Lt. Pink	R-2	40	96	112	144	200
Medium Pink	R-2	40	96	112	144	200
Dark Pink	R-2	40	96	112	144	200
Refer to the Rotary-Cutting Chart on page 62 to cut pieces for side and corner triangles.						

Winter in the Cabin

Quilt Plan

Color photo on page 44.

Color Key

		Reds
		Blues
		Greens
		Blacks
		White

King · Twin · Crib · Double/Queen

Finished size: 10½"

GETTING STARTED

Log Cabin blocks have been a favorite way of using up small scraps of fabric for generations. If you have a collection of old wool pleated skirts, shirts, and blazers that you haven't been able to part with, this quilt offers a good opportunity to use them up. Many 100% cotton plaids that would work well for this quilt are also on the market now.

Color Scheme: Red, blue, green, and black solids and plaids, with a touch of white for contrast. Study the way that the colors change in each row from the center out: green-black, black-red, red-blue, blue-green. Also notice how the plaids and solids alternate on the outside row of the blocks so that no two plaids ever touch each other.

Setting: Side by Side. Log Cabin blocks create interesting patterns when placed side by side. The dramatic Barn Raising design is one of the many that emerges when you rotate the blocks.

Quilt Statistics

Measurements given are for finished sizes.

	Crib	Twin	Dbl/Qn	King
Quilt Size	52" x 73"	73" x 94"	94" x 115"	115" x 115"
Block Layout	4 x 6	6 x 8	8 x 10	10 x 10
Total No. of Blocks	24	48	80	100
Border Width	5"	5"	5"	5"

Materials: 44"-wide fabric

Purchase the required yardage for the quilt size you are making. Fabric requirements are in yards and are based on 42" of usable fabric width after preshrinking.

	Crib	Twin	Dbl/Qn	King
White	1/2	2/3	7/8	1 1/8
Black Solid	5/8	1	1 1/3	2
Black Plaid	5/8	1	1 1/3	2
Red Solid	2/3	1	1 1/3	1 3/4
Red Plaid	2/3	1	1 1/3	1 3/4
Blue Solid	2/3	1	1 1/3	1 3/4
Blue Plaid	2/3	1	1 1/3	1 3/4
Green Solid	1/2	1	1 1/3	2
Green Plaid	1/2	1	1 1/3	2
Border	1 1/8	1 1/2	1 3/4	2
Binding	5/8	3/4	7/8	1
Backing	3 3/8	5 3/4	8 1/2	10 1/4
Piecing for Backing	⊟	‖	⊟	‖‖

Rotary-Cutting Chart

Cut 2"-wide strips across the fabric width. Measurements include ¼"-wide seam allowances.

	Crib	Twin	Dbl/Qn	King
	No. of Strips			
White	6	10	12	17
Black Solid	8	15	20	32
Black Plaid	8	15	20	32
Red Solid	10	15	20	29
Red Plaid	10	15	20	29
Blue Solid	8	15	20	29
Blue Plaid	8	15	20	29
Green Solid	5	15	20	32
Green Plaid	5	15	20	32

Block Assembly

Ninepatch Centers

1. The center of each block is a simple Ninepatch. There are 4 different Ninepatch color combinations required for this quilt: Green/Black, Black/Red, Red/Blue, and Blue/Green. The Ninepatch Center Color Combinations chart on the following page identifies the segments used to make each color combination.

Make eight different strip units as shown. The chart under each strip unit indicates the number of strip units to make and the number of segments to cut for each Ninepatch color combination. You will only cut segments from the solid-colored strip units for one Ninepatch color combination. From each of the strip units containing a plaid strip, you will cut segments for 2 different Ninepatch color combinations. To make ½ of a strip unit, cut the 2" x 42" strips in half to yield 2 strips, 2" x 21"; then sew 21"-long strips together to make the strip unit.

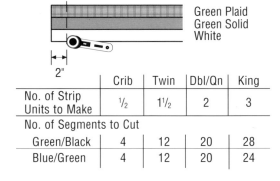

Green Plaid
Green Solid
White

	Crib	Twin	Dbl/Qn	King
No. of Strip Units to Make	½	1½	2	3
No. of Segments to Cut				
Green/Black	4	12	20	28
Blue/Green	4	12	20	24

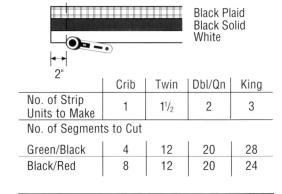

Black Plaid
Black Solid
White

	Crib	Twin	Dbl/Qn	King
No. of Strip Units to Make	1	1½	2	3
No. of Segments to Cut				
Green/Black	4	12	20	28
Black/Red	8	12	20	24

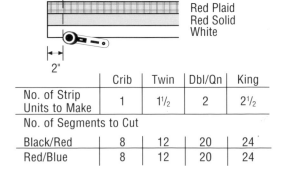

Red Plaid
Red Solid
White

	Crib	Twin	Dbl/Qn	King
No. of Strip Units to Make	1	1½	2	2½
No. of Segments to Cut				
Black/Red	8	12	20	24
Red/Blue	8	12	20	24

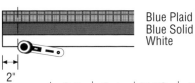

Blue Plaid
Blue Solid
White

2"

	Crib	Twin	Dbl/Qn	King
No. of Strip Units to Make	1	1½	2	2½
No. of Segments to Cut				
Red/Blue	8	12	20	24
Blue/Green	4	12	20	24

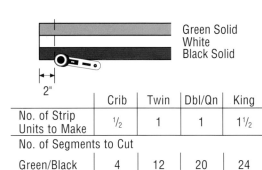

Green Solid
White
Black Solid

2"

	Crib	Twin	Dbl/Qn	King
No. of Strip Units to Make	½	1	1	1½
No. of Segments to Cut				
Green/Black	4	12	20	24

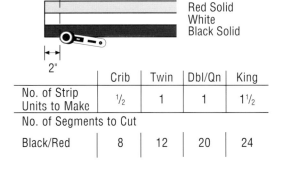

Red Solid
White
Black Solid

2"

	Crib	Twin	Dbl/Qn	King
No. of Strip Units to Make	½	1	1	1½
No. of Segments to Cut				
Black/Red	8	12	20	24

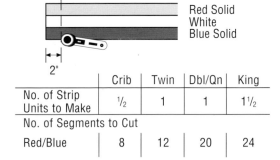

Red Solid
White
Blue Solid

2"

	Crib	Twin	Dbl/Qn	King
No. of Strip Units to Make	½	1	1	1½
No. of Segments to Cut				
Red/Blue	8	12	20	24

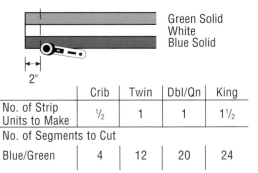

Green Solid
White
Blue Solid

2"

	Crib	Twin	Dbl/Qn	King
No. of Strip Units to Make	½	1	1	1½
No. of Segments to Cut				
Blue/Green	4	12	20	24

2. Sew the segments together as shown to complete the Ninepatch centers so that the white squares form a diagonal row. Press seams to one side.

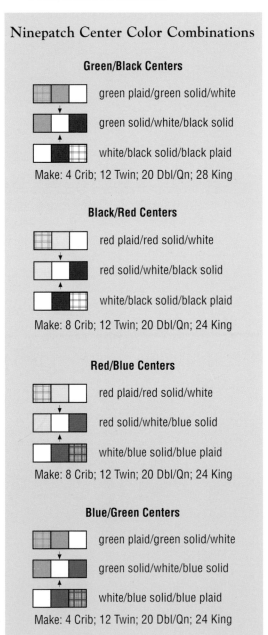

Ninepatch Center Color Combinations

Green/Black Centers

green plaid/green solid/white

green solid/white/black solid

white/black solid/black plaid

Make: 4 Crib; 12 Twin; 20 Dbl/Qn; 28 King

Black/Red Centers

red plaid/red solid/white

red solid/white/black solid

white/black solid/black plaid

Make: 8 Crib; 12 Twin; 20 Dbl/Qn; 24 King

Red/Blue Centers

red plaid/red solid/white

red solid/white/blue solid

white/blue solid/blue plaid

Make: 8 Crib; 12 Twin; 20 Dbl/Qn; 24 King

Blue/Green Centers

green plaid/green solid/white

green solid/white/blue solid

white/blue solid/blue plaid

Make: 4 Crib; 12 Twin; 20 Dbl/Qn; 24 King

Adding the Logs

1. Divide the Ninepatch centers from each color combination into 2 stacks. One stack will be stitched to a solid-colored log first, and the other stack will be stitched to a plaid log first.
2. Place the first stack of Ninepatch centers next to your sewing machine right side down with a white square in the upper right corner. Choose a solid-colored strip to match the solid color on the right side of your Ninepatch centers.
3. Lay the solid-colored strip on the machine right side up. Place the Ninepatch centers right side down on top of the strip. Sew blocks 1/4" from the right-hand edge, as close together as possible without overlapping the edges. Add additional strips as needed until all the blocks in your first stack are sewn to a strip. Trim off any excess strip.

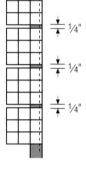

1/4"

1/4"

1/4"

4. Turn the whole thing around and add the solid-colored strip of the second color to the right side. Repeat step 3. Press seams open if you are using wool; otherwise, press seams away from the center.
5. Cut excess fabric between blocks, using a rotary cutter and ruler.
6. Add the solid-colored strips to the two adjacent sides of the Ninepatch centers, matching the colors on each side. Press seams away from the center.

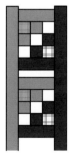

7. Beginning on the same side you started the first row of logs, add corresponding plaid fabrics to each side. Follow the same procedure in steps 3–6 for the second row of logs. Isn't it fun to see the design start to emerge?

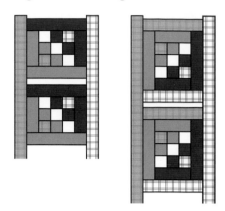

TIP TIP TIP TIP TIP TIP TIP TIP

Sorting Tip
To keep your strips sorted by color, hang them over the back of a chair or on a hanger. If you can get a rhythm going, you will have these blocks done in no time!

8. Repeat this process for the second stack of Ninepatch centers, using plaid fabrics for the first row of logs and corresponding solid colors for the second row of logs.

Quilt Top Assembly and Finishing

1. Arrange the blocks, following the quilt plan on page 64 or the color photo on page 44. Be sure to alternate the blocks with solid-colored outer logs and the ones with plaid outer logs.
2. Sew the blocks together into horizontal rows. Press the seams in opposite directions from row to row. Join the rows, making sure to match the seams between the blocks.
3. Cut the required number of border strips as shown on page 69. Join strips as nec-

essary to make borders long enough for your quilt. Measure, cut, and sew borders to the sides first, then to the top and bottom edges of the quilt top, following directions on pages 23–24 for straight-cut borders.

4. Layer the quilt top with batting and backing; baste. Quilt as desired and bind the edges. Refer to the general directions for quilt finishing, beginning on page 238.

Quilting Suggestion

Border Cutting Chart

		Crib	Twin	Dbl/Qn	King
	Strip Size	No. of Strips			
Border	5¼" x 42"	6	8	10	12

Template Cutting Chart

Templates begin on page 254.

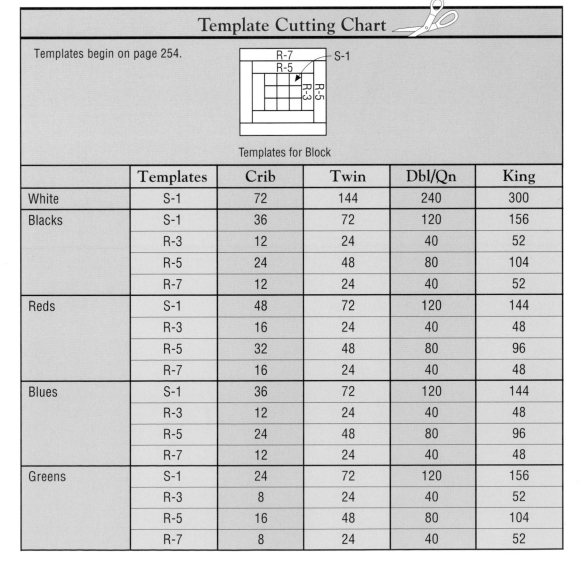

Templates for Block

	Templates	Crib	Twin	Dbl/Qn	King
White	S-1	72	144	240	300
Blacks	S-1	36	72	120	156
	R-3	12	24	40	52
	R-5	24	48	80	104
	R-7	12	24	40	52
Reds	S-1	48	72	120	144
	R-3	16	24	40	48
	R-5	32	48	80	96
	R-7	16	24	40	48
Blues	S-1	36	72	120	144
	R-3	12	24	40	48
	R-5	24	48	80	96
	R-7	12	24	40	48
Greens	S-1	24	72	120	156
	R-3	8	24	40	52
	R-5	16	48	80	104
	R-7	8	24	40	52

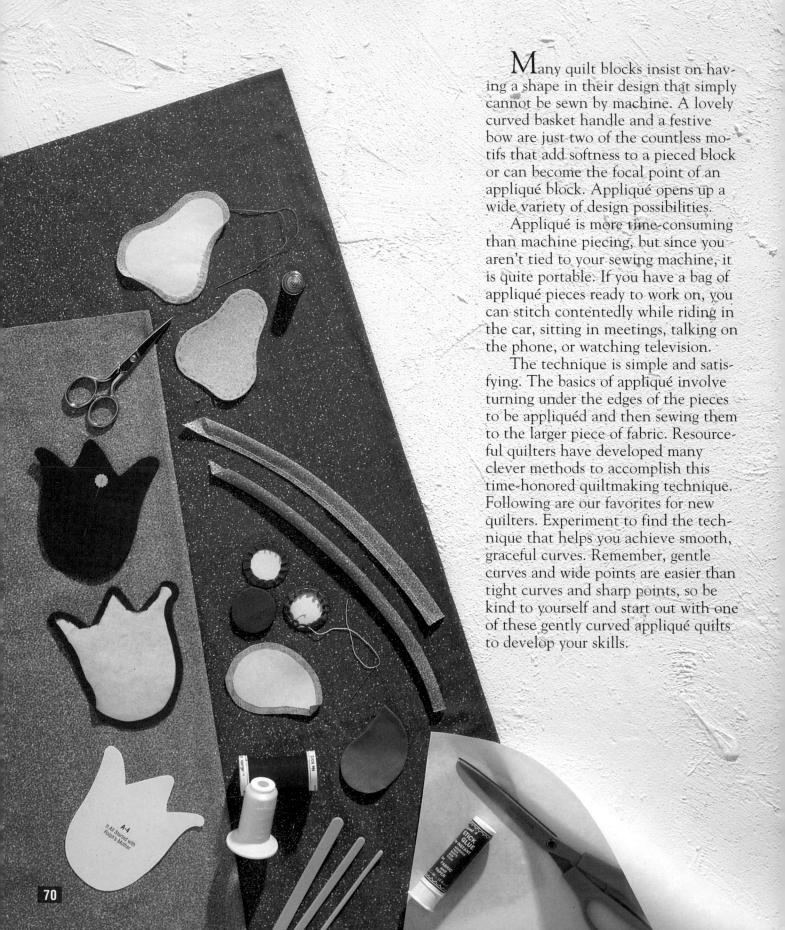

LESSON 6—
Stitching Appliqué

Many quilt blocks insist on having a shape in their design that simply cannot be sewn by machine. A lovely curved basket handle and a festive bow are just two of the countless motifs that add softness to a pieced block or can become the focal point of an appliqué block. Appliqué opens up a wide variety of design possibilities.

Appliqué is more time-consuming than machine piecing, but since you aren't tied to your sewing machine, it is quite portable. If you have a bag of appliqué pieces ready to work on, you can stitch contentedly while riding in the car, sitting in meetings, talking on the phone, or watching television.

The technique is simple and satisfying. The basics of appliqué involve turning under the edges of the pieces to be appliquéd and then sewing them to the larger piece of fabric. Resourceful quilters have developed many clever methods to accomplish this time-honored quiltmaking technique. Following are our favorites for new quilters. Experiment to find the technique that helps you achieve smooth, graceful curves. Remember, gentle curves and wide points are easier than tight curves and sharp points, so be kind to yourself and start out with one of these gently curved appliqué quilts to develop your skills.

Freezer-Paper Appliqué

Many quilters use a paper template as a base to make a smooth, curved edge on an appliqué shape. Freezer paper, which is available in the canning supply section of grocery stores, is a great alternative to regular paper for making paper templates. On one side, it has a thin, shiny coating of plastic that softens and becomes sticky when heated with a warm iron. Pressing freezer paper to fabric with an iron temporarily glues the paper and fabric together. This stickiness, combined with a glue stick, makes it possible to eliminate hand basting.

1. Place a piece of freezer paper on top of the desired shape, dull side up. Use a pencil to trace the appliqué shape onto the paper. Do not add seam allowances. Cut out on the pencil line to create a paper template.

For asymmetrical shapes, the finished design will be reversed from the way the template appears on the page. You will need to trace the reverse of the template onto freezer paper to make a mirror image. For example, to make the mirror-image leaf shapes for the quilt "It All Started with Ralph's Mother," trace Template A-1 as it appears on page 254 to make the right-hand leaf. Then trace the reverse of the shape to make the left-hand leaf.

TIP TIP TIP TIP TIP TIP TIP

Freezer-Paper Tip
If the shape you plan to appliqué is large, you may find it easier to work with stiffer paper. Cut two pieces of freezer paper and layer them together, shiny side against the dull side, and press them together. Be sure to place the dull side of the freezer paper face up against the iron, not the shiny side, when pressing the layers together. Pull the paper off your ironing board cover while it is still hot.

2. Place the shiny side of the freezer-paper template on the wrong side of the fabric, with the sharpest curves on the bias grain. Press firmly with a warm, dry iron (permanent-press setting).

3. Cut the fabric around the freezer paper, allowing a $\frac{1}{8}$" to $\frac{3}{16}$" seam allowance. You do not need to measure the seam allowance—just "eyeball" it.

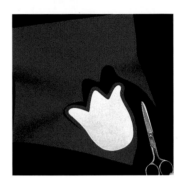

4. Using a glue stick, spread a small amount of glue on the seam allowance of the fabric. Use your fingernail or a Popsicle stick to carefully fold the edges of the fabric over the edges of the paper.

- Start with deep cleavages and inside curves. Clip these areas close to the paper to allow the fabric to stretch over the template.

- On outside curves, fold only a tiny bit of fabric at a time, forming little pleats of fabric over the paper and smoothing the edges carefully to form an even hem. This technique allows you to ease the fullness over the template.

- Points require some encouragement to lie flat and come to a sharp point. First, fold the tip over the paper; then, hold it in place while you fold the right side across the tip. Use a small, sharp scissors to cut away the extra fabric. Next, fold the left seam across the right one and trim it. Put a bit of glue under the folds to hold it all in place.

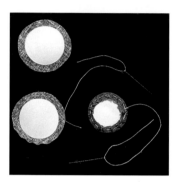

- For circles, ovals, and long, thin leaves, use two pieces of freezer paper to provide a firmer base. See Freezer-Paper Tip on page 71. Cut the template from the layered paper. Use small running stitches to gather the edges of the fabric around the edges of the template. Press.

5. Arrange all the appliqué pieces on the background fabric and pin in place. Set the stitch length on your sewing machine to 6 stitches per inch (or to 5.0 on European machines). Machine baste all the pieces into place. Remove the pins. Machine basting holds the pieces firmly in place and prevents the pins from scratching your hands and tangling with the threads as you appliqué.

6. Appliqué the shapes in place. See page 73 for hand appliqué or page 75 for invisible machine appliqué.

Paper-Patch Appliqué

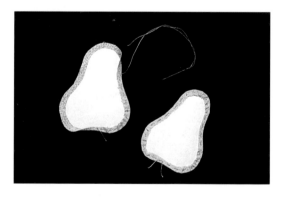

When quilters refer to paper-patch appliqué, they are talking about hand basting the edges of the fabric to the paper shape. This is the surest way to create smooth edges. If you prefer to hand baste, simply follow the steps for freezer-paper appliqué, but omit the glue stick and hand baste the fabric to the paper, using a simple running stitch. Use two layers of freezer paper if you prefer a firmer shape.

The Appliqué Stitch

The traditional appliqué stitch, or blind stitch, is used to sew all appliqué shapes.

1. Cut a single thread, about 20" long, that is the same color as the appliqué fabric, not the background fabric. Thread the needle and tie a knot.

Note: A contrasting thread appears in the following photographs for demonstration purposes only.

2. Hold the needle in your right hand and hold the quilt block in your left hand. (Reverse this if you are left-handed.) Insert the needle from the back side of the block through the background fabric and through the fold, catching only one or two threads of the appliqué fabric. (Your needle may nick the edge of the paper template as it goes through the fabric, which is fine.)

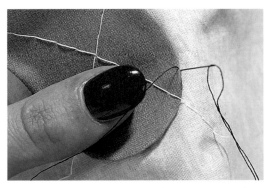

3. Insert the needle in the same spot but through only the background fabric.

4. To start the next stitch, tilt the needle and come up about $\frac{1}{8}$" from the previous stitch through both layers, catching one or two threads of the appliqué fabric. Right-handed people usually find it easier to work counterclockwise, and left-handed people often prefer to work clockwise. Continue sewing around the edges, making your stitches as invisible as possible.

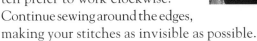
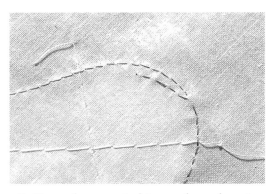

5. To end your stitching, take a few tiny backstitches on the back of your work behind the appliqué. Check to make sure these backstitches do not show on the front side.

6. After you have completed stitching, remove the machine basting. Then working from the back of the quilt block, carefully make a slit in the background fabric behind each shape, trim the background fabric to within $\frac{1}{4}$" of the stitching line. Spray the seam allowance with water and allow it to sit for a few minutes. This will release the fabric from the paper, then gently pull out the paper.

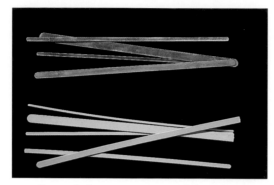

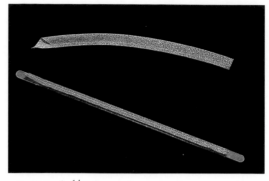

One of the most successful techniques for creating smooth, graceful stems uses metal or plastic strips called bias or Celtic™ bars. Most quilt shops sell bias bars, and hobby and craft stores sell similar bars in a variety of sizes.

1. Cut bias strips $1^1/8$" wide and the length called for in the pattern.

2. Fold the bias strip in half, wrong sides together, and press.

3. Stitch $1/8$" from the raw edges, creating a long tube.

4. Insert a $3/8$" bias bar into the tube. Roll the fabric tube around the bar so that the seam is in the center of one of the flat sides of the bar. Steam-press the seam flat with an iron.

5. Remove the bar. The raw edge is now pressed out of sight on the underside of the tubing, and there are two evenly folded edges to appliqué.

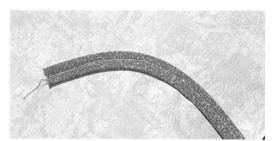

6. Pin the bias tube on the background fabric, gently steam-pressing as you go to ease the fullness on an inside curve. Machine baste in place and appliqué, starting on the inside curve first.

Invisible Zigzag Machine Appliqué

This technique is a quick alternative to hand-appliqué methods and gives surprisingly good results. The key to the success of this method is the use of fine, high-quality 100% cotton thread with a silk finish. Sew each appliqué piece with its own color of thread. If you simply refuse to change thread for every color, use a very fine (.0004m), nylon filament thread as the top thread, and 50-weight cotton thread in the bobbin.

Note: A contrasting thread is used in the following photographs for demonstration purposes only.

1. Follow the freezer-paper method described on pages 71–72 to prepare the shapes. Use two pieces of freezer paper pressed together if you prefer a firmer template.

2. Position the pieces in place and machine baste them to the background fabric.

3. Set your zigzag to a 1mm stitch length and stitch width. Use an open-toe embroidery foot on your machine for better visibility. Slowly stitch around the appliqué shape

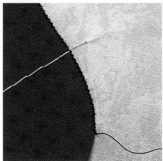

so that the needle takes one stitch in the appliqué piece and one stitch in the background fabric. For points and curves, raise your presser foot and pivot as needed. Zigzag around the appliqué shape, stitching over the first few stitches at the beginning to secure the threads; or backtack two or three stitches at the beginning and end of a line of stitching. Practice on a sample until you become comfortable with this narrow zigzag.

TIP TIP TIP TIP TIP TIP TIP

Pivoting Tip
For inside curves, pivot with the needle down in the appliqué piece. For outside curves, pivot with the needle down in the background fabric.

4. Remove the basting stitches. Working from the back of the quilt block, make a slit in the background fabric behind each shape. Trim the background fabric to within 1/4" of the stitching line. Spray the seam allowance with water and allow it to sit for a few minutes. This will release the fabric from the paper, then gently pull out the template paper, setting paper aside to be reused if needed.

It All Started with Ralph's Mother

By Judy Pollard, 1993, Seattle, Washington, 67$\frac{1}{2}$" x 81$\frac{3}{4}$". The fabrics in this quilt came from a scrap bag handed down by Ralph's mother. Quilted by Virginia Lauth. Directions begin on page 80.

Aunt Boppy's Baskets

By Joan Hanson, 1991, Seattle, Washington, 38$\frac{1}{4}$" x 52$\frac{1}{2}$". Charming May baskets are given a delicate look with lace doilies rescued from an estate sale. Quilted by Anna Mast. Directions begin on page 86.

Fantastic Fans and Beautiful Bows

By Joan Hanson, 1993, Seattle, Washington, 56" x 74". This quilt was inspired by Judy Pollard's Fantastic Fans quilt in *Tea Party Time* by Nancy J. Martin. Quilted by Mrs. John Burkholder. Directions begin on page 91.

Hearts and Gizzards

By Gayle Ducey, 1987, Seattle, Washington, 90" x 100". The inspiration for this design came from a similar quilt made in 1936 by Lucy Conde. Quilted by the Amish in Ohio. Directions begin on page 96.

Quilt Plan

Crib Twin Double Queen King

Crib

Twin

Double

Queen/
King

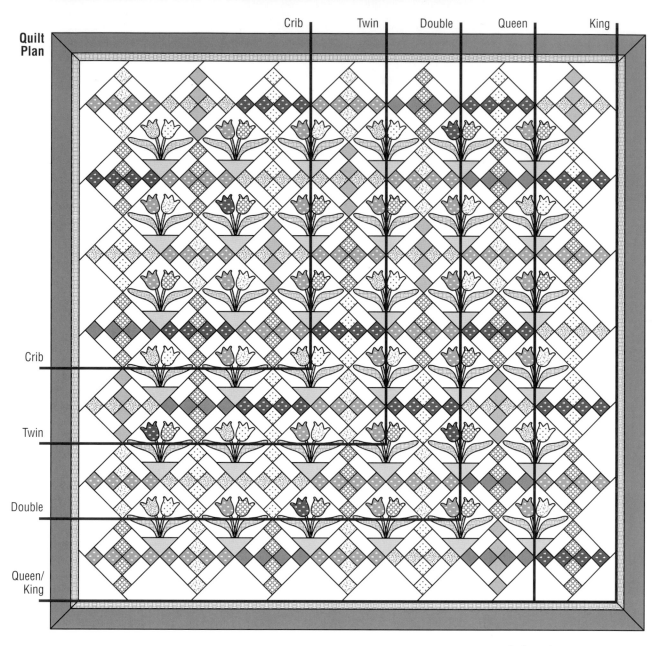

Color photo on page 76.

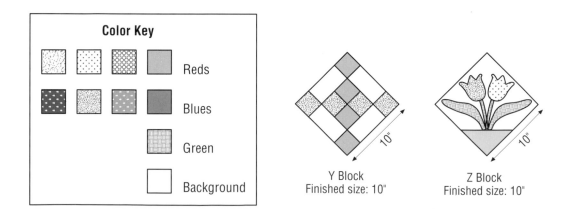

Color Key

Reds

Blues

Green

Background

Y Block
Finished size: 10"

Z Block
Finished size: 10"

GETTING STARTED

Quick-and-easy piecing and appliqué are combined in this whimsical quilt. Fresh scrappy tulips pop out of simple little pots to show that spring is on the way.

Color Scheme: Scrappy reds and blues with green accents. A fifty-year-old scrap bag of fabrics blossomed into this delightful quilt. There are many lines of reproduction prints available today for creating a similar look.

Setting: Alternating Pieced Blocks, diagonally set. In this diagonal set, the pieced Chain blocks link together to form a lattice around the Tulip blocks, blurring the boundaries of each.

Quilt Vital Statistics

Measurements given are for finished sizes.

	Crib	Twin	Double	Queen	King
Quilt Size	53½" x 67½"	67½" x 81¾"	81¾" x 95⅞"	95⅞" x 110"	110" x 110"
No. of Y Blocks	12	20	30	42	49
No. of Z Blocks	6	12	20	30	36
Inner Border Width	1½"	1½"	1½"	1½"	1½"
Outer Border Width	4"	4"	4"	4"	4"

Materials: 44"-wide fabric

Purchase the required yardage for the quilt size you are making. Fabric requirements are in yards and are based on 42" of usable fabric width after preshrinking.
Select assorted reds, blues, and greens totaling the amounts given in the chart.

	Crib	Twin	Double	Queen	King
Background	2¾	3½	5	6½	7¼
Asst. Reds	¾	1	1½	2	2¼
Asst. Blues	⅞	1¼	1¾	2½	2¾
Asst. Greens	⅓	⅔	¾	1	1¼
Inner Border	½	⅝	⅔	¾	¾
Outer Border	1	1¼	1⅜	1⅝	1¾
Binding	⅝	⅔	⅞	⅞	1
Backing	3½	5	7⅜	8⅝	9¾
Piecing for Backing	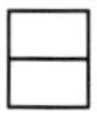 ⊟	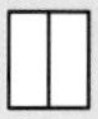 ⊞(vertical)	 ⊟	 ⊟	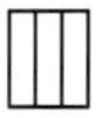 ⫿⫿⫿

Rotary-Cutting Chart

Cut all strips across the fabric width. Measurements include $\frac{1}{4}$"-wide seam allowances.

	Crib	Twin	Double	Queen	King
Background: Side and Corner Triangles					
18" squares	3	4	5	6	6
$9\frac{1}{2}$" squares	2	2	2	2	2
Background: Z Blocks					
$10\frac{1}{2}$" x 42" strips	2	3	5	8	9
Crosscut into $10\frac{1}{2}$" squares	6	12	20	30	36
Background: Y Blocks					
$5\frac{1}{2}$" x 42" strips	4	6	10	14	16
Asst. Blues: Y Blocks					
3" x 42" strips	4	6	10	14	16
Asst. Blues: Z Blocks					
$5\frac{7}{8}$" x 42" strips	1	1	2	3	3
Crosscut into $5\frac{7}{8}$" squares	3	6	10	15	18
Asst. Reds: Y Blocks					
3" x 42" strips	4	6	10	14	16
Asst. Greens: Z Blocks					
$1\frac{1}{8}$" x 5"	12	24	40	60	72

Block Assembly

Y Blocks

1. Sew a 3" red strip and a 3" blue strip to opposite sides of a $5\frac{1}{2}$" background strip as shown to make Strip Unit 1. Press seams toward the red and blue strips. Cut the strip units into 3"-wide segments.

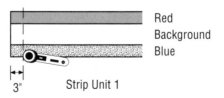

Red
Background
Blue

3"   Strip Unit 1

	Crib	Twin	Double	Queen	King
No. of Strip Units to Make	2	3	5	7	8
No. of Segments to Cut	24	40	60	84	98

2. Sew a 3" red strip and a 3" blue strip together to make Strip Unit 2. Press seams toward the blue strip. Cut the strip into 3"-wide segments.

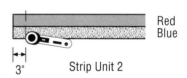

Red
Blue

3"   Strip Unit 2

	Crib	Twin	Double	Queen	King
No. of Strip Units to Make	2	3	5	7	8
No. of Segments to Cut	24	40	60	84	98

3. Sew together 2 segments from Strip Unit 2 as shown to make four-patch units.

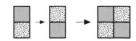

4. Cut the remaining $5\frac{1}{2}$"-wide background strips into 3"-wide segments for background rectangles.

Background

3"

	Crib	Twin	Double	Queen	King
No. of Segments to Cut	24	40	60	84	98

5. Sew the 3" x $5\frac{1}{2}$" background rectangles to the top and bottom of each four-patch unit. Press the seams toward the four-patch unit.

6. Sew the segments from Strip Unit 1 to opposite sides of the four-patch unit. Orient the segments as shown so that the blue and red squares form diagonal lines through the block. Press the seams toward the center.

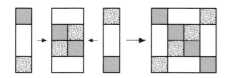

Z Blocks

1. Use cut-off template C-1 on page 256 to remove 1 corner from each $10\frac{1}{2}$" background square. (See page 28 for directions for using cut-off templates.)

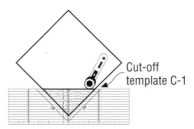

Cut-off template C-1

2. Using $1\frac{1}{8}$" x 5" green pieces, make stems following the bias bar technique on page 74.

3. Make tulips and leaves, using one of the appliqué techniques shown on pages 71–75. Refer to the Template Cutting Chart on page 85 for the number of pieces to cut for the quilt size you are making. Appliqué the pieces onto the background fabric in the following order: stems, leaves, and tulips. "Eye-ball" the position of the pieces. Having them a little off adds to the whimsical look of this quilt. Do not place pieces within $\frac{1}{4}$" of the edge of the block, except for the ends of the leaves and stems. These should be placed even with the diagonal edge so that the ends will be caught in the seam allowance when you add the triangles.

4. Cut the $5\frac{7}{8}$" blue squares once diagonally to yield 2 half-square triangles. Sew a blue triangle to the bottom of each Tulip block. Press the seam toward the blue triangle.

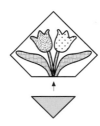

Quilt Top Assembly and Finishing

1. Cut the 18" background squares twice diagonally for side triangles. Cut the 9½" background squares once diagonally for corner triangles. The side and corner triangles are oversized and will be trimmed later.

2. Arrange the blocks into diagonal rows, referring to the quilt plan on page 80. Add the side and corner triangles. Sew the blocks together in diagonal rows, adding a side triangle to each end of a row. Press the seams toward the Y blocks.

3. Sew the rows together, making sure to match the seams between the blocks. Add the corner triangles last.

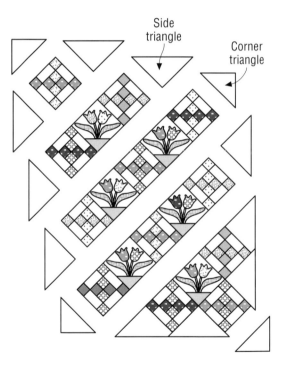

Side triangle

Corner triangle

4. Use a long cutting ruler and a rotary cutter to trim the edges of the quilt. Align the 1¼" mark on your ruler with the points of the Y blocks and trim the quilt edges to 1¼" from these points.

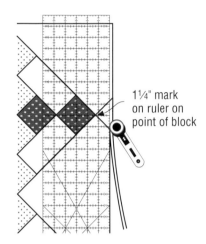

1¼" mark on ruler on point of block

5. Cut the required number of border strips as shown in the chart on page 85. Join strips as necessary to make borders long enough for your quilt. Measure, cut, and sew borders to the quilt top, following directions on pages 24–25 for mitered borders.

6. Layer the quilt top with batting and backing; baste. Quilt as desired and bind the edges. Refer to the general directions for quilt finishing, beginning on page 238.

Quilting Suggestion

Border Cutting Chart

	Strip Size	Crib	Twin	Double	Queen	King
		No. of Strips				
Inner Border	2" x 42"	6	7	9	10	11
Outer Border	4¹/₄" x 42"	7	8	9	11	12

Template Cutting Chart

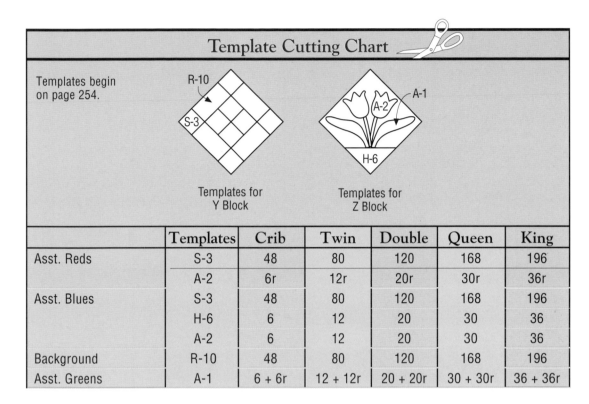

Templates begin on page 254.

Templates for Y Block

Templates for Z Block

	Templates	Crib	Twin	Double	Queen	King
Asst. Reds	S-3	48	80	120	168	196
	A-2	6r	12r	20r	30r	36r
Asst. Blues	S-3	48	80	120	168	196
	H-6	6	12	20	30	36
	A-2	6	12	20	30	36
Background	R-10	48	80	120	168	196
Asst. Greens	A-1	6 + 6r	12 + 12r	20 + 20r	30 + 30r	36 + 36r

Aunt Boppy's Baskets

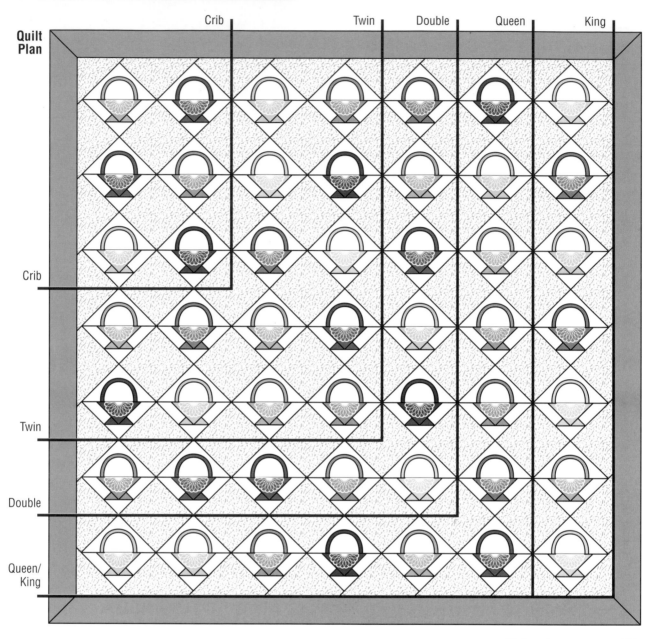

Quilt Plan

Crib · Twin · Double · Queen · King

Crib

Twin

Double

Queen/King

Color photo on page 77.

Basket Block
Finished size: 10"

GETTING STARTED

*B*askets have always been popular quilt designs, ranging from simple Amish baskets to elaborate Baltimore Album appliqué baskets. Crocheted doilies from the 1930s (collected from estate sales) give this humble pieced basket with an appliqué handle a charm all its own. Try other embellishments (laces, handkerchiefs, etc.) stitched into the seam at the top of the basket to give this quilt your own look.

Color Scheme: Multicolored, based on a theme fabric. The solid basket colors were chosen from a wonderful viney floral print.

Setting: Alternating Plain Blocks, diagonally set. By placing an alternating block of the viney print between the Basket blocks, each basket stands on its own without floating over the adjoining basket. Enough of the theme fabric is spread across the quilt to hold all the basket colors together.

Quilt Vital Statistics

Measurements given are for finished sizes.

	Crib	Twin	Double	Queen	King
Quilt Size	$38\frac{1}{4}$" x $52\frac{1}{2}$"	$66\frac{1}{2}$" x $80\frac{3}{4}$"	$80\frac{3}{4}$" x 95"	95" x 109"	109" x 109"
No. of Basket Blocks	6	20	30	42	49
No. of Plain Blocks	2	12	20	30	36
Border Width	5"	5"	5"	5"	5"

Materials: 44"-wide fabric

Purchase the required yardage for the quilt size you are making. Fabric requirements are in yards and are based on 42" of usable fabric width after preshrinking.

	Crib	Twin	Double	Queen	King
Floral Print	$\frac{7}{8}$	$2\frac{1}{4}$	$3\frac{3}{4}$	$4\frac{3}{4}$	$5\frac{1}{4}$
Solid Background	$\frac{3}{4}$	2	$2\frac{1}{2}$	$3\frac{1}{2}$	$4\frac{1}{3}$
Solid Basket Fabrics	$\frac{1}{4}$ each of 6	$\frac{1}{4}$ each of 7	$\frac{1}{4}$ each of 8	$\frac{1}{2}$ each of 7	$\frac{2}{3}$ each of 7
No. of Doilies	3	10	15	21	25
Border	1	$1\frac{1}{2}$	$1\frac{5}{8}$	$1\frac{7}{8}$	2
Binding	$\frac{1}{2}$	$\frac{2}{3}$	$\frac{3}{4}$	$\frac{7}{8}$	1
Backing	$1\frac{3}{4}$	$4\frac{1}{4}$	$5\frac{3}{4}$	$8\frac{1}{2}$	$9\frac{3}{4}$
Piecing for Backing					

Fabric Tip

We are always on the lookout for multi-colored viney prints in a medium scale that we can use for a background theme fabric. They are difficult to find, so if you find one you like, buy LOTS! Buy stock in the company! And, write a thank-you note to the shop owner who ordered it!

Fabric Tip

Choose one of the solid basket colors, combine it with the yardage for the border, and purchase one large piece. Whichever color you choose will become the predominant color in your quilt.

Rotary-Cutting Chart

Cut all strips across the fabric width. Measurements include ¼"-wide seam allowances.

	Crib	Twin	Double	Queen	King
Floral Print for Alternating Plain Blocks					
10½" x 42" strips	1	4	7	10	12
Crosscut into 10½" squares	2	12	20	30	36
Floral Print for Side and Corner Triangles					
17" x 42" strips	1	2	3	3	3
Crosscut into 17" squares	2	4	5	6	6
10" squares*	2	2	2	2	2
*These may be cut from leftover pieces.					
Solid Background for Basket					
10⅞" x 42" strips	1	4	5	7	9
Crosscut into 10⅞" squares	3	10	15	21	25
4⅞" x 42" strips	1	2	2	3	3
Crosscut into 4⅞" squares	3	10*	15	21	25**
2½" x 42" strips	2	5	8	11	13
Crosscut using Template M-1	6 and 6r	20 and 20r	30 and 30r	42 and 42r	49 and 49r
From Each of the Solid Basket Fabrics					
6⅞" squares	1 each	2 each	2 each	3 each	4 each
2⅞" squares	1 each	3 each	4 each	6 each	7 each
**Additional pieces may be cut from leftovers.					

Cutting Tip

When cutting strips for large pieces, you will often have a large enough piece left over to cut some of the smaller pieces. Use up these pieces before you start cutting smaller strips, and you may have a usable piece of fabric left over to make a companion project or add to your fabric collection.

Block Assembly

1. Fold the 2½"-wide background strips in half crosswise, wrong sides together. This is necessary so that you will get mirror-image pieces. Using Template M-1 as a guide and your rotary cutter and ruler, cut the required number of background pieces.

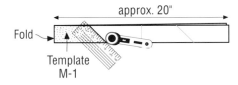

Fold →

Template
M-1

approx. 20"

2. Cut the 6⅞" solid basket squares once diagonally for large basket triangles. Cut the 2⅞" solid basket once diagonally for small basket triangles. Cut the 4⅞" background squares once diagonally for small background triangles.

3. Assemble the lower half of the Basket blocks, following the piecing diagram. The small and large basket triangles should be from the same fabric.

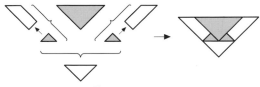

4. Cut the 10⅞" background squares once diagonally to yield half-square triangles. Make the basket handle using one of the appliqué techniques shown on pages 71–75. Refer to the Template Cutting Chart on page 90 for the number of handles to

cut for the quilt size you are making. The handle is too wide and the curve too severe for the bias bar technique. Appliqué the basket handles onto the background half-square triangles.

5. Cut all the doilies in half with your rotary cutter. (You'd think they would ravel apart, but they don't seem to.)

6. Place half doilies in the center of the large basket triangles and pin. Place the triangle with the matching basket handle on top and sew the 2 triangles together with the doily sandwiched between the layers.

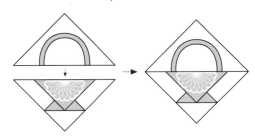

Quilt Top Assembly and Finishing

1. Cut the 17" squares twice diagonally for side triangles. Cut the 10" squares once diagonally for corner triangles. These triangles are oversized and will be trimmed later.

2. Arrange the blocks referring to the quilt plan on page 86. Sew the blocks together into diagonal rows, adding a side triangle to each end of a row. Press the seams toward the plain floral blocks.

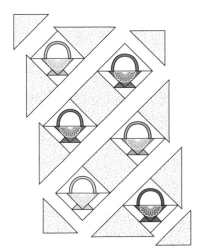

3. Join the rows together, making sure to match the seams between the blocks. Sew the corner triangles last.

4. Trim the edges of the quilt top so that the points of the Basket blocks are 1" from the edge. Align the 1" mark on your ruler with the point of the Basket blocks. Use your rotary cutter to trim the excess fabric.

5. Cut the required number of border strips as shown below. Join strips as necessary to make borders long enough for your quilt. Measure, cut, and sew borders to the quilt top, following directions on pages 24–25 for mitered borders.

6. Layer the quilt top with batting and backing; baste. Quilt as desired and bind the edges. Refer to the general directions for quilt finishing, beginning on page 238.

Quilting Suggestion

Border Cutting Chart

		Crib	Twin	Double	Queen	King
	Strip Size	**No. of Strips**				
Border	5¼ x 42"	5	8	9	11	12

Template Cutting Chart

Templates begin on page 254.

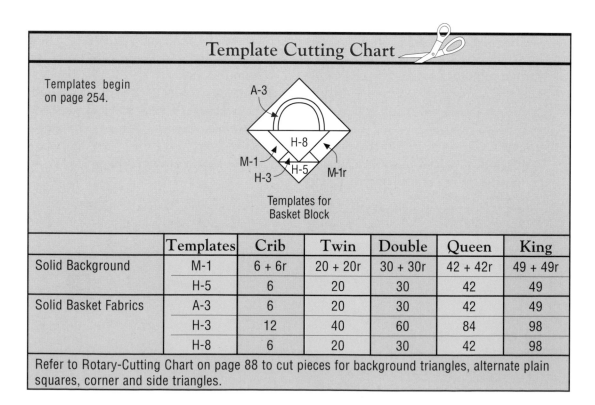

Templates for Basket Block

	Templates	Crib	Twin	Double	Queen	King
Solid Background	M-1	6 + 6r	20 + 20r	30 + 30r	42 + 42r	49 + 49r
	H-5	6	20	30	42	49
Solid Basket Fabrics	A-3	6	20	30	42	49
	H-3	12	40	60	84	98
	H-8	6	20	30	42	98

Refer to Rotary-Cutting Chart on page 88 to cut pieces for background triangles, alternate plain squares, corner and side triangles.

Double/Queen   Crib

Quilt Plan

Crib

Double/ Queen

Color photo on page 78.

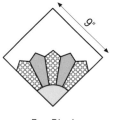

9"

Fan Block
Finished size: 9"

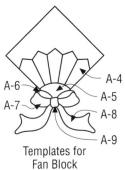

A-4
A-6
A-5
A-7
A-8
A-9

Templates for
Fan Block

GETTING STARTED

Reflections of days gone by are brought to mind by this romantic quilt. It would make a lovely focal point for a girl's bedroom or guest bedroom.

Color Scheme: Pink, green, and periwinkle with yellow accents. A small background print was the basis for this color scheme.

Setting: Stripped Sets. Consider this setting whenever you have odd numbers of blocks. The Fan blocks are set on point with side triangles of background print added to form vertical rows.

Quilt Vital Statistics

Measurements given are for finished sizes.

	Crib	Dbl/Qn
Quilt Size	56" x 74"	82" x 100"
Total No. of Blocks	10	27
Inner Border Width	2"	2"
Middle Border Width	4"	4"
Outer Border Width	3"	3"

Materials: 44"-wide fabric

Purchase the required yardage for the size quilt you are making. Fabric requirements are in yards and are based on 42" of usable fabric width after preshrinking.

Choose a theme fabric that has at least three colors you like.
Collect scraps, fat quarters (18" x 21"), or $1/4$-yard pieces in a variety
of each color. Be sure to get a medium to match up with each dark.

	Crib	Dbl/Qn
Floral Print	$1^3/_4$	$3^1/_8$
Background	1	$2^1/_8$
Total Asst. Mediums & Darks	$1^1/_2$	$2^1/_2$
Inner Border	$^5/_8$	$^3/_4$
Middle Border	$^7/_8$	$1^1/_4$
Outer Border	$^7/_8$	$1^1/_8$
Binding	$^5/_8$	$^7/_8$
Backing	$3^5/_8$	6
Piecing for Backing		

Cutting Chart

Cut all strips across the fabric width. Measurements include $1/4$"-wide seam allowances.

	Crib	Dbl/Qn
Floral Print for Side Triangles		
14" x 42" strips	3	6
Crosscut into 14" squares	7	16
Floral Print for Corner Triangles		
$7^{1}/_{4}$" squares	2	4
Floral Print for Bottom Strip		
$5^{1}/_{2}$" x 42" strips	1	2
Background for Fan Blocks		
$9^{1}/_{2}$" x 42" strips	3	7
Crosscut into $9^{1}/_{2}$" squares	10	27
Assorted Mediums and Darks for Fans and Bows Use templates on pages 254 and 255.		
Template A-4	50	135
Template A-5	10	27
Template A-6	10 + 10r	27 + 27r
Template A-7	10 + 10r	27 + 27r
Template A-8	10 + 10r	27 + 27r
Template A-9	10	27

Block Assembly

1. Sew 5 fan wedges (Template A-4) together, stopping $1/4$" from the edge as shown. Backstitch and press the seams open.

2. Turn the $1/4$"-wide seam allowance at the top of the wedges to the back side and baste with a running stitch.

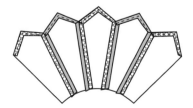

3. Align the raw edges of the fan with the raw edges of the $9^{1}/_{2}$" square; pin or machine baste securely. Appliqué the fan wedges to the background squares, stitching only around the top of the wedges. Remove the basting stitches.

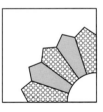

4. Turn the $1/4$" seam allowance of the arc of the fan base (Template A-5) to the back side and baste with a running stitch. Align the raw edge of the fan base with the raw edge of the square, covering the raw edges of the fan. Appliqué in place, stitching only around the arc, and stitching only into the fabric of the fan, not all the way through to the background square. Remove the basting stitches.

 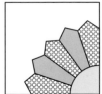

5. From the wrong side of the block, trim away the excess background fabric behind the fan $\frac{1}{4}$" from the stitching line. This reduces the bulk in the block and makes quilting much easier.

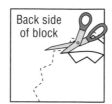

Quilt Top Assembly and Finishing

1. Cut the 14" floral squares twice diagonally for side triangles. Cut the $7\frac{1}{4}$" floral squares once diagonally for corner triangles.
2. Arrange the Fan blocks on point and add side and corner triangles to make vertical columns as shown. Add only side triangles to the short fan columns. Add corner triangles to the top and bottom of each long fan column in addition to the side triangles. For each of the vertical columns, sew the blocks and triangles into diagonal rows. Press the seams away from the Fan blocks. Sew the diagonal rows together to complete the vertical columns.

Side triangles   Corner triangles

Short column   Long column

3. Using one of the appliqué techniques shown on pages 71–75, make all the bow parts and appliqué the bows in numerical order. The bow at the bottom of the long fan columns will be done later.

4. Join the vertical columns together. Press seams to one side. Sew the $5\frac{1}{2}$"-wide floral print strip to the bottom of the quilt top. (For the Double/Queen size, seam the two $5\frac{1}{2}$" strips together to make one long strip.) Trim the excess and press the seam toward the bottom strip.

5. Appliqué the remaining bow(s) to the Fan block(s) in the bottom row.

6. Cut the required number of border strips as shown below. Join strips as necessary to make borders long enough for your quilt. Measure, cut, and sew borders to the quilt top, following directions on pages 24–25 for mitered borders.

7. Layer the quilt top with batting and backing; baste. Quilt as desired and bind the edges. Refer to the general directions for quilt finishing, beginning on page 238.

Quilting Suggestion

Border Cutting Chart			
		Crib	Dbl/Qn
	Strip Size	**No. of Strips**	
Inner Border	2½" x 42"	6	8
Middle Border	4½" x 42"	6	9
Outer Border	3¼" x 42"	7	10

Hearts and Gizzards

Crib   Twin   Double   Queen   King

Crib

Twin

Double

Queen

King

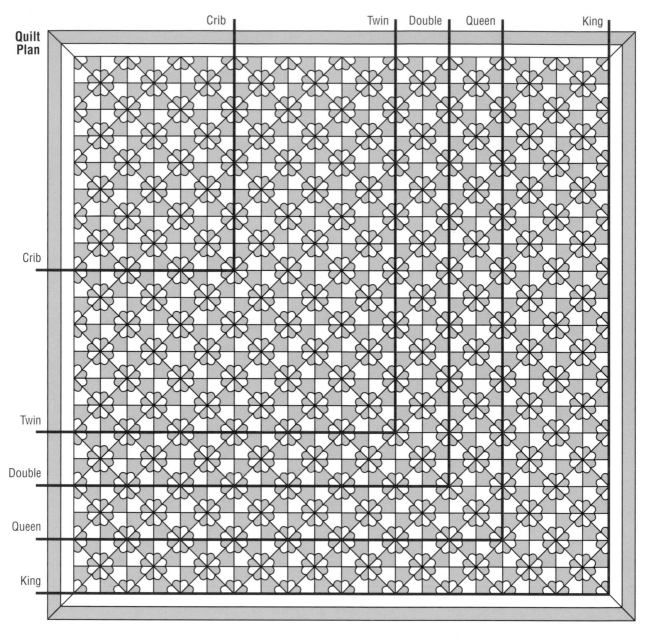

Color photo on page 79.

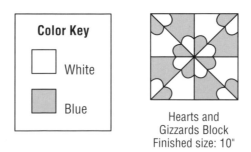

Color Key

□ White

▨ Blue

Hearts and
Gizzards Block
Finished size: 10"

GETTING STARTED

The appeal of this crisp, clean quilt is in the simplicity of its color choice and its repeating positive/negative block. The appliqué is quite simple and would make a great take-along project.

Color Scheme: Blue and white. One of the easiest and most successful color schemes is a two-color quilt using white and another color, in this case blue.

Setting: Side by Side. Placing these blocks next to each other creates this delightful allover design.

Quilt Vital Statistics

Measurements given are for finished sizes.

	Crib	Twin	Double	Queen	King
Quilt Size	40" x 50"	70" x 80"	80" x 90"	90" x 100"	100" x 100"
Block Layout	3 x 4	6 x 7	7 x 8	8 x 9	10 x 10
Total No. of Blocks	12	42	56	72	100
Inner Border Width	2$\frac{1}{2}$"	2$\frac{1}{2}$"	2$\frac{1}{2}$"	2$\frac{1}{2}$"	2$\frac{1}{2}$"
Outer Border Width	2$\frac{1}{2}$"	2$\frac{1}{2}$"	2$\frac{1}{2}$"	2$\frac{1}{2}$"	2$\frac{1}{2}$"

Materials: 44"-wide fabric

Purchase the required yardage for the quilt size you are making. Fabric requirements are in yards and are based on 42" of usable fabric width after preshrinking.

	Crib	Twin	Double	Queen	King
Blue	1$\frac{1}{2}$	4$\frac{1}{8}$	5$\frac{1}{2}$	6$\frac{3}{4}$	9$\frac{1}{2}$
Blue Outer Border	$\frac{1}{2}$	$\frac{3}{4}$	$\frac{7}{8}$	1	1
White	1$\frac{1}{2}$	4$\frac{1}{8}$	5$\frac{1}{2}$	6$\frac{3}{4}$	9$\frac{1}{2}$
White Inner Border	$\frac{1}{2}$	$\frac{3}{4}$	$\frac{7}{8}$	1	1
Binding	$\frac{1}{2}$	$\frac{2}{3}$	$\frac{3}{4}$	$\frac{7}{8}$	$\frac{7}{8}$
Backing	1$\frac{3}{4}$	4$\frac{3}{8}$	5$\frac{1}{2}$	8$\frac{1}{8}$	9
Piecing for Backing	☐	⊟	⊟⊟	⊟	⊟⊟⊟

Note: Yardage for the borders may be combined with yardage for blocks if the same fabric is used; cut lengthwise border strips for seamless borders before cutting strips for block.

Rotary-Cutting Chart

Cut all strips across the fabric width. Measurements include $\frac{1}{4}$"-wide seam allowances.

	Crib	Twin	Double	Queen	King
Blue for Background Triangles					
$5\frac{7}{8}$" x 42" strips	4	14	19	24	34
Crosscut into $5\frac{7}{8}$" squares	24	84	112	144	200
Blue for Cone Shapes					
$3\frac{1}{2}$" x 42" strips	5	16	21	27	37
Crosscut into $3\frac{1}{2}$" squares	48	168	224	288	400
White for Background Triangles					
$5\frac{7}{8}$" x 42" strips	4	14	19	24	34
Crosscut into $5\frac{7}{8}$" squares	24	84	112	144	200
White for Cone Shapes					
$3\frac{1}{2}$" x 42" strips	5	16	21	27	37
Crosscut into $3\frac{1}{2}$" squares	48	168	224	288	400

Block Assembly

1. Cut the $3\frac{1}{2}$" blue squares and white squares once diagonally to yield small half-square triangles.
2. Use trimming template A-10 on page 255 to trim the small half-square triangles into cone-shaped pieces. Trim the triangles as shown so that half of the cone-shaped pieces have the straight grain on the left side and half of the cone-shaped pieces have the straight grain on the right side.

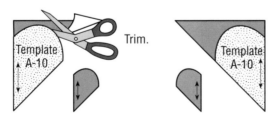

3. Turn the $\frac{1}{4}$" seam allowance at the top of the cone to the back side and baste with a running stitch. If you prefer one of the appliqué methods on pages 71–75, use appliqué template A-11 on page 255 to prepare the top of the cone shape.
4. Cut the $5\frac{7}{8}$" blue squares and white squares once diagonally to yield large half-square triangles.
5. Appliqué the blue cones onto the ends of the large white triangles, and the white cones onto the ends of the large blue triangles. Match the grain lines of the cone pieces with the grain line of the large triangles. Appliqué only the top of the cone; the sides will be caught in the seams when the triangles and squares are sewn together.

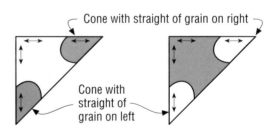

Cone with straight of grain on right

Cone with straight of grain on left

TIP TIP TIP TIP TIP TIP TIP

As you may have noticed, there are a lot of little cones to stitch onto those triangles. If you enjoy handwork, this is a terrific long-term, take-along project to take with you when you are on the go.

6. Working from the wrong side of the triangle, trim the excess fabric behind the cone 1/4" from stitching line.

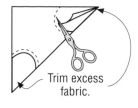
Trim excess fabric.

7. Sew the blue triangles to the white triangles to form a square. Press seams toward the blue triangles.

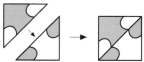

8. Sew 4 squares together as shown to make the Hearts and Gizzards block. Press seams toward the blue triangles when joining 2 blocks and press open the last seam joining the 2 pairs of blocks to reduce bulk.

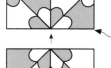
Press last seam open to reduce bulk.

Quilt Top Assembly and Finishing

1. Arrange the blocks as shown in the quilt plan on page 96. Sew the blocks together into horizontal rows. Press the seams in opposite directions from row to row.
2. Sew the rows together, making sure to match the seams between the blocks.
3. Cut the required number of border strips as shown below. Join strips as necessary to make borders long enough for your quilt. Measure, cut, and sew borders to the quilt top, following directions on pages 24–25 for mitered borders.
4. Layer quilt top with batting and backing; baste. Quilt as desired and bind the edges. Refer to the general directions for quilt finishing, beginning on page 238.

Quilting Suggestion

Border Cutting Chart

		Crib	Twin	Double	Queen	King
	Strip Size	No. of Strips				
Inner Border	3" x 42"	4	7	8	9	10
Outer Border	2³⁄₄" x 42"	5	8	9	10	10

Template Cutting Chart

Templates begin on page 254.

Templates for Hearts and Gizzards Block

A-11
H-6

	Templates	Crib	Twin	Double	Queen	King
Blue	H-6	48	168	224	288	400
	A-11	96	336	448	576	800
White	H-6	48	168	224	288	400
	A-11	96	336	448	576	800

Mastering Half-Square Units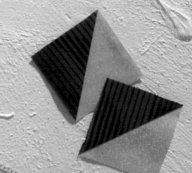

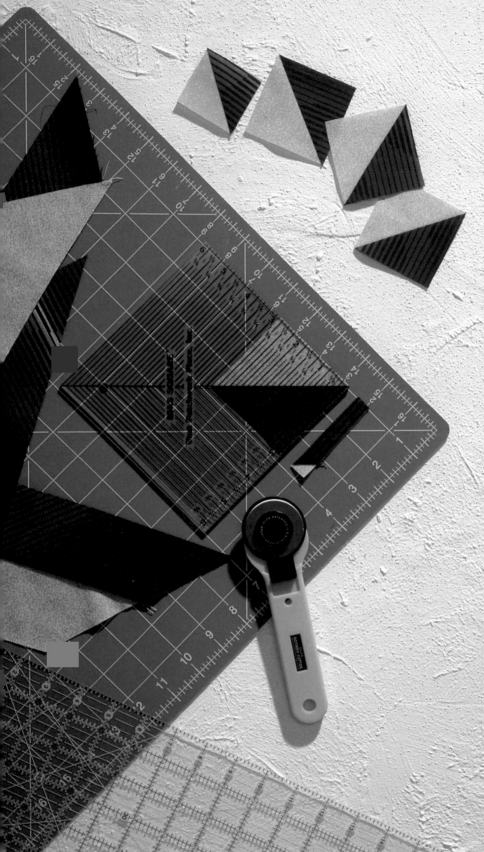

Quilts based on squares and rectangles are the easiest designs to make. But consider the possibilities for pattern and design that occur when you divide some of the squares into two triangles. Two triangles sewn together make up a square, so sewing them into the block is easy; and the triangles open up a whole world of dancing, shimmering designs. The quilts in this section all use squares made up of two triangles called half-square units.

Look carefully at a square made of two triangles. Notice that the seam where the two triangles meet is along the diagonal of the square, and the threads along the seam are on the bias grain of the fabric. During the last few years, many clever quiltmakers have developed several ingenious ways to make sewing these squares quite easy and accurate.

In this lesson, you will find what we think is the easiest, fastest, and most accurate way to make half-square units, along with four beautiful projects based on this method. The basic idea is to cut bias strips, sew the strips into a unit, cut segments from the unit, and cut the segments into squares. The beauty of this method is that you cannot distort the squares when you sew or press them because the sewing and pressing are done before you cut the squares!

Cutting and Sewing the Strips

Cut bias strips $\frac{1}{2}$" wider than the finished short side of the triangle in the half-square unit. For units that finish 3" or larger, cut strips only $\frac{1}{4}$" wider than the finished short side of a triangle.

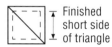
Finished short side of triangle

The instructions for each quilt in this section indicate the size of the fabric piece required. We'll also tell you how wide to cut the strips for each quilt pattern.

1. Layer two contrasting fabrics with right sides facing up. Align the 45° angle of a 6" x 24" ruler with the bottom edge of the lower left corner. Cut along the right edge of the ruler.

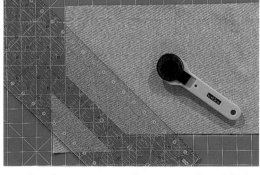

2. Cut bias strips in the required width for the quilt you are making. Align the required measurement on your ruler with the cut edge of the fabric. Make your cuts parallel to the first cut.

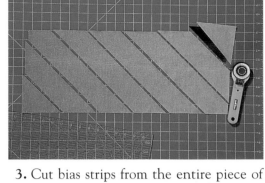

3. Cut bias strips from the entire piece of fabric.

4. Arrange the bias strips into 2 units, alternating the colors in each unit. The bottom left corner of each unit should be a different fabric.

5. Sew the strips with right sides together, offsetting the tops $\frac{1}{4}$" and using an exact $\frac{1}{4}$"-wide seam allowance. Do not make the unit more than 18"–20" wide. Make another unit if you have more strips rather than sewing one very large, wide unit.

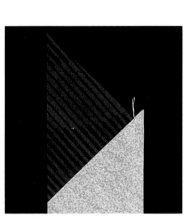

6. Press the seam allowances toward the darker color. Press gently from the back of the fabric first and then on the front to be certain that the seams lie flat without pleats.

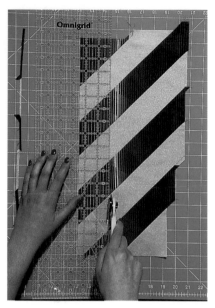

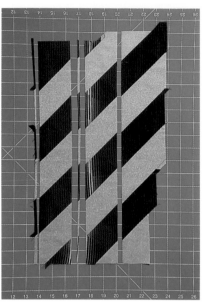

1. Place the diagonal line of the Bias Square ruler on one of the middle seam lines in the unit. Align the long cutting ruler with the edge of the Bias Square ruler, just covering the uneven ends of the strip unit. Move the Bias Square aside and trim the edge of the unit so that it is at a perfect 45° angle to the seam lines. As you trim the edge of the unit, you are actually cutting one side of many squares, so for this method to be accurate, you must retrim the edge of the unit before cutting each segment.

Note: Only a few threads may need to be trimmed at one end while as much as ¹/₂"–1"may have to be trimmed from the other end.

2. Cut a segment ¹/₂" larger than the finished square. For example, if the finished square is 2", add ¹/₂" to that measurement and cut the segment 2¹/₂" wide. As you cut the segment, you are actually cutting the second side of many squares.

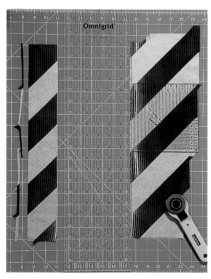

3. Use the Bias Square ruler and long cutting ruler to trim the edge of the unit again so that it is at a 45° angle to the seam lines. Because bias-grain seams have a tendency to shift, you must retrim the edge of the unit before cutting each segment.

4. Continue to cut segments until you have cut the entire unit. Remember to trim the edge before cutting each segment. After you cut the last full-length segment, look at the remaining portion to see if it is wide enough to cut an additional segment. Even though it may not be a full-length segment like the others, you may be able to cut one or more squares from a portion of the segment.

Cutting the Squares

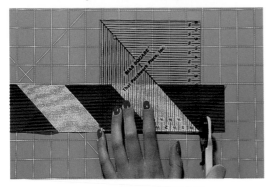

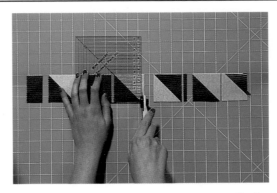

1. Position the edge of the Bias Square ruler on the edge of the segment, with the diagonal line on the seam line. Cut on the right-hand side of the Bias Square ruler.

3. Turn the mat around to place all the right-hand cuts on the left. Reposition the edge of the Bias Square ruler on the edge of the fabric, with the diagonal line on the seam line, and trim the pieces into perfect squares.

What a joy to be able to make perfect half-square units!

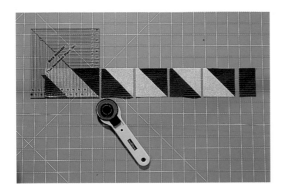

2. Continue cutting squares across the segment, positioning the Bias Square ruler on the edge of the segment with the diagonal line on the seam line before each cut. As you cut on the right side on each seam line, you are cutting the third side of the squares.

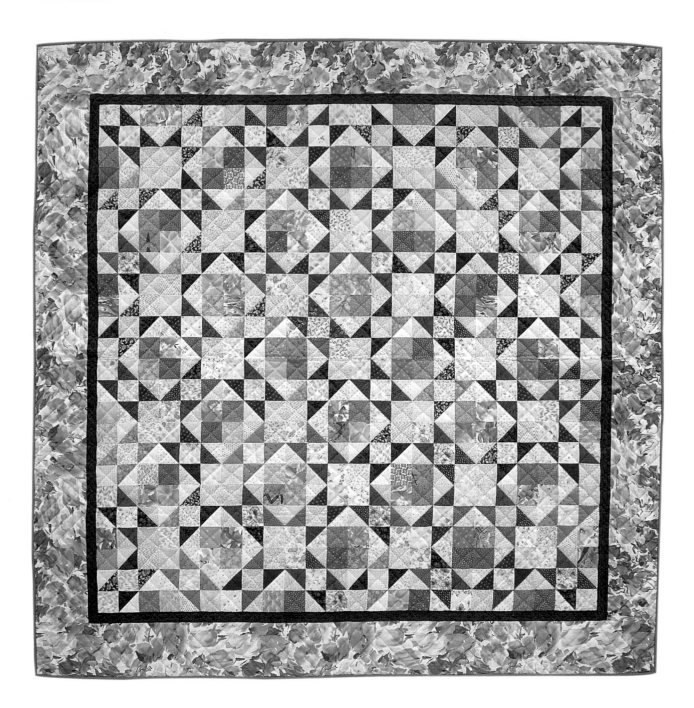

Cheerful Child

By Mary Hickey, 1993, Seattle, Washington, 87" x 87". An impressionistic decorator print inspired the light-hearted color scheme of this jolly quilt. From the collection of the cheerful child, Molly Hickey. Quilted by the Amish. Directions begin on page 108.

Butterflies at the Crossroads

By Connie Nordstrom, 1990, Farmington, New Mexico, 77" x 89¼". A monochromatic color scheme requires skill and artistry to succeed. These butterflies demonstrate Connie Nordstrom's exceptional talent at both. Quilted by Connie Nordstrom. Directions begin on page 112.

Christmas Bear Paw

By Frieda Martinis, 1992, Everett, Washington, 70" x 82". This quilt was made as a Christmas gift for Frieda's daughter. Quilted by Frieda Martinis. (Collection of Margaret Wallace) Directions begin on page 118.

Green Gables

By Connie Nordstrom, 1993, Farmington, New Mexico, 72$^1/_2$" x 84$^3/_4$". This quilt closely resembles Anne's quilt in the video of *Anne of Green Gables*. Quilted by Connie Nordstrom. Directions begin on page 124.

Cheerful Child

Quilt Plan

Crib Twin Double King

Crib

Twin/Double

King

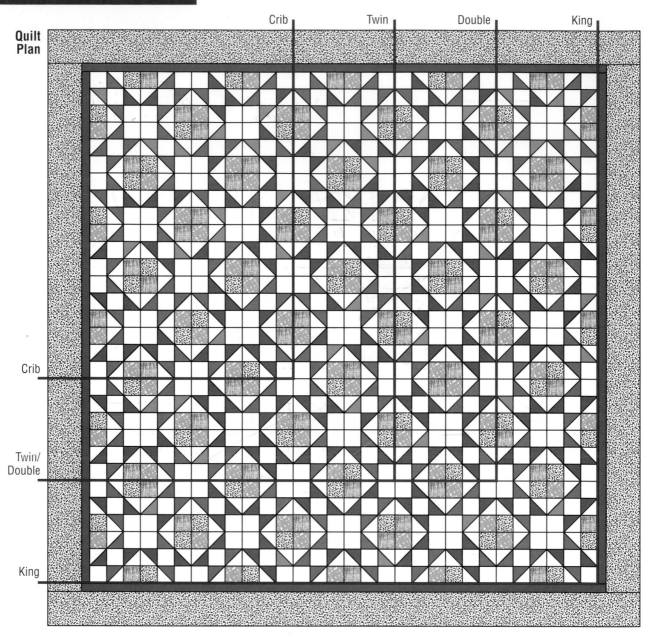

Color photo on page 104.

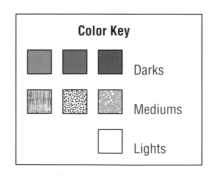

Color Key

Darks

Mediums

Lights

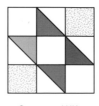

Contrary Wife
Finished size: 9"

GETTING STARTED

The traditional name of this simple block is Contrary Wife. But who could call such an exuberantly cheerful quilt by such a negative name?

Color Scheme: Red, blue, and green with yellow accents. Our sample includes a colorful decorator print, which serves as the theme fabric for all the colors used in the quilt. This print is used in some of the blocks and in the outer border to provide a lovely frame for the quilt.

Setting: Side by Side. Notice that the block is symmetrical from corner to corner rather than from side to side. Making four of the triangles in each block a dark value and rotating the blocks in opposite directions create a lovely secondary star pattern.

Quilt Vital Statistics

Measurements given are for finished sizes.

	Crib	Twin	Dbl/Qn	King
Quilt Size	51" x 69"	69" x 87"	87" x 87"	105" x 105"
Block Layout	4 x 6	6 x 8	8 x 8	10 x 10
Total No. of Blocks	24	48	64	100
Inner Border Width	$1\frac{1}{2}$"	$1\frac{1}{2}$"	$1\frac{1}{2}$"	$1\frac{1}{2}$"
Outer Border Width	6"	6"	6"	6"

Materials: 44"-wide fabric

Purchase the required yardage for the quilt size you are making. Fabric requirements are in yards and are based on 42" of usable fabric width after preshrinking.
Select fabrics in a variety of colors totaling the amounts given below.

	Crib	Twin	Dbl/Qn	King
Lights	$1\frac{1}{2}$	$2\frac{7}{8}$	4	6
Mediums	$\frac{5}{8}$	1	$1\frac{1}{3}$	2
Darks	$\frac{7}{8}$	$1\frac{1}{2}$	$2\frac{1}{8}$	$3\frac{1}{8}$
Inner Border	$\frac{1}{2}$	$\frac{5}{8}$	$\frac{5}{8}$	$\frac{3}{4}$
Outer Border	$1\frac{1}{4}$	$1\frac{5}{8}$	$1\frac{3}{4}$	$2\frac{1}{8}$
Binding	$\frac{5}{8}$	$\frac{2}{3}$	$\frac{3}{4}$	$\frac{7}{8}$
Backing	$3\frac{1}{4}$	$5\frac{1}{4}$	$7\frac{3}{4}$	$9\frac{1}{4}$
Piecing for Backing				

7 LESSON

Rotary-Cutting Chart

Cut all strips across the fabric width. Measurements include $\frac{1}{4}$"-wide seam allowances.

	Crib	Twin	Dbl/Qn	King
Lights for Half-Square Units				
12" x 42" pieces	2*	4*	5	7
Lights for Squares				
3½" x 42" strips	7	14	18	28
Crosscut into 3½" squares	72	144	192	300
Mediums for Squares				
3½" x 42" strips	5	9	12	19
Crosscut into 3½" squares	48	96	128	200
Darks for Half-Square Units				
12" x 42" pieces	2*	4*	5	7

*To get a greater variety of color in these smaller quilts, use 12" x 21" pieces to make the half-square units.

Block Assembly

1. Using the 12" x 42" light and dark pieces, follow the directions on pages 101–103 for "Mastering Half-Square Units." Cut and sew the required number of half-square units as shown in the chart below for the quilt size you are making.

   Cut the bias strips 3¼" wide.
   Cut the segments 3½" wide.
   Cut the squares 3½" x 3½".

	Crib	Twin	Dbl/Qn	King
No. of Half-Square Units	96	192	256	400

2. Assemble the half-square units and 3½" squares, following the piecing diagram. Place the light squares in a diagonal row, and the medium squares in the remaining opposite corners.

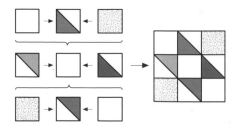

Piecing Tip

Arrange all the half-square units in a stack with the triangles pointing in the same direction. Place a light square on each half-square unit and arrange each pair in a stair-stepped stack. Chain-piece the light squares to the dark edges of the half-square units.

Pressing Tip

Press the seams of the outer rows away from the half-square unit, and the seams of the middle row toward the center square. This will allow you to aim for the X when sewing the rows together. (See page 34.)

Quilt Top Assembly and Finishing

1. Arrange the blocks, rotating them as necessary and referring to the quilt plan on page 108. Sew the blocks together into horizontal rows. Press the seams in opposite directions from row to row.

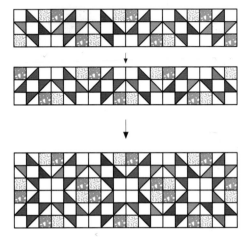

2. Sew the rows together, making sure to match the seams between the blocks.

3. Cut the required number of border strips as shown below. Join strips as necessary to make borders long enough for your quilt. Measure, cut, and sew borders to the sides first, then to the top and bottom edges of the quilt top, following directions on pages 23–24 for straight-cut borders.

4. Layer the quilt top with batting and backing; baste. Quilt as desired and bind the edges. Refer to the general directions for quilt finishing, beginning on page 238.

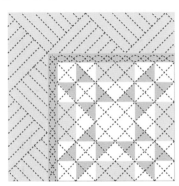

Quilting Suggestion

Border Cutting Chart					
		Crib	Twin	Dbl/Qn	King
	Strip Size	No. of Strips			
Inner Border	2" x 42"	6	8	9	11
Outer Border	6¼" x 42"	6	8	9	11

Template Cutting Chart					
Templates begin on page 254.					
	Templates	Crib	Twin	Dbl/Qn	King
Lights	S-4	72	144	192	300
	H-4	96	192	256	400
Mediums	S-4	48	96	128	200
Darks	H-4	96	192	256	400

Templates for Contrary Wife

Butterflies at the Crossroads

Quilt Plan

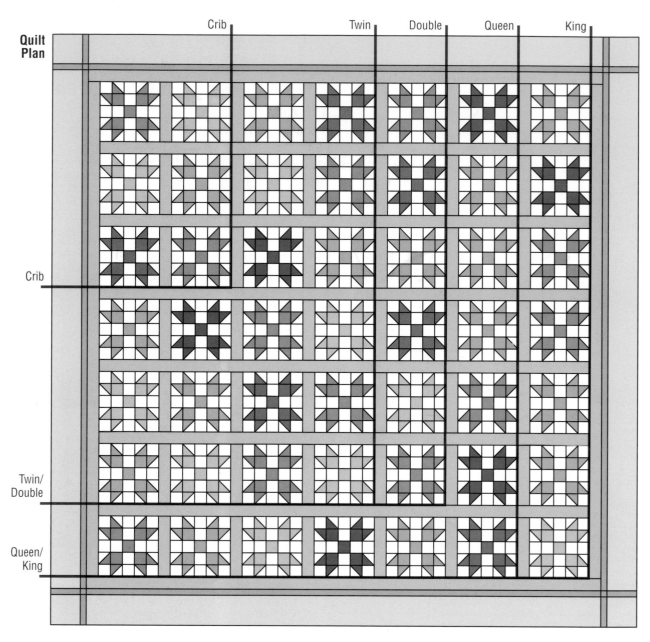

Crib Twin Double Queen King

Crib

Twin/
Double

Queen/
King

Color photo on page 105.

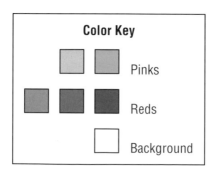

Color Key

Pinks

Reds

Background

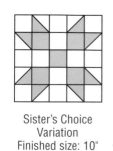

Sister's Choice
Variation
Finished size: 10"

GETTING STARTED

On the prairie, the colors of sky, trees, and grasses stretch across the vast landscape to the horizon. During the long winters, the gray sky fades into the white of the snow-covered countryside. The letters of the early women homesteaders describe what a joy it was to imagine butterflies, free and fragile, fluttering in the tall grasses, while they patched images of butterflies during the dreary winters. "Butterflies at the Crossroads" reaches out to us from a distant time, reminding us of the grace and beauty in simple pleasures.

Color Scheme: Pink and red. A variety of soft pinks and deep reds create this quilt's timeless beauty, reminding us that a carefully chosen monochromatic color scheme can be stunning. When choosing fabrics for this quilt, look for ones with soft, subtle color variations.

Setting: Simple Sashing. The simple sashing separates each block and adds to the enduring charm of this old-fashioned treasure. Since the sashing fabric plays such an important role in unifying the quilt, choose it carefully. Look for a medium color value that ties the colors in the blocks together but doesn't overpower them.

Quilt Vital Statistics

Measurements given are for finished sizes.

	Crib	Twin	Double	Queen	King
Finished Size	40¼" x 52½"	64¾" x 89¼"	77" x 89¼"	89¼" x 101½"	101½" x 101½"
Block Layout	2 x 3	4 x 6	5 x 6	6 x 7	7 x 7
Total No. of Blocks	6	24	30	42	49
Sashing Width	2¼"	2¼"	2¼"	2¼"	2¼"
Inner Border Width	2¼"	2¼"	2¼"	2¼"	2¼"
Middle Border Width	1¼"	1¼"	1¼"	1¼"	1¼"
Outer Border Width	5½"	5½"	5½"	5½"	5½"

7 LESSON

Materials: 44"-wide fabric

Purchase the required yardage for the size quilt you are making. Fabric requirements are in yards and are based on 42" of usable fabric width after preshrinking.

Each pink or red fat quarter will yield 3 blocks.

	Crib	Twin	Double	Queen	King
Background	¾	2½	3¼	4½	5¼
Assorted Pinks and Reds No. of fat quarters	2	8	10	14	18
Sashing & Inner Border	⅔	1⅝	2	2⅝	3
Middle Border	⅜	½	⅝	⅝	⅝
Outer Border	⅞	1⅜	1½	1⅔	1¾
Binding	½	⅔	¾	⅞	⅞
Backing	1¾	5⅜	5⅜	8	9
Piecing for Backing	▢	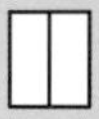 ▯▯	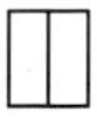 ▯▯	 ▤	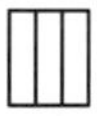 ▯▯▯

Rotary-Cutting Chart

Cut all strips across the fabric width. Measurements include ¼"-wide seam allowances.

	Crib	Twin	Double	Queen	King
Background for Half-Square Units					
9" x 21" pieces	2	8	10	14	17
Background for Squares					
2½" x 42" strips	3	12	15	21	25
Crosscut into 2½" squares	48	192	240	336	392
Background for Strip Units					
2½" x 21" strips	2	8	10	14	18
2½" x 10" strips	4	16	20	28	36
Assorted Pinks and Reds — From each fat quarter, cut:					
9" x 21" piece	1	1	1	1	1
2½" x 21" strips	2	2	2	2	2
2½" x 10" strips	1	1	1	1	1
Sashing Strips*					
2¾" x 42" strips	2	12	16	23	27
Crosscut into 2¾" x 10½" strips	3	18	24	35	42

*Use remainder of full-length strips for horizontal sashing strips.

Block Assembly

1. Use the 2½" x 21" and 2½" x 10" strips cut from the same pink or red fabric to make 3 ninepatch center units. Sew matching 2½" x 21" pink or red strips to opposite sides of a background strip as shown to make Strip Unit 1; cut 6 segments, each 2½" wide.

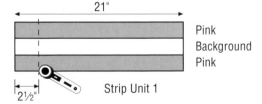

Strip Unit 1

2. Sew a 2½" x 10" strip of pink or red between 2 background strips as shown to make Strip Unit 2; cut 3 segments, each 2½" wide.

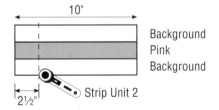

Background
Pink
Background

Strip Unit 2

3. Using segments that contain the same pink or red fabric, sew 2 segments from Strip Unit 1 to opposite sides of a segment from Strip Unit 2.

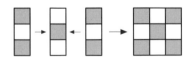

Repeat steps 1–3 with matching strips cut from each of the fat quarters to make the number of blocks required for the quilt size you are making.

4. Pair a 9" x 21" piece of pink or red with a 9" x 21" piece of background fabric and follow the directions on pages 101–103 for "Mastering Half-Square Units."

    Cut the bias strips $2\frac{1}{2}$" wide.
    Cut the segments $2\frac{1}{2}$" wide.
    Cut the squares $2\frac{1}{2}$" x $2\frac{1}{2}$".

You should be able to cut 24 half-square units from a pair of 9" x 21" pieces, enough for 3 blocks. You will need 8 matching half-square units for each block.

5. Following the piecing diagram, assemble the ninepatch centers, half-square units, and $2\frac{1}{2}$" background squares. Be sure to use units with matching pink or red fabrics for each block.

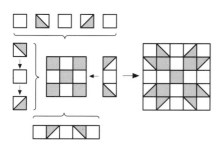

Quilt Top Assembly and Finishing

1. Arrange the blocks, with sashing strips between the blocks, as shown. Sew into horizontal rows. Press the seams toward the sashing strips. Measure the length of the rows.

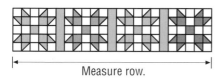

Measure row.

2. Piece remaining sashing strips together end to end to make one long continuous piece of sashing. Cut horizontal sashing strips to fit the length of the rows made in step 1. Sew the rows together, alternating rows of blocks and long horizontal sashing strips.

3. Cut the required number of border strips as shown in the chart on page 117. Join inner border strips as necessary to make borders long enough for your quilt. Measure, cut, and sew the inner border to the sides first, then to the top and bottom edges of the quilt top, following directions on pages 23–24 for straight-cut borders.

4. For middle and outer borders, measure the length and width of the quilt top through the center, including the inner border just added. Join strips for middle borders as necessary and cut borders to fit quilt-top measurements. Repeat with outer border strips.

5. Sew a middle border strip to a corresponding outer border strip.

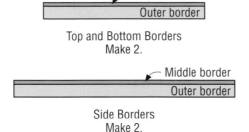

Top and Bottom Borders
Make 2.

Side Borders
Make 2.

6. Cut the following pieces from the middle border fabric:
   4 rectangles, each $1^3/_4$" x $5^3/_4$"
   4 rectangles, each $1^3/_4$" x 7"
   Cut 4 squares from the outer border fabric, each $5^3/_4$" x $5^3/_4$".

7. Assemble 4 corner squares as shown.

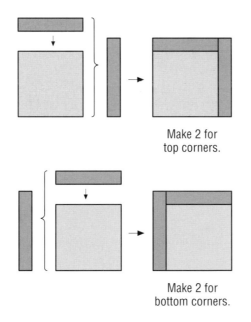

Make 2 for
top corners.

Make 2 for
bottom corners.

8. Sew the side borders to opposite sides of the quilt top. Sew the pieced corner squares to each end of the top and bottom borders. Be sure to orient the squares as shown. Sew the top and bottom borders to the top and bottom edges of the quilt top.

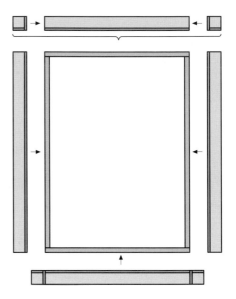

9. Layer the quilt top with batting and backing; baste. Quilt as desired and bind the edges. Refer to the general directions for quilt finishing, beginning on page 238.

Quilting Suggestion

Border Cutting Chart

	Strip Size	Crib	Twin	Double	Queen	King
		No. of Strips				
Inner Border	$2^3/_4" \times 42"$	4	7	7	9	9
Middle Border	$1^3/_4" \times 42"$	4	7	8	9	9
Outer Border	$5^3/_4" \times 42"$	4	7	8	9	10

Template Cutting Chart

Templates begin on page 254.

H-3

S-2

Templates for
Sister's Choice Variation

	Templates	Crib	Twin	Double	Queen	King
Background	S-2	72	288	360	504	588
	H-3	48	192	240	336	392
Pinks and Reds	S-2	30	120	150	210	245
	H-3	48	192	240	336	392

Christmas Bear Paw

Crib Twin Double/Queen King

Crib

Twin

Double/Queen

King

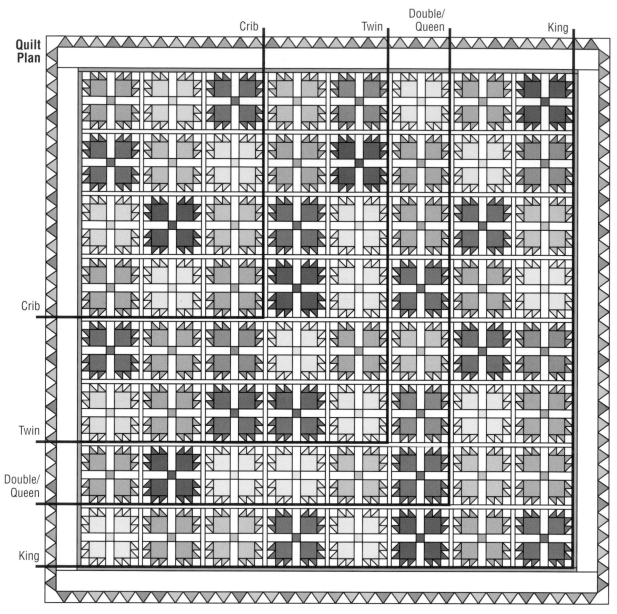

Color photo on page 106.

Color Key

Reds

Greens

White

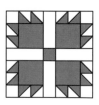

Bear Paw
Finished size: 10½"

GETTING STARTED

*A*nyone with a collection of reds and greens will enjoy using them in this festive holiday quilt. Then, what a treat it would be each year to bring out this lovely quilt for the holiday season.

Color Scheme: Complementary. Traditional Christmas reds and greens are placed on a crisp, clean, white background.

Setting: Simple Sashing. The simple sashing separates the Bear Paw points so they don't touch each other.

Quilt Vital Statistics

Measurements given are for finished sizes.

	Crib	Twin	Dbl/Qn	King
Quilt Size	46" x 58"	70" x 82"	82" x 94"	106" x 106"
Block Layout	3 x 4	5 x 6	6 x 7	8 x 8
Total No. of Blocks	12	30	42	64
Sashing Width	1"	1"	1"	1"
Inner Border Width	1"	1"	1"	1"
Middle Border Width	$3\frac{1}{4}$"/$3\frac{1}{2}$"*	$3\frac{1}{2}$"/$3\frac{3}{4}$"*	$3\frac{1}{2}$"/$4\frac{1}{4}$"*	$4\frac{1}{2}$"
Outer Pieced Border Width	2"	2"	2"	2"

*Widths of middle border vary to accommodate outer pieced border.

Materials: 44"-wide fabric

Purchase the required yardage for the quilt size you are making. Fabric requirements are in yards and are based on 42" of usable fabric width after preshrinking.
Each $\frac{1}{2}$ yard of holiday print will yield five blocks.
Smaller pieces can be used for a scrappier look.

	Crib	Twin	Dbl/Qn	King
White	2	$3\frac{1}{4}$	5	$6\frac{3}{4}$
Assorted Holiday Prints No. of $\frac{1}{2}$-yard pieces (18" x 42")	3	6	9	13
Inner Border	$\frac{3}{8}$	$\frac{1}{2}$	$\frac{1}{2}$	$\frac{5}{8}$
Middle Border*	$\frac{3}{4}$	1	$1\frac{1}{4}$	$1\frac{5}{8}$
Binding	$\frac{5}{8}$	$\frac{2}{3}$	$\frac{3}{4}$	$\frac{7}{8}$
Backing	3	$4\frac{3}{8}$	$5\frac{3}{4}$	$9\frac{3}{8}$
Piecing for Backing				

*In our quilt, the white fabric was also used for the middle border. If you wish to use the same fabric for the background and the middle border, combine the yardage and purchase one large piece.

Rotary-Cutting Chart

Cut all strips across the fabric width. Measurements include ¼"-wide seam allowances.

	Crib	Twin	Dbl/Qn	King
White for Half-Square Units				
18" x 21" pieces	3	6	9	13
White for Vertical Sashing Strips*				
1½" x 42" strips	2	4	5	7
Crosscut into 1½" x 11" strips	5	11	15	20
White for Horizontal Sashing Strips				
1½" x 42" strips	3	7	11	16
White for Rectangles				
5" x 42" strips	3	6	9	13
Crosscut into 2" x 5" rectangles	48	120	168	256
*If you have any 18" leftover strips, you can use them to cut the 1½" x 10½" segments.				
Asst. Holiday Prints — From each ½-yard piece, cut:				
18" x 21" piece	1	1	1	1
3½" squares for blocks	20	20	20	20
2" squares for blocks	5	5	5	5
Save remainder from each ½-yard piece for cutting border triangles.				

Block Assembly

1. Using the 18" x 21" background and holiday print pieces, follow the directions on pages 101–103 for "Mastering Half-Square Units."

   Cut the bias strips 2" wide.
   Cut the segments 2" wide.
   Cut the squares 2" x 2".

   You should be able to cut 80 half-square units from a pair of 18" x 21" pieces, enough for 5 blocks. You will need 16 matching half-square units for each block.

2. Using matching half-square units, 2" and 3½" squares, along with the background pieces, complete the blocks, following the piecing diagram. Press the seams toward the darks as you go.

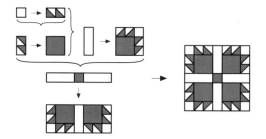

Quilt Top Assembly and Finishing

1. Arrange the blocks and vertical sashing strips between them as shown. Sew into horizontal rows. Press the seams toward the sashing strips.

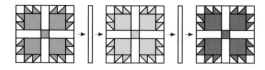

2. Join horizontal sashing strips as necessary to make strips long enough for your quilt. Sew rows of blocks, alternating with horizontal sashing strips, as shown. Press the seams toward the sashing strips.

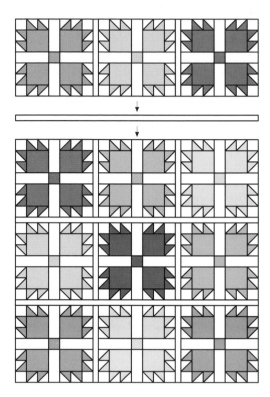

3. Cut the required number of inner border strips as shown in the chart below. Join the strips as necessary to make borders long enough for your quilt. Measure, cut, and sew borders to the sides first, then to the top and bottom edges of the quilt top, following directions on pages 23–24 for straight-cut borders.

4. Cut the required number of middle border strips as shown in the chart below. Notice that the width of the side borders are different from the top and bottom borders for the crib, twin, and double/queen size. This is another example of coping with a unique situation. See "Coping with Borders" on page 143. For this quilt we did not add another border to reach a desired dimension; we merely increased or decreased the width of the middle border. We did this to make the pieced outer border fit the quilt. The differences in the dimensions of the border are not large enough to be very noticeable in the finished quilt.

Straight-Cut Border Cutting Chart

	Strip Size	Crib	Twin	Dbl/Qn	King
		No. of Strips			
Inner Border	1½" x 42"	4	7	8	10
Middle Border					
Crib					
Sides	3¾" x 42"	2	—	—	
Top/Bottom	4" x 42"	3	—	—	—
Twin					
Sides	4" x 42"	—	4	—	—
Top/Bottom	4¼" x 42½"	—	4	—	—
Dbl/Qn					
Sides	4" x 42"	—	—	4	—
Top/Bottom	4¾" x 42"	—	—	5	—
King					
Sides/Top/Bottom	5" x 42"	—	—	—	10

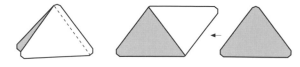

5. Label the middle border strips and keep the sides separate from the top and bottom strips so that you can sew them onto the appropriate sides of the quilt. Join the strips of the same width together as necessary to make borders long enough for the sides or top and bottom. Measure, cut, and sew borders to the sides first, then to the top and bottom edges of the quilt.

6. Cut triangles from white and assorted holiday print fabrics as indicated in the border cutting chart below.

7. Sew the triangles together as shown, alternating white and holiday print triangles and beginning and ending each border strip with a holiday print triangle. Refer to the border piecing chart below for the number of triangles needed for each border for the quilt size you are making.

Border Tip

It can be difficult to get pieced borders to come out evenly with the same number of units on opposite sides of the quilt. Add to this the bias seams used in the triangles, and the size can vary even more. To adjust the size of the pieced border to match the quilt, either take in or let out a few seams just slightly until it fits.

Pieced Outer Border Cutting Chart

	Templates	Crib	Twin	Dbl/Qn	King
Side Borders					
White	M-2	34	50	58	66
Assorted Holiday Prints	M-2	36	52	60	68
Top and Bottom Borders					
White	M-2	26	42	50	66
Assorted Holiday Prints	M-2	28	44	52	68
Corner Triangles					
White	M-3	4	4	4	4

Pieced Outer Border Piecing Chart

	Crib	Twin	Dbl/Qn	King
	No. of Pieces in each Border			
Side Borders				
White	17	25	29	33
Holiday Prints	18	26	30	34
Top and Bottom Borders				
White	13	21	25	33
Holiday Prints	14	22	26	34

8. Sew the pieced borders to the quilt top, adding the corner triangles last.

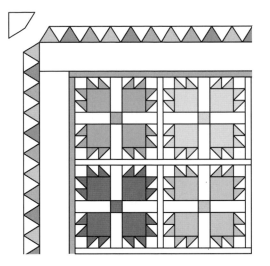

Quilting Suggestion

9. Layer the quilt top with batting and backing; baste. Quilt as desired and bind the edges. Refer to the general directions for quilt finishing, beginning on page 238.

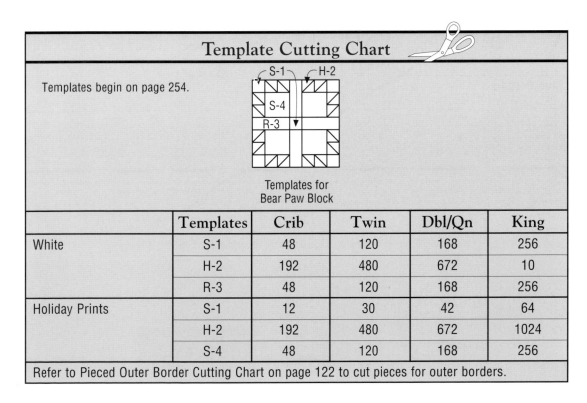

Template Cutting Chart

Templates begin on page 254.

Templates for
Bear Paw Block

	Templates	Crib	Twin	Dbl/Qn	King
White	S-1	48	120	168	256
	H-2	192	480	672	10
	R-3	48	120	168	256
Holiday Prints	S-1	12	30	42	64
	H-2	192	480	672	1024
	S-4	48	120	168	256

Refer to Pieced Outer Border Cutting Chart on page 122 to cut pieces for outer borders.

Quilt Plan

Crib   Twin   Double   Queen   King

Crib

Twin/ Double

Queen

King

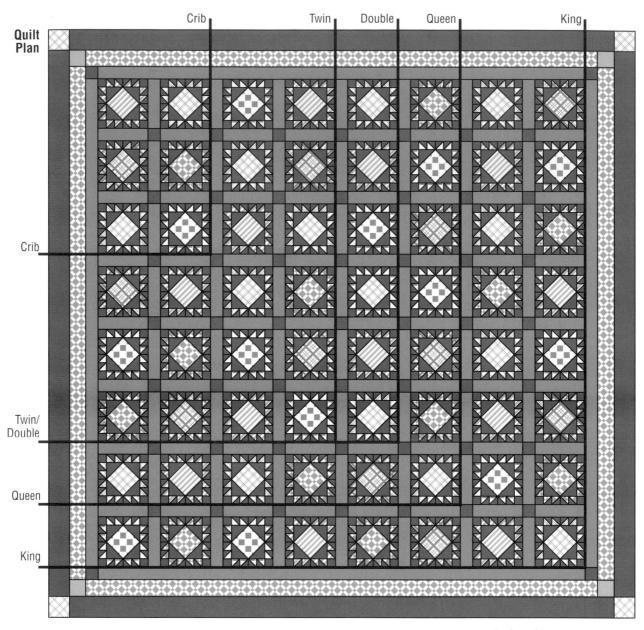

Color photo on page 107.

Color Key

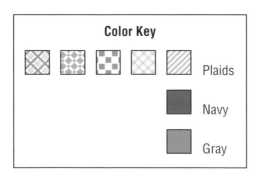

Plaids

Navy

Gray

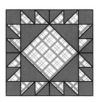

King's Crown
Finished size: 9"

GETTING STARTED

Quilts have always been a source of comfort, providing a warmth far deeper than can be felt just from the fabric and batting. In the endearing story of Anne of Green Gables, after Anne Shirley arrived at Green Gables, Marilla took a while to warm to Anne's irrepressible ways. One night, she covered Anne in a heavy, old quilt. In our interpretation of Anne's quilt, we used plaids that are reminiscent of Marilla's old dresses and Matthew's worn shirts.

Color Scheme: Navy and muted plaids with gold and white accents. A navy background forms a dramatic stage for the assortment of muted plaids used in this vivid quilt. Notice how the splashes of gold and white add sparkle to the deep, rich palette.

Setting: Sashing and Cornerstones. The sashing and cornerstones separate and frame the blocks. While the cornerstones echo the background color, the sashings are a muted navy, maintaining the rich continuity of the quilt.

Quilt Vital Statistics

Measurements given are for finished sizes.

	Crib	Twin	Double	Queen	King
Quilt Size	38³/₄" x 50"	61¼" x 83³/₄"	72½" x 83³/₄"	83³/₄" x 95"	106¼" x 106¼"
Block Layout	2 x 3	4 x 6	5 x 6	6 x 7	8 x 8
Total No. of Blocks	6	24	30	42	64
Sashing Width	2¼"	2¼"	2¼"	2¼"	2¼"
Inner Border Width	2¼"	2¼"	2¼"	2¼"	2¼"
Middle Border Width	3"	3"	3"	3"	3"
Outer Border Width	4"	4"	4"	4"	4"

Note: The quilt in the photo on page 107 was made using a different plaid for each block. If you want every block to be different, you will need at least a 6" x 42" strip of each plaid. Since shops do not sell fabric in ¹/₆-yard increments, ¹/₄-yard lengths or fat quarters (18" x 22") will work, plus you will have scraps left over for other projects.

To take advantage of quick cutting and piecing techniques, directions are given below for making a quilt with fewer fabrics, using ¹/₃-yard pieces (12" x 42"). Be sure to look for 100% cotton plaids.

Materials: 44"-wide fabric

Purchase the required yardage for the quilt size you are making. Fabric requirements are in yards and are based on 42" of usable fabric width after preshrinking.

	Crib	Twin	Double	Queen	King
Navy	1¼	2½	3¼	4¼	6¼
Assorted Plaids Number of ¹/₃-yard pieces	2	5	6	9	13
Gray for Sashing*	³/₈	⁷/₈	1¼	1½	2¼
Gray for Inner Border*	³/₈	⁵/₈	²/₃	³/₄	1
Middle Border	⁵/₈	³/₄	³/₄	1	1¹/₈

Materials (cont.)					
	Crib	Twin	Double	Queen	King
Outer Border	$2/3$	1	$1^{1}/8$	$1^{1}/4$	$1^{3}/8$
Binding	$1/2$	$2/3$	$3/4$	$7/8$	1
Backing	$1^{5}/8$	$5^{1}/8$	$5^{1}/8$	$7^{1}/2$	$9^{3}/8$
Piecing for Backing	□	⊔	⊔	⊟	⊔⊔

*Combine the yardage requirements for the sashings and the inner border if you are using the same fabric. Then cut long border strips first from the lengthwise grain and sashing strips from remaining width of fabric.

Rotary-Cutting Chart

Cut all strips across the fabric width. Measurements include $1/4$"-wide seam allowances.

	Crib	Twin	Double	Queen	King
Plaids for Half-Square Units					
12" x 24" pieces	2	—	—	—	—
12" x 30" pieces	—	5	6	9	13
Plaid for Center Squares					
Cut $4^{3}/4$" strips from remaining 12"-wide pieces					
Crosscut into $4^{3}/4$" squares	6	24	30	42	64
Navy for Half-Square Units					
12" x 24" pieces	2	—	—	—	—
12" x 30" pieces	—	5	6	9	13
Navy for Background Squares					
Cut 2" strips from remaining 12"-wide pieces					
Crosscut into 2" squares	24	96	120	168	256
Navy for Background Triangles					
$3^{7}/8$" x 42" strips	2	5	6	9	13
Crosscut into $3^{7}/8$" squares	12	48	60	84	128
Navy for Cornerstones					
$2^{3}/4$" x 42" strips	—	1	2	2	4
Crosscut into $2^{3}/4$" squares	2*	15*	20	30*	49
*If necessary, cut additional squares from navy scraps.					
Gray for Sashing					
$9^{1}/2$" x 42" strips	1	3	4	5	8
Crosscut into $2^{3}/4$" x $9^{1}/2$" strips	7	38	49	71	112

Block Assembly

1. Using the 12" x 30" pieces of plaid and navy, (12" x 24" pieces for crib size), follow the directions on pages 101–103 for "Mastering Half-Square Units." Each pair of 12" x 30" fabrics should yield an ample amount of half-square units for 5 blocks Each pair of 12" x 24" pieces will yield enough for 3 blocks. You will need 16 matching half-square units for each block.

   Cut the bias strips 2" wide.
   Cut the segments 2" wide.
   Cut the squares 2" x 2".

2. Cut the $3^{7}/8$" background squares once diagonally. Assemble the half-square units, triangles, and squares as shown in the piecing diagram. Match the plaid in the center square and the plaid in the half-square units for each block.

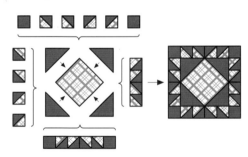

Sashings and Borders

1. Arrange the blocks with sashing strips between the blocks as shown. Sew together into horizontal rows. Press the seams toward the sashing strips.

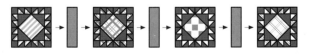

2. Sew sashing strips and cornerstones together in horizontal rows, beginning and ending each row with a sashing strip. Press the seams toward the sashing strips.

3. Sew the rows together, alternating rows of blocks and rows of sashing and cornerstones as shown in the quilt plan on page 124.

4. Cut the required number of corner squares and border strips as shown in the chart on page 128. Join strips as necessary to make borders long enough for your quilt. For each border, measure the width and length of the quilt through the center; cut border strips to those lengths. Sew the borders to the sides first. Add corner squares to each end of the top and bottom border strips and sew in place.

5. Layer the quilt top with batting and backing; baste. Quilt as desired and bind the edges. Refer to the general directions for quilt finishing, beginning on page 238.

Quilting Suggestion

Border Cutting Chart

	Crib	Twin	Double	Queen	King
Gray for Inner Border $2^{3}/_{4}$" x 42" strips	3	6	7	8	10
Navy for Corner Squares $2^{3}/_{4}$" x $2^{3}/_{4}$" squares (S-10)	4	4	4	4	4
Middle Border $3^{1}/_{2}$" x 42" strips	4	7	7	9	10
Plaid for Corner Squares (matching) $3^{1}/_{2}$" x $3^{1}/_{2}$" squares (S-4)	4	4	4	4	4
Outer Border $4^{1}/_{2}$" x 42" strips	4	7	8	9	10
Plaid for Corner Squares (matching) $4^{1}/_{2}$" x $4^{1}/_{2}$" squares (S-5)	4	4	4	4	4

Template Cutting Chart

Templates begin on page 254.

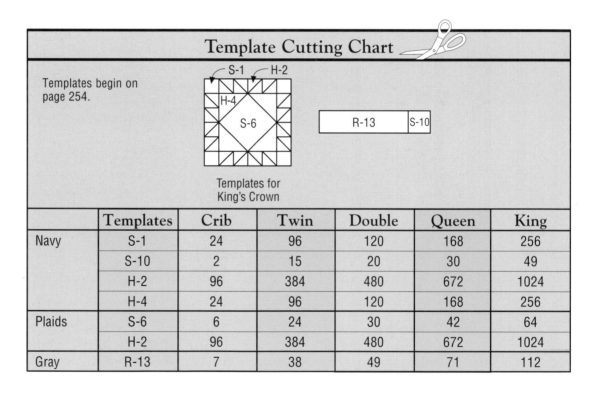

Templates for King's Crown

	Templates	Crib	Twin	Double	Queen	King
Navy	S-1	24	96	120	168	256
	S-10	2	15	20	30	49
	H-2	96	384	480	672	1024
	H-4	24	96	120	168	256
Plaids	S-6	6	24	30	42	64
	H-2	96	384	480	672	1024
Gray	R-13	7	38	49	71	112

Assembling Quarter-Square Units

In the previous lesson, you learned a quick way to make squares made up of two triangles called half-square units. What if you were to cut the completed square in half on the diagonal? With a single slice of your rotary cutter, you would create two triangles, each made up of two smaller triangles! The small petals of the Lily block in "Line Dancing Lilies" on page 137 are all made using this technique.

When you cut half-square units in half and reassemble the pieces, you create a wonderful design unit called a quarter-square unit. With these triangles, you can make intricate patterns accurately and easily. The star points in the "Garland Star" (page 155) and the "Starberry" (page 146) quilts are both constructed using quarter-square units sewn together to make a square.

By sewing the strip units and matching darks to darks and lights to lights, you can also create a soft illusion of transparency as shown in the inner border of the Exampler Quilt on pages 246 and 247.

To make quarter-square units, cut bias strips ⁷/₈" wider than the finished long side of the triangle.

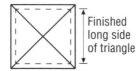

To allow for the seam allowance required to sew the quarter-square units together, the measurement for bias strips is larger than the one given for cutting bias strips in Lesson 7. Strips are cut narrower on larger units, but don't worry, we will tell you how wide to cut the strips for each quilt.

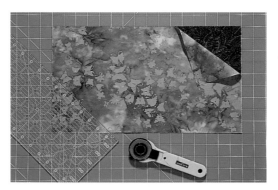

1. Layer contrasting fabrics with right sides facing up. Align the 45° angle of a 6" x 24" ruler with the bottom edge of the lower left corner. Cut along the right edge of the ruler.

2. Cut bias strips from the entire piece of fabric in the required width for the quilt you are making. Make cuts parallel to the first cut.

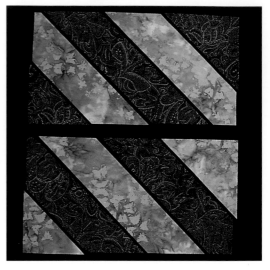

3. Arrange the strips into 2 units, alternating the colors in each unit.

4. Sew the strips with right sides together, offsetting the tops ¹/₄" and using an exact ¹/₄"-wide seam allowance. Do not create a unit that is more than 18"–20" wide. Make another unit if you have more strips rather than sewing one very large, wide unit. Press the seam allowances toward the darker color. Press gently from the back of the fabric and then on the front to be certain that the seams lie flat without pleats.

Cutting the Segments

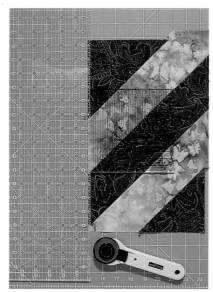

1. Place the diagonal line of the Bias Square ruler on one of the middle seam lines in the unit. Align the long cutting ruler with the edge of the Bias Square ruler, just covering the uneven ends of the strip unit. Trim the edge of the unit so that it is at a perfect 45° angle to the seam lines. As you trim the edge of the unit, you are actually cutting one side of many squares, so for this method to be accurate, you must trim the edge of the unit before cutting each segment.

Note: Only a few threads may need to be trimmed at one end while as much as $1/2$"–1" may need to be trimmed from the other end.

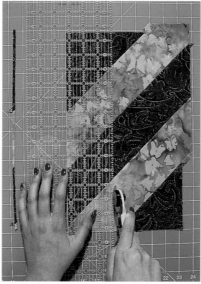

2. Cut a segment $7/8$" larger than the finished square. For example, if the finished long side of the triangle is $2^3/8$" (as in the "Line Dancing Lilies" quilt), add $7/8$" to that measurement and cut the segments $3^1/4$" wide. As you cut each segment, you are actually cutting the second side of many squares.

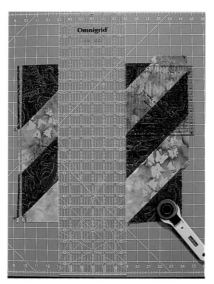

3. Trim the edge of the unit again so that it is at a 45° angle to the seam lines (see step 1 at left). Remember, this is the step that creates accurate squares.

4. Continue to trim the edges and cut segments until you have cut the entire unit. Remember to trim the edge before cutting each segment.

Cutting Half-Square Units

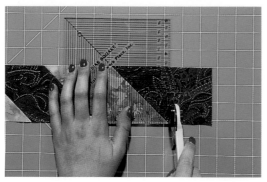

1. Position the edge of the Bias Square ruler on the edge of the segment, and the diagonal line of the ruler on the seam line. Cut on the right-hand side of the Bias Square ruler.

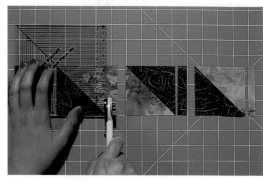

3. Turn the mat around to place all the right-hand cuts on the left. Reposition the edge of the Bias Square ruler on the edge of the fabric, with the diagonal line on the seam line, and trim the pieces to perfect squares.

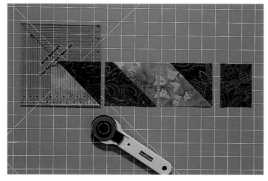

2. Continue cutting squares across the segment, positioning the Bias Square ruler on the edge of the segment with the diagonal line on the seam line before each cut. As you cut on the right side on each seam line, you are cutting the third side of the squares.

Cutting and Sewing Quarter-Square Units

1. Place your ruler diagonally on the square, perpendicular to the seam line, and cut the square in half. Notice that you have 2 triangles that are mirror images of each other. You must cut another square in half to get the required pieces to make a quarter-square unit.

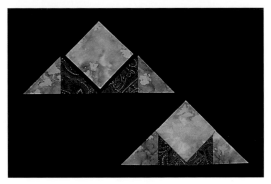

3. For the "Line Dancing Lilies" quilt, a square is sewn between the quarter-triangle segments to form the petals of the lilies.

Now, give yourself a pat on the back for being so incredibly clever!

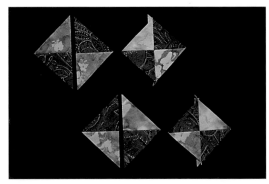

2. Take the identical quarter-triangle segment from each square; rotate one so that the diagonal cuts are facing each other and sew them together to make a quarter-square unit. Repeat with the other 2 segments to make a second quarter-square unit.

Line Dancing Lilies

By Mary Hickey, 1993, Seattle, Washington, 86" x 102⅝". The blocks for this quilt were inspired by Marsha McCloskey's Meadow Lily quilt and were generously made by friends at In The Beginning Quilts in 1986. Quilted by Susie Eerb. Directions begin on page 137.

Starberry

By Mary Hickey, 1993, Seattle, Washington, 94½" x 94½". Stars hovering over a strawberry field create a lovely image. Quilted by Mrs. Marion Yoder. Directions begin on page 146.

Garland Star

By Judy Pollard, 1990, Seattle, Washington, 81$\frac{1}{4}$" x 94". Quilts set with long strips of beautiful chintz fabrics were popular in the United States as well as in England in the mid-1800s. Judy took her inspiration from these old-time favorites. Quilted by an Amish quilter. Directions begin on page 155.

**Quilt
Plan**

Wall

Double

Color photo on page 134.

Lily Block
Finished size: 11⁷⁄₈"

*F*or as long as quilters have been stitching little patches together, they have loved making floral patterns. These prim and proper Lily blocks become vibrant when sewn in a group of four, and the addition of checkerboard borders makes them positively exuberant!

Color Scheme: Red, green, and white. Cranberry reds, cool greens, and pure white create a simple, complementary color combination that enhances the Lily blocks. Found in the bottom of an old trunk, a treasured bit of chintz with a viney twig design has a worthy place in this cheerful quilt. Choose a special stripe or border print for the first border in this quilt and key your other choices to it.

Setting: Medallion. A medallion setting enables you to turn a few special blocks into a respectably sized quilt and provides a focal point to showcase the blocks. Turning the central medallion on point adds interest and energy to the quilt. The large triangles surrounding the medallion can be made with a lively print to add color and interest or with a solid to emphasize a finely quilted design.

Note: We have provided charts for making the quilt in two sizes: the central medallion and its borders for the wall size, and the quilt shown in the color photo on page 134 for the double size. Since some of the pieces in the Lily block are unusual measurements, we have given strip-cutting instructions for only the quarter-square units (the tiny red and white triangles) and suggest that you use the templates for all other parts of the block (or measure the templates and then decide what size to make your strips). We have provided quick-cutting instructions for the other parts of the quilt.

Quilt Vital Statistics		
Measurements given are for finished sizes.		
	Wall	**Double**
Quilt Size	$37^{1}/_{2}$" x $37^{1}/_{2}$"	86" x $102^{5}/_{8}$"
No. of Lily Blocks	4	10
Inner Print Border Width*	$2^{1}/_{2}$"	$2^{1}/_{2}$"
Inner Green Border Width*	$1^{1}/_{4}$"	$1^{1}/_{4}$"
Inner Checkerboard Border Width	3"	3"
Inner Side Border Width	—	$5^{1}/_{2}$"
Outer Checkerboard Border Width	—	3"
Outer Green Border Width	—	5"
*See Coping with Borders on page 143.		

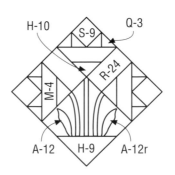

Materials: 44"-wide fabric

Purchase the required yardage for the quilt size you are making. Fabric requirements are in yards and are based on 42" of usable fabric width after preshrinking.
Purchase at least three different shades of greens totaling the amount given for stems, leaves, the triangles in the blocks, and the checkerboard borders.

	Wall	Double
Light Red	$3/8$	$1/2$
Dark Red	$3/8$	$1/2$
White	1	$3^1/2$
Chintz Print*	$1/2$	$1/2$
Solid Green*	$3/8$	$1^7/8$
Asst. Green Prints*	$3/4$	2
Light Green Print	—	$1^7/8$
Binding	$3/8$	$7/8$
Backing	$1^1/4$	$7^3/4$
Piecing for Backing		

*See Coping with Borders on page 143 before purchasing yardage.

Cutting Chart

Cut all strips across the fabric width. Measurements include $1/4$"-wide seam allowances.
Note: *Cut only the number of pieces indicated and use the scraps for cutting templates. Templates begin on page 254.*

Wall Quilt

From light red, cut:
1 piece, 9" x 18", for quarter-square units, **OR** cut 12 Template Q-3
6 Template M-4 for the flower

From dark red, cut:
1 piece, 9" x 18", for quarter-square units, **OR** cut 12 Template Q-3
6 Template M-4 for the flower

From white, cut:
2 pieces, each 9" x 18", for quarter square units, **OR** cut 24 Template Q-3
4 squares, each $7^5/8$" x $7^5/8$"
12 Template S-9
8 Template R-24
5 strips, each 2" x 42", for checkerboard border

From chintz print, cut:
4 strips, each 3" x 42", for inner border (See "Coping with Borders," page 143 before cutting borders.)

From solid green, cut:
4 strips, each $1^7/8$" x 42", for middle border (See "Coping with Borders," page 143 before cutting borders.)

From assorted green prints, cut a total of:
5 strips, each 2" x 42", for checkerboard border
12 Template H-10 for flower base
4 Template H-9 for corner of block
4 and 4r Template A-12 for leaves
12 bias strips, each $1^1/8$" x 8", for stems

Double Quilt

From light red, cut:
1 piece, 9" x 30", for quarter-square units, **OR** cut 30 Template Q-3
15 Template M-4 for the flower

From dark red, cut:
1 piece, 9" x 30", for quarter-square units, **OR** cut 30 Template Q-3
15 Template M-4 for the flower

From white, cut:
2 pieces, each 9" x 30", for quarter-square units, **OR** cut 60 Template Q-3
2 squares, each 28" x 28"; cut once diagonally to yield 4 half-square triangles
10 squares, each $7^5/8$" x $7^5/8$"
30 Template S-9
20 Template R-24
15 strips, each 2" x 42", for checker-board border

From chintz print, cut:
4 strips, each 3" x 42", for medallion inner border (See "Coping with Borders," page 143, before cutting borders.)

From solid green, cut:
4 strips, each $1^7/8$" x 42", for medallion middle border (See "Coping with Borders," page 143, before cutting borders.)
10 strips, each $5^1/4$" x 42", for outer border

From assorted green prints, cut a total of:
15 strips, each 2" x 42", for checker-board border
30 Template H-10 for flower base
10 Template H-9 for corner of block
10 and 10r Template A-12 for leaves
30 bias strips, each $1^1/8$" x 8", for stems

From light green print, cut:
2 squares, each $18^1/4$" x $18^1/4$"
4 squares, each $9^3/8$" x $9^3/8$"
2 strips, each $2^1/2$" x 18", for side coping strips
5 strips, each 6" x 42", for side borders

Cutting Tip
To make cutting a large square (such as 30") easier, fold the fabric in half and press a crease. Fold it in half again and press another crease. Lay your 15" square ruler on the folded fabric as shown and use your rotary cutter to cut off the raw edges on two sides. (Do not cut the folds.) If you do not have a 15" square ruler, use the lines on your cutting mat.

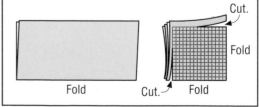

Block Assembly

1. Using the 9" x 18" pieces of white and red for the wall size, or the 9" x 30" pieces of white and red for the double size, follow directions on pages 130–33 for "Assembling Quarter-Square Units."

   Cut the bias strips 3¼" wide.
   Cut the segments 3¼" wide.
   Cut the squares 3¼" x 3¼".
   Cut the squares in half on the diagonal.

	Wall	Double
No. of Half-Square Units	12	30
No. of Quarter-Square Segments	24	60

Cut on the diagonal perpendicular to seam line.

Note: If you cut triangles using Template Q-3, sew a light red or dark red triangle to a white triangle as shown.

2. Use cut-off template C-2 on page 256 to cut one corner of each of the 7⅝" white squares as shown. See page 28 for using cut-off templates.

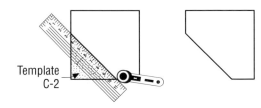

3. Prepare leaves, using one of the appliqué techniques shown on pages 71–75. Use 1⅛" x 8" green strips to make bias stems following directions on page 74. Arrange leaves and stems on the white cut-off square, following the placement guide on page 265. Machine baste in place and appliqué.

4. Assemble the Lily blocks, following the the piecing diagram.

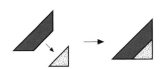

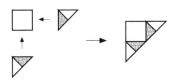

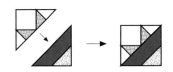

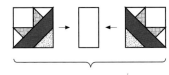

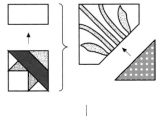

5. Sew 4 Lily blocks together, carefully matching the seams at the center.

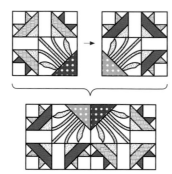

6. Before cutting the inner and middle border strips for the medallion see "Coping with Borders" on page 143. Depending on your particular coping needs, the width of the inner and middle borders may vary from those given in the cutting chart. Cut the required number of inner and middle border strips as shown in the cutting chart on pages 139–40, but cut the strips in the widths you need for your quilt if they differ from those given in the cutting chart.

7. Measure, cut, and sew borders to the center medallion, following directions on pages 24–25 for mitered borders.

8. To make the checkerboard border, sew the 2" strips of green and white in pairs as shown. Press the seams toward the green strip. Cut the strip unit into 2"-wide segments.

	Wall	Double
No. of Strip Units to Make	5	16
No. of Segments to Cut	92	310

9. Join 21 segments to make each of the side borders, and 25 segments for each of the top and bottom borders.

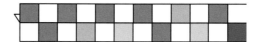

10. Sew the pieced borders to the sides first, then to the top and bottom edges of the quilt top.

11. If you are making the wall quilt, skip to step 9 on page 145. If you are making the double quilt, continue with "Set Pieces and Outer Borders" on pages 144–45.

Coping with Borders

Medallion quilts often require the use of additional borders, sometimes called coping strips, to get pieced borders to fit evenly around the edges. It is called a coping strip because it allows you to make the components of the quilt fit together perfectly. It copes with all the special needs of the other fabrics and various size pieces.

The center medallion of 4 Lily blocks should finish to $23^3/4$" x $23^3/4$", not including seam allowances. To make the checkerboard border come out evenly around the four sides, we need to enlarge the center by $7^3/4$" so that it finishes to $31^1/2$". That means we need to add something that finishes to $3^7/8$" on each side of the center. Follow along with us as we explain how we coped to make the center medallion large enough to fit the checkerboard border.

Because of the width of the design in the chintz print we selected we could only get a $2^1/2$"-wide finished border. That was not enough to reach the desired $31^1/2$".

We coped with the situation by adding another border all the way around that finishes to $1^3/8$" wide—our coping strips. With the addition of both borders ($2^1/2$" + $1^3/8$ "= $3^7/8$") on all four sides, our center square now finishes to $31^1/2$" x $31^1/2$" (not including seam allowances). Remember to add seam allowances when cutting strips; we cut 3"-wide strips from the chintz print for a $2^1/2$"-wide finished border, and $1^7/8$"-wide strips from the solid green fabric for the $1^3/8$"-wide coping strips.

Each situation will be different and will depend on your fabric. For example, if the fabric you selected for the inner chintz border has a design that is wide enough so that you can cut strips $4^3/8$" wide, you will not need to add an additional border to reach the $31^1/2$" desired size. A $4^3/8$"-wide cut strip will finish to $3^7/8$", which is exactly what you need on all sides of the center medallion.

31½"
Finished size
(not including seam allowances)

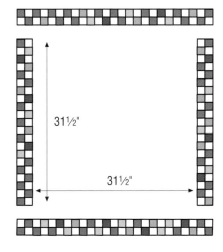

31½"

31½"

Set Pieces and
Outer Borders

1. Cut the white 28" squares once diagonally. Sew the long sides of the triangles to opposite sides of the center medallion first, then to the remaining two sides.

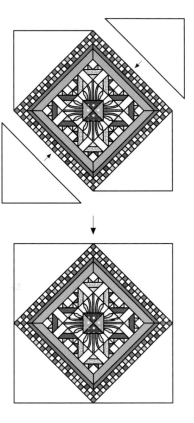

Piecing Tip
To sew a triangle to a square accurately, without stretching the bias edges, carefully fold the long side of the triangles in half and place a pin at the center. Fold each side of the medallion in half, place a pin at the center. Match the center of a triangle to the center of a side. Pin along the edges and stitch.

2. After adding the large triangles, trim the sides of the center medallion to ¼" from the point of the Lily blocks. Align one ruler with the edges of one of the corners. Place your 6" x 24" ruler adjacent to the first ruler, with the ¼"mark on the ruler on the point of the Lily block. Use your rotary cutter to trim the excess. Trim all four sides in this manner.

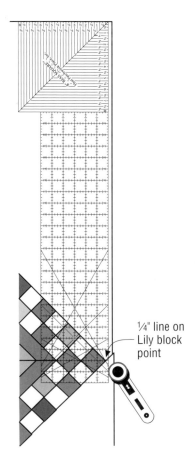

¼" line on Lily block point

3. Cut the light green 18¼" squares twice diagonally for side triangles, and the light green 9⅜" squares once diagonally for corner triangles. Sew the remaining Lily blocks and side and corner triangles as shown to make the top and bottom block units. If necessary, trim the sides to within ¼" from the point of the Lily blocks. See step 2 on page 144.

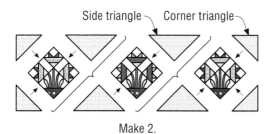

Make 2.

4. Add the 2½" x 18" coping strips to each end of the block units and trim excess.

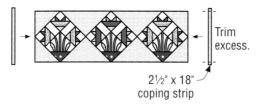

2½" x 18"
coping strip

5. Center the point of the middle Lily block with the point of the medallion; sew the block units to the top and bottom of the center section. Trim the sides of the block units if necessary so that they are even with the center section.

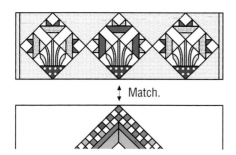

6. Cut the required number of light green border strips as shown in the cutting chart on page 140. Join strips as necessary to make borders long enough for your quilt. Measure, cut, and sew borders to the sides of the quilt top.

7. Sew the remaining two-patch segments together to make the checkerboard border. Join 58 segments for each of the side borders, and 47 for each of the top and bottom borders.

8. Sew the pieced borders to the sides first, then to the top and bottom edges.

9. Cut the required number of solid green outer border strips as shown in the cutting chart on page 140. Join strips as necessary to make borders long enough for your quilt. Measure, cut, and sew borders to the quilt top, following directions on pages 23–24 for straight-cut borders.

10. Layer the quilt top with batting and backing; baste. Quilt as desired and bind the edges. Refer to the general directions for quilt finishing, beginning on page 238.

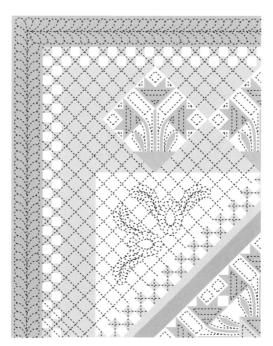

Quilting Suggestion

Starberry

Quilt Plan

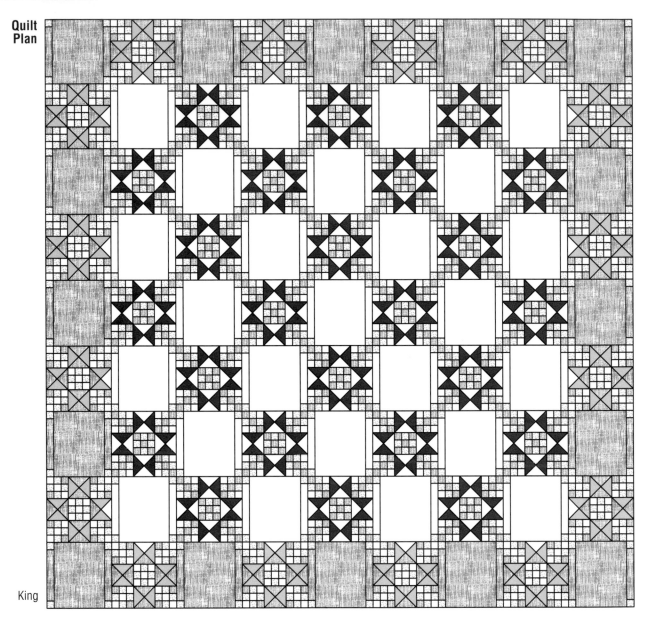

King

Color photo on page 135.

Color Key

- ☐ White Floral
- ☐ Pink
- ■ Rose
- ☐ Medium Blue
- ☐ Dark Blue

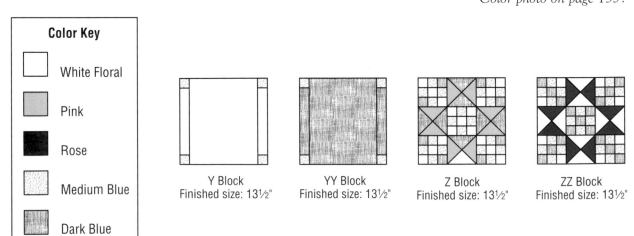

Y Block
Finished size: 13½"

YY Block
Finished size: 13½"

Z Block
Finished size: 13½"

ZZ Block
Finished size: 13½"

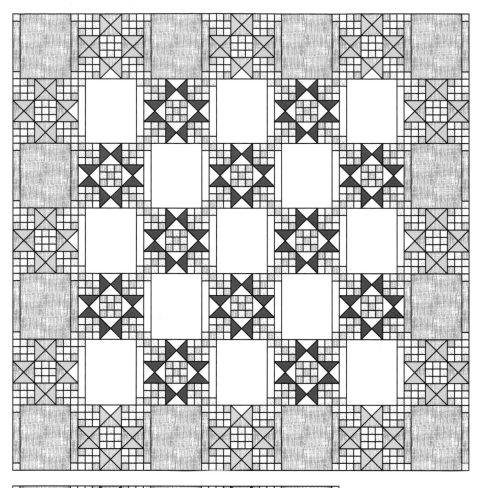

Double

Twin

A chain of blue squares links the stars in this grand quilt. The design is similar to the traditional Double Irish Chain quilt, but the addition of triangle stars gives the quilt added excitement and sparkle.

Color Scheme: Rose and blue. A romantic English floral background serves as the theme fabric. The center blocks borrow their rose stars and blue Ninepatch units from the English floral. In the border, the dark and light colors are reversed, creating an interesting positive-negative effect.

Setting: Alternating Pieced Blocks. In the alternating block setting, one elaborate block has Ninepatch units and stars while its simple partner has one small square in each corner. These small squares play a vital role in the pattern, pulling the chain across the surface of the quilt and linking the fancy blocks to each other. The generous size of the blocks make this design a good choice for a large quilt.

Quilt Vital Statistics

Measurements given are for finished sizes.

	Twin	Double	King
Quilt Size	67$\frac{1}{2}$" x 94$\frac{1}{2}$"	94$\frac{1}{2}$" x 94$\frac{1}{2}$"	121$\frac{1}{2}$" x 121$\frac{1}{2}$"
Block Layout	5 x 7	7 x 7	9 x 9
No. of Y Blocks	8	13	25
No. of YY Blocks	10	12	16
No. of Z Blocks	10	12	16
No. of ZZ Blocks	7	12	24

Materials: 44"-wide fabric

Purchase the required yardage for the quilt size you are making. Fabric requirements are in yards and are based on 42" of usable fabric width after preshrinking.

	Twin	Double	King
Pink	1$\frac{3}{8}$	1$\frac{3}{8}$	1$\frac{7}{8}$
Rose	$\frac{3}{4}$	1$\frac{3}{8}$	2$\frac{1}{2}$
White Floral	3$\frac{3}{8}$	5$\frac{1}{8}$	7$\frac{5}{8}$
Medium Blue	1$\frac{1}{2}$	2$\frac{1}{8}$	3$\frac{1}{8}$
Dark Blue	3$\frac{1}{2}$	4$\frac{1}{4}$	4$\frac{3}{4}$
Binding	$\frac{3}{4}$	$\frac{7}{8}$	1
Backing	5$\frac{3}{4}$	8$\frac{1}{2}$	10$\frac{3}{4}$
Piecing for Backing			

Rotary-Cutting Chart

Cut all strips across the fabric width. Measurements include ¼"-wide seam allowances.

	Twin	Double	King
Pink for Quarter-Square Units in Z Blocks			
21" x 21" squares	4	4	5
Rose for Quarter-Square Units in ZZ Blocks			
21" x 21" squares	2	4	7
White Floral for Quarter-Square Units in Z and ZZ Blocks			
21" x 21" squares	3	5	8
White Floral for Y Blocks			
11" x 42" strips	1	2	3
11" x 42" strips	3	5	9
Crosscut into 11" x 14" pieces	8	13	25
White Floral for Ninepatch Units			
2" x 42" strips	12	17	25
Medium Blue for Y and YY Blocks			
2" x 42" strips	4	6	9
Medium Blue for Ninepatch Units			
2" x 42" strips	18	27	43
Dark Blue for YY Blocks			
11" x 42" strips	1	2	2
11" x 42" strips	4	4	6
Crosscut into 11" x 14" pieces	10	12	16
Dark Blue for Ninepatch Units			
2" x 42" strips	11	17	28
Dark Blue for Quarter-Square Units for Z Blocks			
21" x 21" squares	3	3	4

Block Assembly

Y and YY Blocks

1. Sew the 2" medium blue strips to opposite sides of the 11" x 42" white floral strips; sew the 2" medium blue strips to opposite sides of the 11" x 42" dark blue strips. To make $\frac{1}{2}$ of a strip unit, cut the 2" x 42" strips in half to yield 2 strips, each 2" x 21", then sew 21" strips together to make the strip unit. Press the seams toward the 2" strips. Cut the strip units into 2"-wide segments.

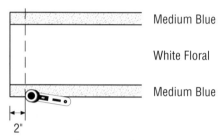

Medium Blue

White Floral

Medium Blue

2"

	Twin	Double	King
No. of Strip Units to Make	1	1½	2½
No. of Segments to Cut	16	26	50

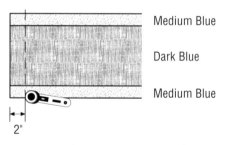

Medium Blue

Dark Blue

Medium Blue

2"

	Twin	Double	King
No. of Strip Units to Make	1	1½	2
No. of Segments to Cut	20	24	32

2. Sew the medium blue and white floral segments to both sides of the 11" x 14" white floral pieces, and the medium blue and dark blue segments to both sides of the 11" x 14" dark blue pieces.

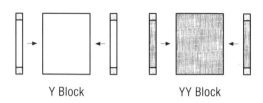

Y Block   YY Block

Z and ZZ Blocks

1. Using the 21" squares, follow the directions on pages 130-33 for "Assembling Quarter-Square Units."

   For the Z blocks, layer the pink and the dark blue squares and 1 pink square with a white floral square; one set of quarter-square units in the Z blocks has 1 white and 1 dark blue triangle in it, while the other sets have 2 dark blue triangles. For the ZZ blocks, layer the rose and the white floral squares.

   Cut the bias strips 5".
   Cut the segments $5\frac{3}{8}$" wide.
   Cut the squares $5\frac{3}{8}$" x $5\frac{3}{8}$".

No. of Squares to Cut

	Twin	Double	King
Pink/Dark Blue	35	42	56
Pink/White Floral	5	6	8
Rose/White Floral	28	48	96

Cut the squares in half on the diagonal and assemble quarter-square units as shown.

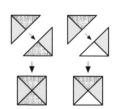

Quarter-Square Units   Quarter-Square Unit
for Z Block   for ZZ Block

2. Sew the 2"-wide strips together to make strip units for each type of Ninepatch unit as shown below and on page 152. Press the seams as indicated. Cut the strip units into 2"-wide segments and join the segments, following the piecing diagrams.

For Z Blocks — Center 2-color Ninepatch Units

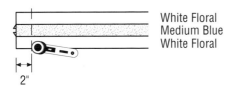

White Floral
Medium Blue
White Floral

	Crib	Double	King
No. of Strip Units to Make	1	1½	2
No. of Segments to Cut	20	24	32

For Z Blocks — Corner 3-color Ninepatch Unit

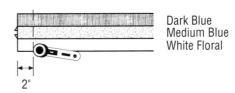

Dark Blue
Medium Blue
White Floral

	Crib	Double	King
No. of Strip Units to Make	4	5	6½
No. of Segments to Cut	80	96	128

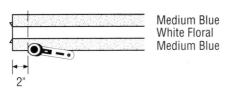

Medium Blue
White Floral
Medium Blue

	Crib	Double	King
No. of Strip Units to Make	½	1	1
No. of Segments to Cut	10	12	16

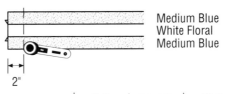

Medium Blue
White Floral
Medium Blue

	Crib	Double	King
No. of Strip Units to Make	2	2½	3½
No. of Segments to Cut	40	48	64

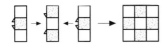

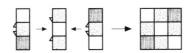

For ZZ Blocks — Center 2-color Ninepatch Units

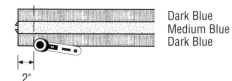

Dark Blue
Medium Blue
Dark Blue

2"

	Crib	Double	King
No. of Strip Units to Make	1	1½	2½
No. of Segments to Cut	14	24	48

For ZZ Blocks — Corner 3-color Ninepatch Units

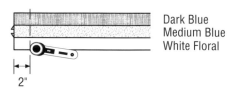

Dark Blue
Medium Blue
White Floral

2"

	Crib	Double	King
No. of Strip Units to Make	2½	5	10
No. of Segments to Cut	56	96	192

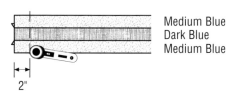

Medium Blue
Dark Blue
Medium Blue

2"

	Crib	Double	King
No. of Strip Units to Make	½	1	1½
No. of Segments to Cut	7	12	24

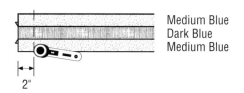

Medium Blue
Dark Blue
Medium Blue

2"

	Crib	Double	King
No. of Strip Units to Make	1½	2½	5
No. of Segments to Cut	28	48	96

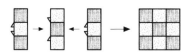

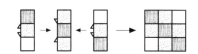

3. Assemble the quarter-square units, center and corner ninepatch units following the piecing diagram for each block. Pay careful attention to the orientation and coloration of the units as you arrange them.

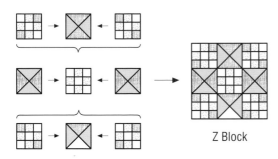

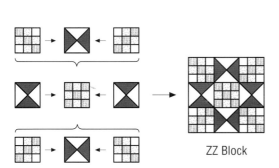

Z Block

ZZ Block

Quilt Top Assembly and Finishing

1. Arrange the blocks referring to the quilt plan on pages 146–47. Sew the blocks together into horizontal rows. Press the seams toward the Y and YY blocks. Sew the rows together, making sure to match the seams between the blocks.

2. Layer the quilt top with batting and backing; baste. Quilt as desired and bind the edges. Refer to the general directions for quilt finishing, beginning on page 238.

Quilting Suggestion

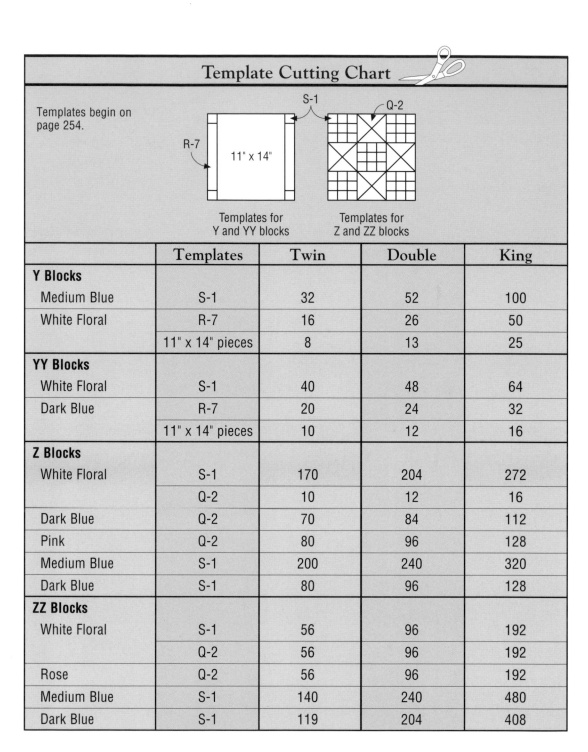

Template Cutting Chart

Templates begin on page 254.

Templates for Y and YY blocks

Templates for Z and ZZ blocks

	Templates	Twin	Double	King
Y Blocks				
Medium Blue	S-1	32	52	100
White Floral	R-7	16	26	50
	11" x 14" pieces	8	13	25
YY Blocks				
White Floral	S-1	40	48	64
Dark Blue	R-7	20	24	32
	11" x 14" pieces	10	12	16
Z Blocks				
White Floral	S-1	170	204	272
	Q-2	10	12	16
Dark Blue	Q-2	70	84	112
Pink	Q-2	80	96	128
Medium Blue	S-1	200	240	320
Dark Blue	S-1	80	96	128
ZZ Blocks				
White Floral	S-1	56	96	192
	Q-2	56	96	192
Rose	Q-2	56	96	192
Medium Blue	S-1	140	240	480
Dark Blue	S-1	119	204	408

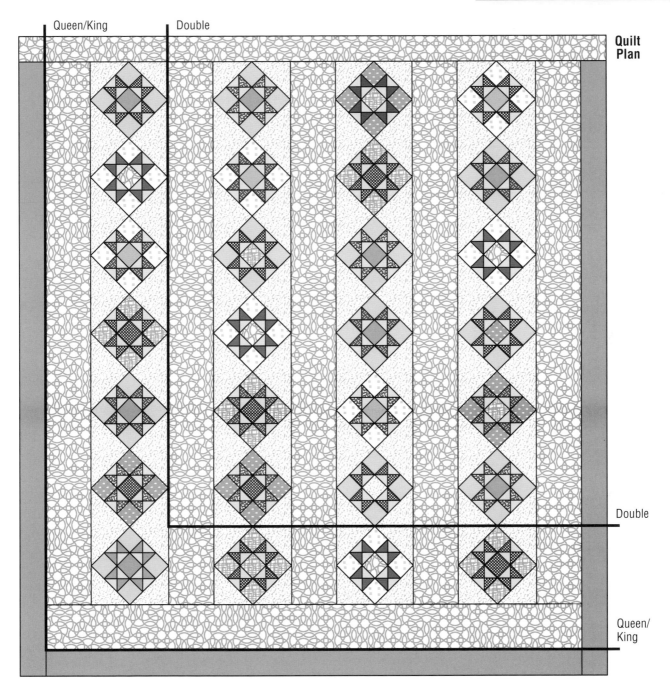

Queen/King   Double   **Quilt Plan**

Double

Queen/King

Color photo on page 136.

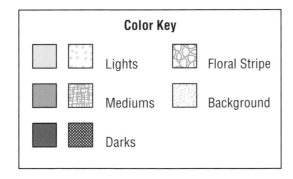

Color Key

Lights

Mediums

Darks

Floral Stripe

Background

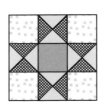

Variable Star Block
Finished size: 9"

Getting Started

Sometimes a fabric comes along that begs to be used in a quilt. The elegant striped floral decorator fabric used in this quilt is just such a fabric. Its rich color palette offers many color choices for the scrappy Variable Star blocks.

Color Scheme: Theme fabric with scrappy stars. The colors for the stars are drawn from the floral fabric used in this quilt. Choose one color that will dominate plus one or two secondary colors; the remainder of your color choices will be accents. As you choose the fabrics, keep this color ratio in mind.

Setting: Strippy. Scrappy star blocks are set diagonally with side and corner triangles, then wide vertical sashing is placed between the columns.

Quilt Vital Statistics

Measurements given are for finished sizes.

	Double	Qn/King
Quilt Size	$81^{1}/_{4}$" x 94"	$102^{1}/_{4}$" x $106^{3}/_{4}$"
Total No. of Blocks	18	28
Sashing/Inner Border Width	$8^{1}/_{2}$"	$8^{1}/_{2}$"
Outer Border Width	$4^{1}/_{2}$"	$4^{1}/_{2}$"

Materials: 44"-wide fabric

Purchase the required yardage for the quilt size you are making. Fabric requirements are in yards and are based on 42" of usable fabric width after preshrinking.
Select a variety of lights, mediums, and darks to total the amounts given below.

	Double	Qn/King
Assorted Lights	$1^{1}/_{2}$	2
Assorted Mediums	$1^{1}/_{2}$	2
Assorted Darks	$1^{1}/_{2}$	2
Light Print Background	$2^{1}/_{4}$	3
Floral Stripe*	$2^{3}/_{4}$–5	3–6
Binding	$^{3}/_{4}$	1
Backing	$5^{3}/_{4}$	$9^{1}/_{8}$
Piecing for Backing	▯▯	⊟

*Yardage for floral stripe includes sashing and the outer border fabric and is based on cutting along the lengthwise grain; amount will vary, depending on the number of stripes repeated across the width of the fabric.

Note: Lightweight decorator fabrics are often a good source of wonderful floral-stripe fabrics, and they are often 54"–60" wide. The floral-stripe fabric determined the width of the sashing/inner border used in our quilt. This measurement may vary, depending on your fabric. To help you figure your fabric requirements, count the number of floral stripes repeated across your fabric and determine how long the vertical sashings need to be for the quilt you are making. Add additional yardage if you want to add a horizontal stripe at the bottom of the quilt or cut the outer border from the floral stripes.

Rotary-Cutting Chart

Cut all strips across the fabric width unless otherwise instructed.
Measurements include ¼"-wide seam allowances.

	Double	Qn/King
Assorted Mediums for Background Squares		
3½" x 42" strips	7	11
Crosscut into 3½" squares	72*	112*
*You will need 4 matching background squares for each block.		
Assorted Mediums for Center Squares		
3½" x 42" strips	2	3
Crosscut into 3½" squares	18	28
Assorted Lights for Quarter-Square Units		
12" x 12" squares	9	14
Assorted Darks for Quarter-Square Units		
12" x 12" squares	9	14
Light Print Background for Corner and Side Triangles		
14" x 14" squares	8	12
7¼" x 7¼" squares	6	8

Block Assembly

Refer to the general directions for "Assembling Quarter-Square Units" on pages 130–33.

1. Pair the 12" light and dark squares. Cut the squares diagonally from corner to corner. Then cut bias strips 3⅞" wide as shown.

2. Sew the bias strips together, alternating lights and darks as shown to make pieced squares. Offset the ends of the strips ¼". (See page 130.)

Note: For more variety, make one square from a light and dark pair, then trade the remaining light or dark strips with strips from another pair. Remember, you need 4 half-square units for each block to make the quarter-square units.

3. Trim the edge of the pieced square as shown. Cut 1 segment, 3⅞" wide.

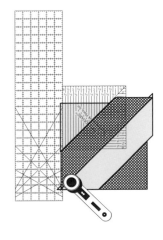 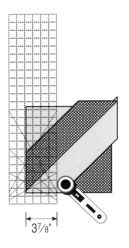

3⅞"

Garland Star

4. Turn the remaining portion of the pieced square 180°. Trim the uneven edge and cut another 3⅞"-wide segment.

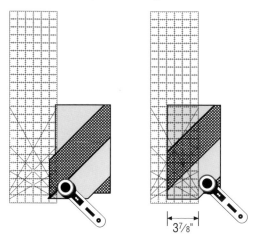

5. Cut 2 half-square units, 3⅞" x 3⅞" from each 3⅞"-wide segment. Cut the squares once diagonally to yield quarter-square segments.

6. Sew the quarter-square segments together as shown to make quarter-square units.

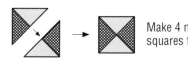

Make 4 matching squares for each block.

7. Assemble the quarter-square units, 3½" background squares, and center squares, following the piecing diagram, to make the Variable Star blocks.

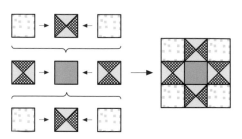

Quilt Top Assembly and Finishing

1. Cut the 14" squares twice diagonally for side triangles. Cut the 7¼" squares once diagonally for corner squares.
2. Arrange the blocks and side and corner triangles into vertical columns as shown. Sew the blocks and triangles into diagonal rows. Press the seams toward the triangles. Join the rows together to complete the columns.

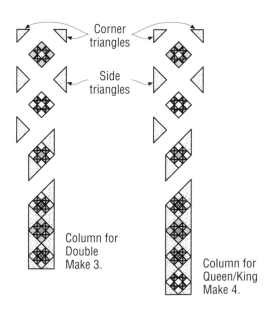

Corner triangles

Side triangles

Column for Double Make 3.

Column for Queen/King Make 4.

3. Measure the length of the columns and cut 4 vertical sashing strips to that measurement if you're making the Double quilt, or 5 vertical sashing strips if you're making the Queen/King. Cut them from the lengthwise grain of the fabric as wide as the stripe in your fabric, adding $^1/_2$" for seam allowances. Sew the vertical columns and sashing strips as shown. Measure the width of the quilt through the center to determine the length of the strip required for the bottom sashing strip. Cut a strip the same width as the vertical sashing strips to this length and sew to the bottom of the quilt top.

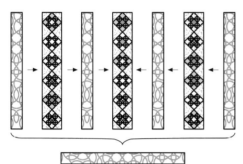

4. The finished width of the outer border in our quilt is $4^1/_2$" (cut width is $4^3/_4$"). If the stripe of the fabric you used for your sashing is narrower or wider than the $8^1/_2$" stripe we used, you may want to change the width of the outer border to have your quilt finish to a specific size.

Refer to the directions on pages 23–24 for straight-cut borders. Cut outer border strips from the lengthwise grain of the fabric in the desired width for your quilt. Measure, cut, and sew outer borders to the bottom first, then to the sides, and finally to the top edge. In our quilt, the top outer border was cut from the same floral-stripe fabric used for the sashing strips.

5. Layer the quilt top with batting and backing; baste. Quilt as desired and bind the edges. Refer to the general directions for quilt finishing, beginning on page 238.

Quilting Suggestion

Template Cutting Chart

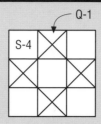

Templates begin on page 254.

Templates for
Variable Star Block

	Templates	Double	Qn/King
Asst. Mediums for Outer Squares	S-4	72	112
Asst. Mediums for Center Squares	S-4	18	28
Asst. Darks for Star Points	Q-1	144	224
Asst. Lights for Star-Point Background	Q-1	144	224
Refer to the Rotary-Cutting Chart on page 157 and step 1 on page 158 for cutting side and corner triangles.			

Conquering Half-Rectangle Units

Have you ever walked by a magnificent quilt in a show and said, "I love that quilt but those skinny triangles are impossible to match. Besides, if I can't be skinny, why should my triangles"? But take a closer look at those skinny triangles. A light one and a dark one sewn together make a rectangle. If you cut strips on a slightly different bias angle and sew them into strip units, you can cut rectangles from the strip units the same way you cut half-square units. We call this fantastic design element a "half-rectangle unit." While other quilters may think sewing skinny triangles is difficult, using our system should help you sew this fascinating shape easily and quickly.

By sewing the tip of the skinny triangle to the tip of a half square, you can create the illusions of curves and circles. If the skinny triangles meet simple patches, they add spectacular vibrancy and energy to the quilt.

The basic method is similar to the one for making half-square units. The only real differences are that you fold the fabrics in half before cutting the strips and you use a BiRangle ruler to establish the cutting angle. And, of course, you cut the segments into rectangles rather than squares.

If you have always avoided these skinny triangles, here is your chance to learn to make them. Be brave, get out your BiRangle, fold those fabrics, and slice up the strips.

Making half-rectangle units is a bit trickier than making half-square or quarter-square units. For the quilts in this section, half-rectangle units must be cut so that you end up with units that are mirror images of each other. To do this you fold the fabric in half before cutting the strips and keep the down-facing strips separate from the up-facing strips. The quilts in this section require different size pieces of fabric to make the half-rectangle units. We'll tell you what to cut for each quilt.

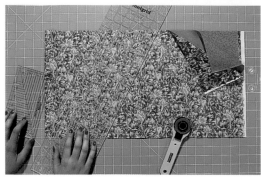

3. Hold the long ruler in place and slide the BiRangle out of the way.

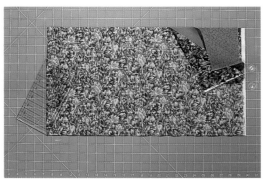

1. Layer the two fabrics together with right sides face up. Fold the fabrics in half and place the fold on the left. Place the BiRangle ruler with the diagonal line on the fold.

4. The first cut must be made so that it bisects the corner of the folded fabric. To do this easily, walk around to the other side of your table or turn your mat around so that you can cut along the right-hand side of the ruler.

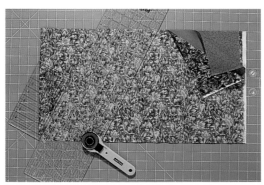

2. Align your long cutting ruler with the side of the BiRangle.

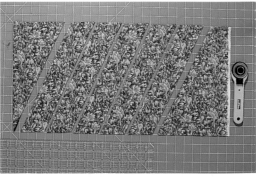

5. Walk back to the other side of the table and cut strips parallel to the first cut. All of the quilts in this book use a 2$\frac{1}{2}$" strip width.

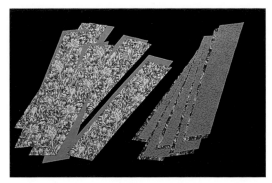

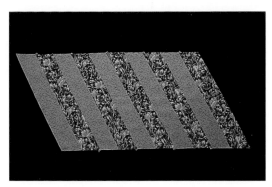

6. Sort the strips into two sets, the up-facing ones and the down-facing ones. The up-facing strips are sneaky and love to confuse you, so place them in the kitchen for now.

9. Sew the pairs of strips into a strip unit, again offsetting the tops $1/4$". Make strip units of 10 strips rather than one large wide unit with all the strips. Press the seams toward the darker color.

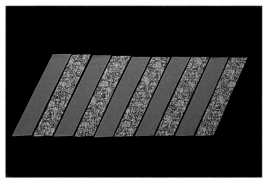

7. Arrange the down-facing strips, right side down, in a unit, alternating the colors.

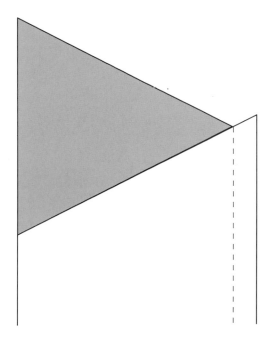

8. Sew the strips together in pairs, offsetting the tops of the strips $1/4$". Since a little time now will save you a great deal of fabric, fuss a little to offset the tops of the strips $1/4$". Use the illustration to the right like a little carpenter's jig. Lay one of the strips on the drawing and then place the other one on top. Be sure the edges of the fabrics are on the lines of the drawing.

Cutting the Segments

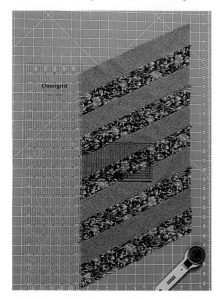 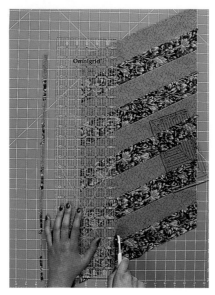 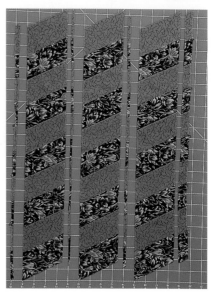

1. Place the diagonal line of the BiRangle ruler on one of the seam lines in the unit. Align the long cutting ruler with the edge of the BiRangle ruler, just covering the uneven ends of the strip unit. Trim the edge of the unit. Each time you trim the edge of the unit, you are actually cutting one side of many rectangles.

Note: Only a few threads will need to be trimmed at one end while as much as 1"—sometimes more—will have to be trimmed from the other end.

2. Cut a segment the unfinished size of the long side of the half-rectangle unit. For all the quilts in this book, cut segments $3\frac{1}{2}$" wide. As you cut the segment, you are actually cutting the second side of each rectangle.

3. Trim the edge of the unit again, referring to step 1 if necessary, and cut another segment. Continue to trim the edge of the unit and cut segments until you have cut the entire unit.

Now clear your mind and focus your eyes on the next step.

Cutting the Half-Rectangle Units

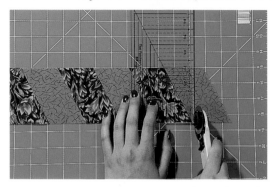

1. Place the bottom edge of the BiRangle ruler on the edge of the segment, and the diagonal line of the ruler on the seam line. Cut on the right-hand side of the BiRangle ruler.

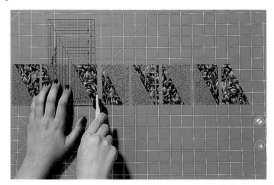

3. Turn your cutting mat around so that all your right-hand cuts are on the left. Reposition the diagonal line of the BiRangle ruler on the seam line and the edge of the BiRangle on the edge of the cut segment; trim. There is usually about $\frac{1}{4}$" of fabric to trim. As you trim, you are cutting the fourth and last side of each half-rectangle unit.

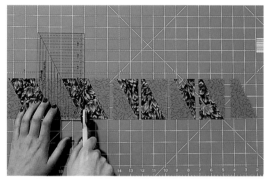

2. Move the BiRangle ruler to the next seam line. Cut on the right side of every seam line. Continue this process until you have cut the entire segment. As you cut, you are cutting the third side of each rectangle.

The quilts in this book require mirror-image half-rectangle units. The unit on the left was cut from the down-facing strips and the unit on the right was cut from the up-facing strips.

Now, go to the kitchen, have a cup of coffee, and get the other set of strips.

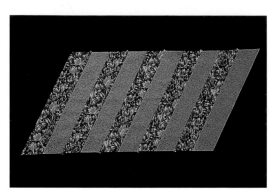

1. Sew the up-facing strips into a strip unit, offsetting them ¼" as shown on page 163. The angle of the strips will be facing in the opposite direction. Use the illustration below as the carpenter's jig for this set.

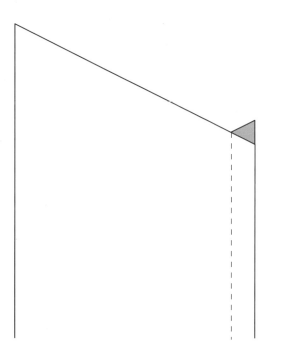

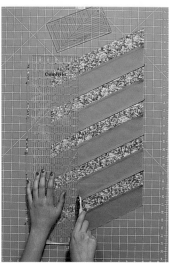

2. To cut the segments, place the strip unit *face down* on your cutting mat and follow directions for "Cutting the Segments" on page 164.

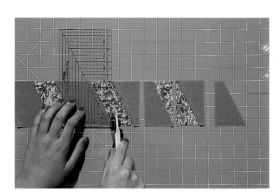

3. To cut the half-rectangle units, place segments *face down* and follow directions for "Cutting the Half-Rectangle Units" on page 165.

TIP TIP TIP TIP TIP TIP TIP

If you are left-handed, you may find it easier to follow the diagrams with the book turned upside down.

The Incredibly Cool Cosmic Rocket Ship

By Joan Hanson, 1993, Seattle, Washington, 67¹/₂" x 85". The universe beckons the child in all of us as we gaze through the windows at this delightful quilt. From the collection of Derek Hanson. Quilted by Laura Raber. Directions begin on page 169.

Women in the Men's Club

By Joan Hanson and Mary Hickey, 1993, Seattle, Washington, 70¹/₂" x 70¹/₂". Stars linking the fifty-four signatures of the women of the 103rd Congress honor their remarkable accomplishments and their ability to break through the gender barrier to serve our country. Quilted by Hazel Montague. Directions begin on page 177.

Jiggle and Jump

By Mary Hickey (with a little help from Joan), 1993, Seattle, Washington, 48" x 48". Color and energy bounce from block to block in this vibrant quilt. Quilted by Joan Hanson. Directions begin on page 184.

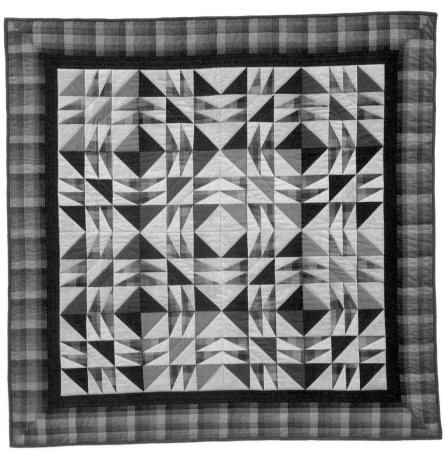

The Incredibly Cool Cosmic Rocket Ship

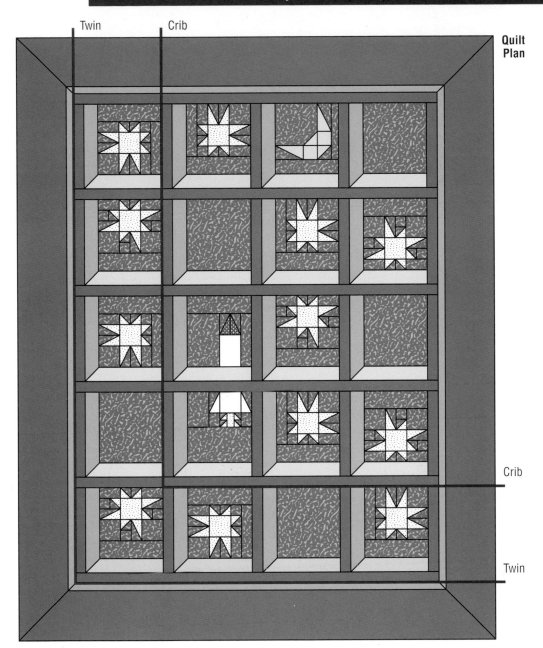

Twin   Crib

Quilt Plan

Crib

Twin

9 LESSON

Color photo on page 167.

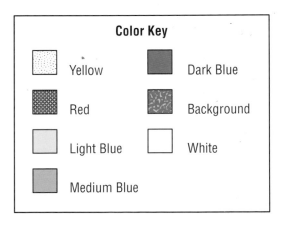

Color Key

Yellow		Dark Blue	
Red		Background	
Light Blue		White	
Medium Blue			

Moon Block
Finished size: 9" x 10"

Star Block
Finished size: 9" x 10"

Rocket Ship Block (top)
Finished size: 9" x 10"

Rocket Ship Block (bottom)
Finished size: 9" x 10"

GETTING STARTED

The child in each of us is the inspiration for this out-of-this-world quilt. When you gaze out through your window at the night sky, what do you see? I see the man in the moon looking at me! Any child would be delighted to sleep under this magical quilt and blast off into dreamland to explore the universe. This design is for an advanced beginner.

Color Scheme: Predominately blue with yellow, red, and white accents. The light to medium to dark blues in the window sections give the illusion of the moonlight streaming through the window.

Setting: Simple Sashing. Narrow dark blue sashing strips help create the illusion of a set of windows when combined with the lighter blue Attic Window strips.

Quilt Vital Statistics

Measurements given are for finished sizes.

	Crib	Twin
Quilt Size	47" x 63½"	67½" x 85"
Block Layout	3 x 4	4 x 5
No. of Star Blocks	7	12
No. of Plain Blocks	2	5
Rocket Block (Top)	1	1
Rocket Block (Bottom)	1	1
No. of Moon Blocks	1	1
Sashing Width	1½"	1½"
Inner Border Width	1"	1"
Outer Border Width	3"	7"

Materials: 44"-wide fabric

Purchase the required yardage for the quilt size you are making. Fabric requirements are in yards and are based on 42" of usable fabric width after preshrinking.

	Crib	Twin
Background	1½	2
Yellow for Stars	½	¾
Blue for Moon	Scraps	Scraps
Red for Rocket Ship	Scraps	Scraps
White for Rocket Ship	Scraps	Scraps
Light Blue for Window	½	⅞
Medium Blue For Window	½	1
Dark Blue for Sashing	1¼	1⅝
Red Inner Border	⅓	½
Blue Outer Border	¾	1⅞
Binding	⅝	¾
Backing	3⅛	5¼
Piecing for Backing	 ⊟	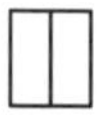 ⊞

Rotary-Cutting Chart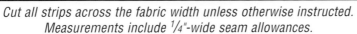

Cut all strips across the fabric width unless otherwise instructed.
Measurements include ¼"-wide seam allowances.

	Crib	Twin
Background for Half-Square Units		
9" x 18" piece	1	—
9" x 30" piece	—	1
Background for Plain Blocks		
9½" x 10½" rectangles	2	5
Background for Half-Rectangle Units		
4½" x 42" piece	1	—
9" x 42" piece	—	1
Background for Rocket Ship		
Template B-1	2 + 2r	2 + 2r
1⅞" x 1⅞" squares	2	2
2" x 2½" rectangles	2	2
Background for Moon		
Template B-2	1 + 1r	1 + 1r
2½" x 2½" square	1	1
6½" x 6½" square	1	1
Yellow for Half-Square Units		
9" x 18" piece	1	—
9" x 30" piece	—	1
Yellow for Half-Rectangle Units		
4½" x 42" piece	1	—
9" x 42" piece	—	1
Yellow for Star Centers		
3½" x 3½" squares	7	12
Yellow for Rocket Ship		
1⅞" x 1⅞" squares	2	2
Red for Rocket Ship		
Template B-1	1 + 1r	1 + 1r
White for Rocket Ship		
Template B-1	1 + 1r	1 + 1r
1½" x 2½" rectangle	1	1
3½" x 3½" square	1	1
3½" x 5" rectangle	1	1
Blue for Moon		
Template B-2	1 + 1r	1 + 1r
2½" x 2½" squares	4	4

Rotary-Cutting (cont.)	Crib	Twin
Light Blue for Bottom Window Frame		
$11\frac{1}{2}$" x 42" strips	1	2
Crosscut into $2\frac{1}{2}$" x $11\frac{1}{2}$" strips	12	20
Medium Blue for Side Window Frame		
$12\frac{1}{2}$" x 42" piecess	1	2
Crosscut into $2\frac{1}{2}$" x $12\frac{1}{2}$" strips	12	20
Dark Blue for Sashing		
Cut the following piecess from the lengthwise grain of the fabric:		
Horizontal Sashing		
2" x $39\frac{1}{2}$" strips	5	—
2" x 52" strips	—	6
Vertical Sashing		
2" x $12\frac{1}{2}$" strips	16	25

Block Assembly

Star Blocks

1. Using the 9" x 18" (or 9" x 30" for the twin size) pieces of yellow fabric and background fabric, follow the directions on pages 100–103 for "Mastering Half-Square Units."

   Cut the bias strips 2" wide.
   Cut the segments 2" wide.
   Cut the squares 2" x 2".

   Cut 28 squares for the Crib size and 52 squares for the Twin size.

2. Using the $4\frac{1}{2}$" x 42" pieces of yellow fabric and background fabric (9" x 42" for twin size), follow the directions on pages 162–66 for "Conquering Half-Rectangle Units."

   Cut the angled strips $2\frac{1}{2}$" wide.
   Cut the segments $3\frac{1}{2}$" wide.
   Cut the rectangles 2" x $3\frac{1}{2}$".

   Cut 10 left-angled rectangles and 10 right-angled rectangles for the Crib size, cut 17 left-angled rectangles and 17 right-angled rectangles for the Twin size.

3. Create each star individually, starting with a yellow center square. Lay out the half-square units and half-rectangle units to form short and long star points on 2, 3, or all 4 sides of the center square. The illustrations below are just two examples of how to arrange the star points. Refer to the color photo on page 167 for more options.

   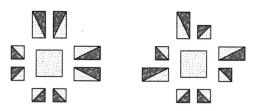

4. Add background pieces around the star to fill in the corners. Cut several pieces in the following sizes, and keep them handy as you work.

   $3\frac{1}{2}$" x $3\frac{1}{2}$" squares
   2" x $3\frac{1}{2}$" rectangles
   2" x 2" squares

Arrange the background pieces around the star points as shown, sew the units together in rows, then join the rows. Press the seams toward the darker fabric. You can make all stars the same or vary them from block to block.

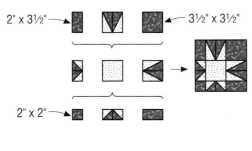

2" x 3½" →   ← 3½" x 3½"

2" x 2" →

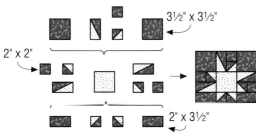

3½" x 3½"

2" x 2"

2" x 3½"

5. Cut and sew additional pieces of background to the block so that the block is 9½" x 10½" (including seam allowances). Add the background pieces to different sides of the blocks. Look at the Star blocks in the quilt plan on page 169 for some of the ways that background pieces were added to the stars.

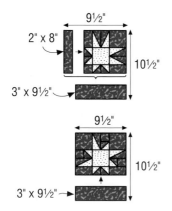

9½"

2" x 8"

10½"

3" x 9½"

9½"

10½"

3" x 9½"

Measurements include seam allowances.

TIP TIP TIP TIP TIP TIP TIP

Rocket Ship Blocks

1. With right sides together, align the diagonal edge of the skinny red triangles and skinny background triangles, matching the ends of the pieces as shown. Sew ¼" from the raw edges. Press the seams toward the background.

Trim the points even with the straight edges of the rectangle.

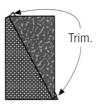

Trim.

2. Assemble the top of the rocket ship following the piecing diagram.

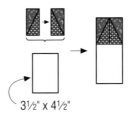

3½" x 4½"

3. Sew the skinny white triangles and skinny background triangles, following directions in step 1 above.

9 LESSON

The Incredibly Cool Cosmic Rocket Ship   173

4. Draw a diagonal line from corner to corner on the back of both of the 1⅞" yellow squares. Place a yellow square on top of a 1⅞" background square, right sides together. Sew ¼" away on each side of the drawn pencil line. Cut on the pencil line. Press the seams toward the background. This is a quick way to piece half-square units when you only need a few.

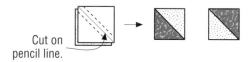

Cut on pencil line.

5. Assemble the bottom of the rocket ship following the piecing diagram.

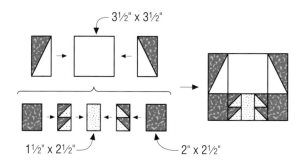

3½" x 3½"

1½" x 2½"　　　　2" x 2½"

6. Cut and sew background pieces as shown to complete the Rocket Ship blocks.

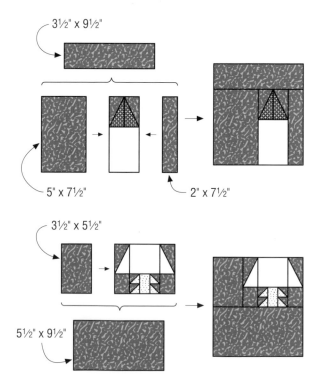

3½" x 9½"

5" x 7½"　　　2" x 7½"

3½" x 5½"

5½" x 9½"

Moon Block

1. Place a 2½" square of moon fabric on one corner of the 6½" square of background fabric, right sides together. Sew from corner to corner as shown. Trim the seam allowance to ¼" and press toward the triangle.

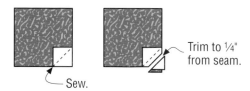

Trim to ¼" from seam.

Sew.

2. Place a 2½" square of moon fabric on top of a 2½" square of background fabric, right sides together. Sew from corner to corner as shown. Trim the seam allowance to ¼" and press toward the moon fabric.

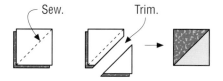

Sew.　　　Trim.

3. Sew the skinny moon triangles to the skinny background triangles as shown in step 1 on page 173.

4. Assemble the Moon block following the piecing diagram.

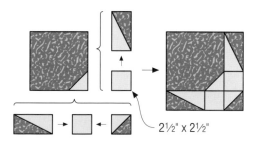

2½" x 2½"

5. Cut and sew background pieces as shown to complete the Moon block.

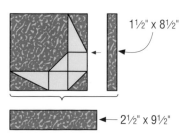

1½" x 8½"

2½" x 9½"

Attic Window Frames

1. Sew the 12½" medium blue strips to the left side, and the 11½" light blue strips to the bottom of all the pieced blocks as well as the plain blocks.

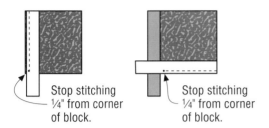

Stop stitching ¼" from corner of block.

Stop stitching ¼" from corner of block.

2. Miter the corner of the strips. (See pages 24–25 in the borders section for mitered-corner instructions.) Press seams toward the window frames.

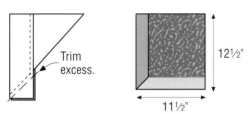

Trim excess.

12½"

11½"

Quilt Top Assembly and Finishing

1. Arrange the blocks into rows, with vertical sashing strips between the blocks as shown. Sew into horizontal rows. Press the seams toward the sashing strips.

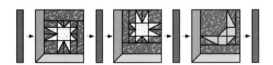

2. Sew rows together, adding horizontal sashing strips between the rows and at the top and bottom edges of the quilt. Press the seam allowances toward the sashing strips.

3. Cut the required number of border strips as indicated in the chart below. Join strips as necessary to make borders long enough for your quilt. Measure, cut, and sew borders to the quilt top, following directions on pages 24–25 for mitered borders.

4. Layer the quilt top with batting and backing; baste. Quilt as desired and bind the edges. Refer to the general directions for quilt finishing, beginning on page 238.

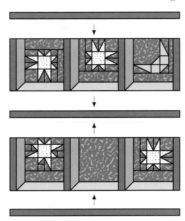

Quilting Suggestion

Border Cutting Chart			
		Crib	Twin
	Strip Size	No. of Strips	
Red Inner Border	1½" x 42"	5	7
Blue Outer Border	3¼" x 42"	6	–
	7¼" x 42"	–	8

Template Cutting Chart

Templates begin on page 254.

Templates for Star Block | Templates for Rocket Ship Block (top) | Templates for Rocket Ship Block (bottom) | Templates for Moon Block

	Templates	Crib	Twin
Star Blocks			
Yellow*	B-1	14 + 14r	24 + 24r
	H-2	28	48
	S-4	7	12
Background*	B-1	14 + 14r	24 + 24r
	H-2	28	48
	S-1	7	14
	S-4	7	12
	R-2	14	24
Rocket Ship Blocks			
Red	B-1	1 and 1r	1 and 1r
White	B-1	1 and 1r	1 and 1r
	S-4	1	1
	R-27	1	1
Yellow	H-1	4	4
	R-1	1	1
Background	B-1	2 + 2r	2 + 2r
	H-1	4	4
	R-16	2	2
	R-26	1	1
Moon Block			
Light Blue	B-2	1 + 1r	1 + 1r
	S-2	2	2
	H-3	2	2
Background	B-2	1 + 1r	1 + 1r
	S-8**	1	1
	H-3	1	1

*The number of pieces needed will vary depending on how you arrange the star points. See step 3 on page 172 for some examples.

**Use cut-off template C-3 on page 256 to remove one corner of S-8. Sew light blue piece H-3 to the cut-off corner of the square.

Refer to the Rotary-Cutting Chart on pages 171–72 to cut pieces for the plain blocks, window frames, and sashing.

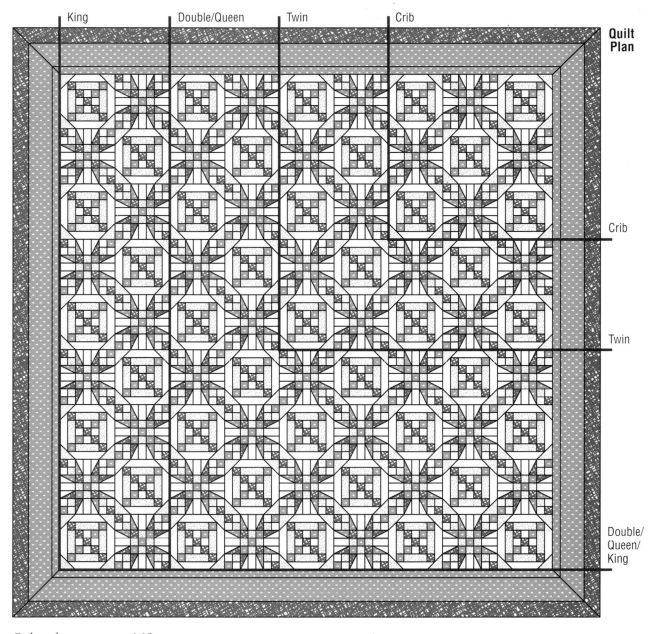

King   Double/Queen   Twin   Crib

Quilt Plan

Crib

Twin

Double/ Queen/ King

Color photo on page 168.

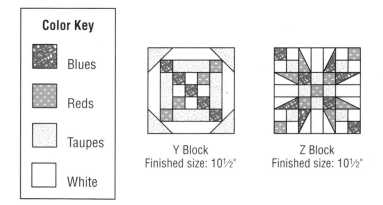

Color Key

■ Blues

■ Reds

□ Taupes

□ White

Y Block
Finished size: 10½"

Z Block
Finished size: 10½"

GETTING STARTED

Many generations of American women have made quilts to express their political views. During the First World War, quilts were made to raise funds for the Red Cross. People would make a contribution to sign their name on a red-and-white quilt. Women today are taking a more active role in our nation's politics. In the past several years, women have been elected to high offices in record numbers. To honor these women, we designed this quilt and asked the women of the 103rd Congress to sign patches for the quilt. In the tradition of the Red Cross quilts, we are donating this quilt so it can be used to raise funds for the Red Cross. **Color Scheme:** Red, white, and blue with taupe. Patriotic red, white, and blue make up the basic color scheme of this quilt with taupe added for softness. Notice how the ninepatch centers of the Y blocks use lighter blues and reds to reduce the competition between the two blocks. **Setting:** Alternating Pieced Blocks. These two blocks are based on a 49-patch grid. A secondary design emerges where the blocks intersect and blurs the boundaries of each block. Since there are four spaces in each Y block for signatures, this makes a wonderful friendship quilt.

Quilt Vital Statistics

Measurements given are for finished sizes.

	Crib	Twin	Dbl/Qn	King
Quilt Size	49$\frac{1}{2}$" x 49$\frac{1}{2}$"	70$\frac{1}{2}$" x 70$\frac{1}{2}$"	91$\frac{1}{2}$" x 112$\frac{1}{2}$"	112$\frac{1}{2}$" x 112$\frac{1}{2}$"
Block Layout	3 x 3	5 x 5	7 x 9	9 x 9
No. of Y Blocks	5	13	32	41
No. of Z Blocks	4	12	31	40
Inner Border Width	1$\frac{1}{2}$"	1$\frac{1}{2}$"	1$\frac{1}{2}$"	1$\frac{1}{2}$"
Middle Border Width	4$\frac{1}{2}$"	4$\frac{1}{2}$"	4$\frac{1}{2}$"	4$\frac{1}{2}$"
Outer Border Width	3"	3"	3"	3"

Materials: 44"-wide fabric

Purchase the required yardage for the quilt size you are making. Fabric requirements are in yards and are based on 42" of usable fabric width after preshrinking.

For a scrappy effect, purchase assorted reds, blues, and taupes totaling the amounts given below. One fabric of each color can also be used and may be easier for the smaller sizes.

	Crib	Twin	Dbl/Qn	King
White	1	2$\frac{1}{4}$	4$\frac{3}{4}$	6
Assorted Reds	$\frac{1}{2}$	1	1$\frac{3}{4}$	2$\frac{1}{4}$
Assorted Blues	$\frac{1}{2}$	1	1$\frac{3}{4}$	2$\frac{1}{4}$
Assorted Taupes	$\frac{3}{4}$	1$\frac{1}{2}$	2$\frac{7}{8}$	3$\frac{1}{2}$
Inner Border	$\frac{1}{2}$	$\frac{1}{2}$	$\frac{3}{4}$	$\frac{3}{4}$
Middle Border	$\frac{7}{8}$	1$\frac{1}{4}$	1$\frac{2}{3}$	1$\frac{3}{4}$
Outer Border	$\frac{2}{3}$	$\frac{7}{8}$	1$\frac{1}{4}$	1$\frac{1}{4}$
Binding	$\frac{1}{2}$	$\frac{3}{4}$	$\frac{7}{8}$	1
Backing	3$\frac{1}{8}$	4$\frac{1}{4}$	8$\frac{1}{8}$	10
Piecing for Backing				

Rotary-Cutting Chart

Cut all strips across the fabric width unless otherwise instructed.
Measurements include ¼"-wide seam allowances.

	Crib	Twin	Dbl/Qn	King
White for Y Blocks				
2" x 42" strips	6	13	30	38
Red for Y Blocks				
2" x 42" strips	1	3	7	9
Blue for Y Blocks				
2" x 42" strips	2	4	9	12
Taupe for Y Blocks				
5" x 42" strips	2	4	8	10
Crosscut into 2" x 5" rectangles	10	26	64	82
3⅞" x 42" strips	1	3	7	9
Crosscut into 3⅞" squares	10	26	64	82
White for Z Blocks				
3½" x 42" strips	1	3	7	8
Crosscut into 2" x 3½"	16	48	124	160
2" x 42" strips	2	6	14	16
4½" x 42" strips	2	—	—	—
12" x 42" pieces	—	2	4	6
Red for Z Blocks				
2" x 42" strips	2	4	9	10
4½" x 42" strips	1	—	—	—
12" x 42" pieces	—	1	2	3
Blue for Z Blocks				
2" x 42" strips	1	3	7	8
4½" x 42" strips	1	—	—	—
12" x 42" pieces	—	1	2	3
Taupe for Z Blocks				
2" x 42" strips	3	6	14	16

Block Assembly

Y Blocks

1. Sew 2"-wide strips of white, red, and blue together as shown to make 2 different strip units for the Ninepatch centers. To make ½ of a strip unit, cut the 2½" x 42" strips in half to yield 2 strips, each 2½" x 21", then sew 21" long strips together to make the strip unit. Press the seams away from the white strips. Cut the strip units into 2"-wide segments.

Red
White
Blue

	Crib	Twin	Dbl/Qn	King
No. of Strip Units to Make	½	1½	3½	4½
No. of Seg-ments to Cut	10	26	64	82

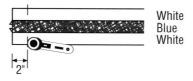

White
Blue
White

	Crib	Twin	Dbl/Qn	King
No. of Strip Units to Make	½	1	2	2½
No. of Seg-ments to Cut	5	13	32	41

2. Sew the segments together as shown to make the Ninepatch centers. Before you stitch, double check to make sure the blue squares are in a diagonal row.

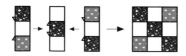

3. Sew a 2" red strip and a 2" blue strip to opposite sides of a 5" taupe strip as shown to make a strip unit for the side units. Press the seams toward the red and blue strips. Cut the strip units into 2"-wide segments.

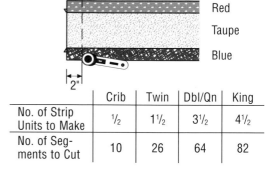

Red
Taupe
Blue

	Crib	Twin	Dbl/Qn	King
No. of Strip Units to Make	½	1½	3½	4½
No. of Seg-ments to Cut	10	26	64	82

4. Sew the 2" x 5" taupe rectangles to the top and bottom of the Ninepatch centers. Then add the 2"-wide segments from step 3 to opposite sides as shown. Notice that the red and blue squares in the side units are positioned in opposite diagonal corners so that the blue squares are in a diagonal row.

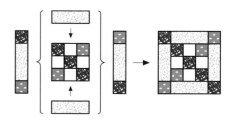

5. Use Template M-8 on page 261 to cut pieces from 2" white strips as shown. See page 28 for cutting shapes with templates. You should be able to cut 6 pieces from each 42" long strip. Sew a white piece to each side of the block.

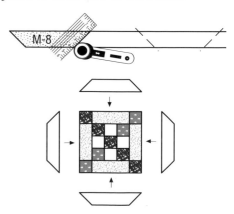

6. Cut the $3^7/8$" taupe squares once diagonally to yield half-square triangles. Sew a triangle to each corner to complete the Y blocks.

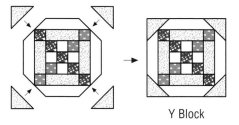

Y Block

Z Blocks

1. Sew 2"-wide strips of taupe, red, and blue together as shown to make 2 different strip units for the ninepatch centers. Press seams away from the taupe strips. Cut strip units into 2"-wide segments.

Red
Taupe
Blue

	Crib	Twin	Dbl/Qn	King
No. of Strip Units to Make	$1/2$	$1^1/2$	$3^1/2$	4
No. of Segments to Cut	8	24	62	80

Taupe
Red
Taupe

	Crib	Twin	Dbl/Qn	King
No. of Strip Units to Make	$1/2$	1	2	2
No. of Segments to Cut	4	12	31	40

2. Sew the segments together following the piecing diagram. In this block the red squares are in a diagonal row.

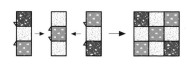

3. Sew 2"-wide strips of taupe, red, and blue together as shown to make 3 different strip units for the four-patch corner units. Press the seams toward the dark strips. Cut the strip units into 2"-wide segments.

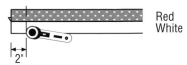

Red
White

	Crib	Twin	Dbl/Qn	King
No. of Strip Units to Make	$1/2$	$1^1/2$	$3^1/2$	4
No. of Segments to Cut	8	24	62	80

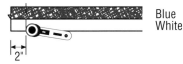

Blue
White

	Crib	Twin	Dbl/Qn	King
No. of Strip Units to Make	$1/2$	$1^1/2$	$3^1/2$	4
No. of Segments to Cut	8	24	62	80

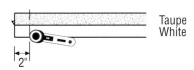

Taupe
White

	Crib	Twin	Dbl/Qn	King
No. of Strip Units to Make	1	$2^1/2$	$6^1/2$	8
No. of Segments to Cut	16	48	124	160

4. Sew the segments together, following the piecing diagram, to make Red/Taupe and Blue/Taupe four-patch units.

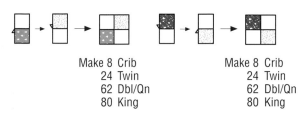

Make 8 Crib
24 Twin
62 Dbl/Qn
80 King

Make 8 Crib
24 Twin
62 Dbl/Qn
80 King

5. Using the $4^1/2$" x 42" pieces of red, blue, and white for the crib size (12" x 42" for other sizes), follow the directions on pages 162–66 for "Conquering Half-Rectangle Units." Pair the red and white fabrics to make red-and-white half-rectangle units, and pair the blue and white fabrics to make blue-and-white half-rectangle units.

Cut the angled strips $2^1/2$" wide.
Cut the segments $3^1/2$" wide.
Cut the rectangles 2" x $3^1/2$".

Cut	Red	Crib	Twin	Dbl/Qn	King
		8	24	62	80
	Blue	8	24	62	80

Cut	Red	Crib	Twin	Dbl/Qn	King
		8	24	62	80
	Blue	8	24	62	80

6. Arrange the Ninepatch centers, four-patch units, 2" x $3^1/2$" white rectangles, and half-rectangle units so that the blue squares and blue points are positioned diagonally in one direction and the red squares and red points are positioned diagonally in the opposite direction. Sew the units together, following the piecing diagram.

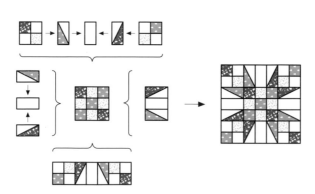

Quilt Top Assembly and Finishing

1. Arrange the blocks, referring to the quilt plan on page 177. Rotate the blocks so that the blue squares and blue star points are running diagonally from upper left to lower right, and the red squares and red star points from upper right to lower left. Sew the blocks into horizontal rows. Press the seams toward the Y blocks.

2. Cut the required number of border strips as shown in the chart on page 183. Join strips as necessary to make borders long enough for your quilt. Measure, cut, and sew borders to the quilt top, following directions on pages 24–25 for mitered borders.

3. Layer the quilt top with batting and backing; baste. Quilt as desired and bind the edges. Refer to the general directions for quilt finishing, beginning on page 238.

Quilting Suggestion

Border Cutting Chart

	Strip Size	Crib	Twin	Dbl/Qn	King
			No. of Strips		
Inner Border	2" x 42"	4	6	9	10
Middle Border	5" x 42"	5	7	10	11
Outer Border	3¼" x 42"	5	8	11	12

Template Cutting Chart

Templates begin on page 254.

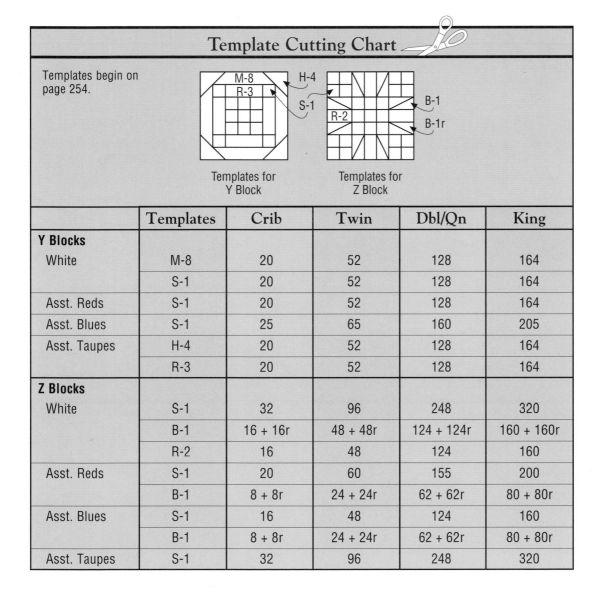

Templates for Y Block

Templates for Z Block

	Templates	Crib	Twin	Dbl/Qn	King
Y Blocks					
White	M-8	20	52	128	164
	S-1	20	52	128	164
Asst. Reds	S-1	20	52	128	164
Asst. Blues	S-1	25	65	160	205
Asst. Taupes	H-4	20	52	128	164
	R-3	20	52	128	164
Z Blocks					
White	S-1	32	96	248	320
	B-1	16 + 16r	48 + 48r	124 + 124r	160 + 160r
	R-2	16	48	124	160
Asst. Reds	S-1	20	60	155	200
	B-1	8 + 8r	24 + 24r	62 + 62r	80 + 80r
Asst. Blues	S-1	16	48	124	160
	B-1	8 + 8r	24 + 24r	62 + 62r	80 + 80r
Asst. Taupes	S-1	32	96	248	320

Jiggle and Jump

Quilt Plan

Crib   Twin   Double/Queen   King

Crib

Twin

Double/
Queen/
King

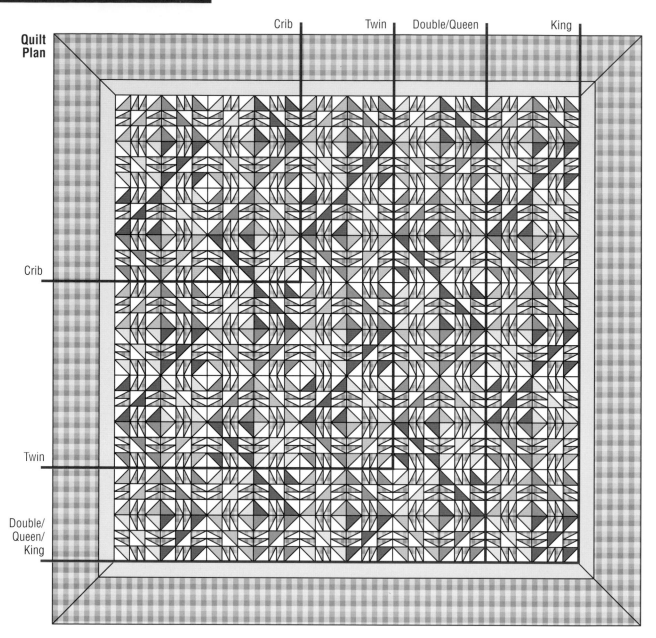

Color photo on page 168.

Color Key

☐	Magenta	◼	Teal
◼	Plum	▦	Plaid
◼	Turquoise	☐	Background

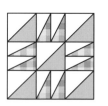

Give and Take Block
Finished size: 9"

GETTING STARTED

Color and energy leap from block to block in this intriguing design. Think of each block split in half along the diagonal. One side of the block has dark triangles on a light background, and the other half has light triangles on a dark background, creating an engaging positive/negative design. The tips of the triangles carry the pattern across the surface, bouncing colors first in one direction and then in another. Since the design moves across the block seam lines, much of the viewer's enjoyment of the quilt relies on perfectly matched points. Thus, the quilt provides a wonderful exercise in precision point sewing as well as a place to play with colors.

Color Scheme: Turquoise, teal, plum, and magenta with yellow and orange accents. A lovely Madras plaid sets the stage for the dramatic color combination. Soft aqua backgrounds and four strong shades of teal, turquoise, plum, and magenta energize the quilt. Bits of muted yellow and orange peeking through the plaid soften and warm the striking teals and magentas.

Setting: Side by Side. While the blocks are set side by side, rotating each block transforms the design, creating a dynamic secondary pattern. Try several different block arrangements before sewing your blocks together.

Quilt Vital Statistics

Measurements given are for finished sizes.

	Crib	Twin	Double	Queen	King
Quilt Size	48" x 48"	66" x 84"	84" x 102"	90" x 108"	114" x 114"
Block Layout	4 x 4	6 x 8	8 x 10	8 x 10	10 x 10
Total No. of Blocks	16	48	80	80	100
Inner Border Width	$1^1/_2$"	$1^1/_2$"	$1^1/_2$"	3"	3"
Outer Border Width	$4^1/_2$"	$4^1/_2$"	$4^1/_2$"	6"	9"

Materials: 44"-wide fabric

Purchase the required yardage for the quilt size you are making. Fabric requirements are in yards and are based on 42" of usable fabric width after preshrinking.

	Crib	Twin	Double	Queen	King
Plaid	$^7/_8$	$2^1/_4$	$3^1/_4$	$3^1/_4$	$4^1/_4$
Background	$1^7/_8$	$4^1/_4$	$6^1/_4$	$6^1/_4$	$8^1/_4$
Teal	$^3/_8$	$^3/_4$	1	1	$1^1/_4$
Turquoise	$^3/_8$	$^3/_4$	1	1	$1^1/_4$
Plum	$^3/_8$	$^3/_4$	1	1	$1^1/_4$
Magenta	$^3/_8$	$^3/_4$	1	1	$1^1/_4$
Inner Border	$^1/_3$	$^1/_2$	$^5/_8$	1	$1^1/_8$
Outer Border	$^7/_8$	$1^1/_4$	$1^1/_2$	$2^1/_8$	$3^1/_4$
Binding	$^1/_2$	$^2/_3$	$^7/_8$	$^7/_8$	1
Backing	$3^1/_8$	$5^1/_8$	$7^1/_2$	$8^1/_8$	$10^1/_8$
Piecing for Backing					

Rotary-Cutting Chart

Cut all strips across the fabric width. Measurements include ¹/₄"-wide seam allowances.

	Crib	Twin	Double	Queen	King
Plaid for Half-Rectangle Units 12" x 42" pieces	2	6	9	9	12
Background for Half-Rectangle Units 12" x 42" pieces	2	6	9	9	12
Background for Half-Square Units 9" x 42" pieces	4	8	12	12	16
Teal for Half-Square Units 9" x 42" pieces	1	2	3	3	4
Turquoise for Half-Square Units 9" x 42" pieces	1	2	3	3	4
Plum for Half-Square Units 9" x 42" pieces	1	2	3	3	4
Magenta for Half-Square Units 9" x 42" pieces	1	2	3	3	4

Block Assembly

1. Using the 9" x 42" pieces of each of the four colors—teal, turquoise, plum, and magenta—pair one of each color with a 9" x 42" background piece and follow the directions on pages 100–103 for "Mastering Half-Square Units."

   Cut the bias strips 3¹/₄" wide.
   Cut the segments 3¹/₂" wide.
   Cut the squares 3¹/₂" x 3¹/₂".

	Crib	Twin	Double	Queen	King
From each color you will need	20	60	100	100	125

	Crib	Twin	Double	Queen	King
Total No. of Squares to Cut	80	240	400	400	500

2. Using the 12" x 42" plaid pieces and the 12" x 42" background pieces, follow the directions on pages 162–66 for "Conquering Half-Rectangle Units."

   Cut the angled strips 2¹/₂" wide.
   Cut the segments 3¹/₂" wide.
   Cut the rectangles 2" x 3¹/₂".

Cut

	Crib	Twin	Double	Queen	King
	64	192	320	320	400

Cut

	Crib	Twin	Double	Queen	King
	64	192	320	320	400

3. Using matching half-square units and the plaid half-rectangle units, assemble the blocks following the piecing diagram. Carefully pin each point of matching. See "Sword Pins" on page 34.

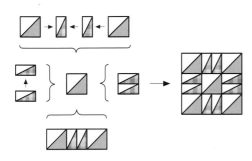

	Crib	Twin	Double	Queen	King
No. of Blocks in Each Color	4	12	20	20	25

Quilt Top Assembly and Finishing

1. Spend some time arranging and rearranging your blocks to see all the different designs that appear or refer to the quilt plan on page 184. Choose an arrangement that you enjoy.

2. Sew the blocks together into horizontal rows, carefully pinning each point of matching. Press the seams in opposite directions from row to row.

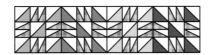

3. Sew the rows together, again carefully pinning each point of matching.

4. Cut the required number of border strips as shown in the chart on page 188. Join strips as necessary to make borders long enough for your quilt. Measure, cut, and sew borders to the quilt top, following directions on pages 24–25 for mitered borders.

5. Layer the quilt top with batting and backing; baste. Quilt as desired and bind the edges. Refer to the general directions for quilt finishing, beginning on page 238.

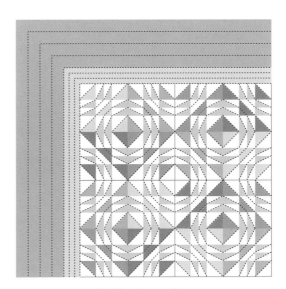

Quilting Suggestion

Border Cutting Chart

	Strip Size	Crib	Twin	Double	Queen	King
				No. of Strips		
Inner Border	2" x 42"	4	7	9	—	—
	$3\frac{1}{2}$" x 42"	—	—	—	9	10
Outer Border	$4\frac{3}{4}$" x 42"	5	8	10	—	—
	$6\frac{1}{4}$" x 42"	—	—	—	11	—
	$9\frac{1}{4}$" x 42"	—	—	—	—	12

Template Cutting Chart

Templates begin on page 254.

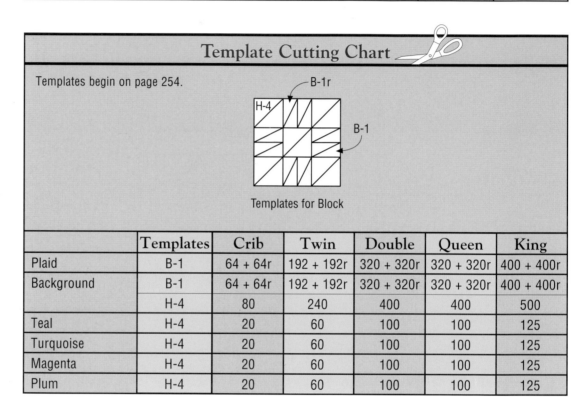

Templates for Block

	Templates	Crib	Twin	Double	Queen	King
Plaid	B-1	64 + 64r	192 + 192r	320 + 320r	320 + 320r	400 + 400r
Background	B-1	64 + 64r	192 + 192r	320 + 320r	320 + 320r	400 + 400r
	H-4	80	240	400	400	500
Teal	H-4	20	60	100	100	125
Turquoise	H-4	20	60	100	100	125
Magenta	H-4	20	60	100	100	125
Plum	H-4	20	60	100	100	125

Devising Diamonds ✣

Quilt patterns that repeat a single shape to create a larger design provide quiltmakers with an opportunity to play with color in an intriguing way. Diamonds create an exceptionally attractive design when the colors are graded from light to dark and from color to color.

Quiltmakers have been sewing Diamond Star or Lone Star quilts since the late 1700s. Since the piecing used to be considered difficult and the fabrics were costly, Lone Star quilts served as "best quilts" and were reserved as bedcovers to honor a special guest or momentous occasion. In contrast, by cutting strips with a rotary cutter, sewing the strips together, and then cutting rows of diamonds from the sewn strips, you can make splendid Star quilts quickly and accurately.

The "Garden Trellis" quilt on page 194 creates a wonderful illusion of a woven trellis by utilizing pairs of bias strips cut in elongated diamond shapes. The strips form a simple, easy-to-piece, X-shaped block. Alternating the Cross blocks with a Snowball block links the Xs and moves the design over the entire surface of the quilt. Thoughtful color placement and careful pinning as the blocks are sewn to each other produce the beautiful illusion.

The star is made up of small diamonds sewn together to form eight large diamonds. When the eight large diamonds are sewn together, the star appears in all its glory. The instructions that follow guide you in making Lone Stars in almost the same way you create a Ninepatch except that the squares are slanted.

 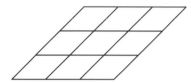

1. Begin by making sure that the cut edges of your fabrics are straight and at a perfect right angle with the fold. See page 27 for a reminder on how to do this.

2. Cut strips of each color in the width indicated in the chart for the quilt size you are making.

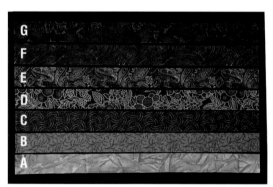

3. Arrange the strips in groups in the order you want them to appear in the star. Letter the strips according to their position in the star. Start with the center color as A and proceed to the tips of the star. Use the letters to guide you in arranging the strip units.

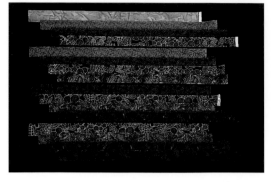

4. Sew the strips together in alphabetical order, offsetting the strips about the width of a strip. Press all seams in each unit toward the strip with the highest letter (with A the lowest).

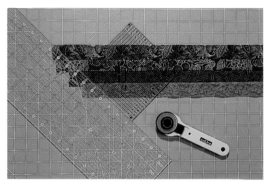

5. Place a strip unit on your cutting board and position the diagonal line of a Bias Square ruler on one of the middle seam lines. Align a long cutting ruler at the edge of the square, just covering the uneven ends of the strip unit. Holding the long cutting ruler in place, move the square out of the way and cut along the edge of the ruler.

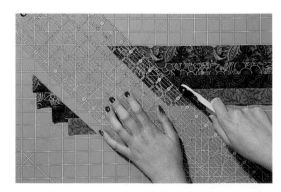

6. Cut segments parallel to the first cut the same width as the strips. For example, if you cut strips 1 1/2" wide, then cut the segments 1 1/2" wide.

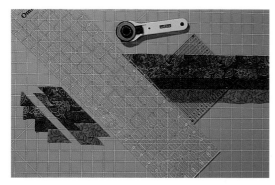

7. Trim the edge after every second or third cut to make sure the edge is at a perfect 45° angle to the seam lines.

8. Using one segment from each strip unit, arrange the diamond segments into large diamonds. Handle the segments carefully to avoid stretching the bias edges.

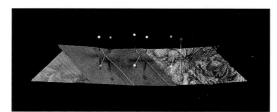

9. Place 2 of the diamond segments right sides together. Insert a pin through one of the seams of the first diamond segment $1/4$" from the raw edge. Separate the 2 segments slightly so you can see the seam of the second segment. Push the pin right through the seam $1/4$" from the edge of that diamond segment and pull it tight to establish the proper point of matching. Leave the end of the pin loose like a sword. Place a pin on either side of the sword pin, about $1/8$" away.

10. Sew the segments together in pairs, using $1/4$" seams. Remove the sword pin at the last minute just before the needle can hit it. Perfectly matched diamond tips are the hall-mark of a good Lone Star, so pin each seam carefully.

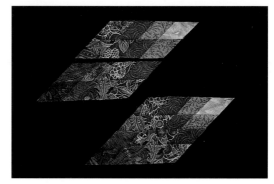

11. Sew the pairs to each other, matching the seams between the diamonds.

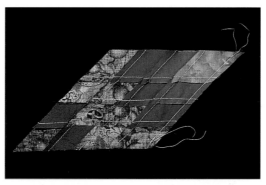

12. Sew the large diamonds into pairs. Match and pin all the seams. Sew from the center of the star to **within $1/4$" of the outer edge;** backstitch.

13. Sew the pairs of diamonds into groups of 4, again sewing from the center to within $1/4$" of the outer edge; backstitch.

14. Baste the two halves of the star together, matching all points. Sew this seam from one side of the star to the other, starting and stopping ¹⁄₄" from the inside corners. Press the seams between the large diamonds on the reverse side of the star in the same direction.

Background

Background triangles and squares for the "Glowing Star" quilt on page 195 are cut slightly oversized to give the illusion that the star is floating on the background. However, the triangles and squares for the "Shining Star" quilt on page 213 are not oversized. The points of the stars for this quilt touch the sashing strips that surround each block.

The following example illustrates inserting oversized triangles and squares. Follow the same directions for constructing either quilt. The only difference will be the amount of fabric that extends beyond the points of the diamonds.

1. Cut 1 square in the size indicated for the quilt size you are making. Cut the square twice diagonally to yield 4 quarter-square triangles. These will be set into the sides of the star.

2. Cut 4 squares in the size indicated for the quilt size you are making. These will be set into the corners of the star. Arrange the star and background pieces on your work surface. Sew the background pieces one at a time, starting with the side triangles.

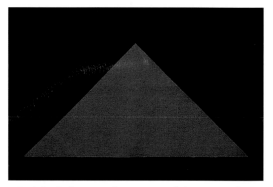

3. Mark the inside corner of the triangle on the wrong side of the fabric.

4. Pin the inside corner of the triangle to the inside corner between the two diamonds. Align the raw edge of the triangle and the diamond, being careful not to stretch the bias edges of the triangle. Sew from the outer edge to ¹⁄₄" from the inside corner; backstitch.

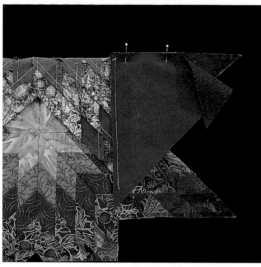

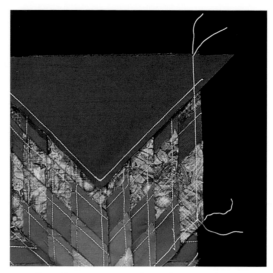

5. Pin the triangle to the adjacent diamond. Sew from the outer edge to $\frac{1}{4}$" from the inside corner. This time you will sew on the side with the diamonds. Repeat for remaining side triangles. Press the seams toward the diamonds.

7. Pin the square to the adjacent diamond, aligning the raw edges. Sew from the outer edge to $\frac{1}{4}$" from the inside corner on the side with the diamonds. Repeat for remaining squares. Press the seams toward the diamonds.

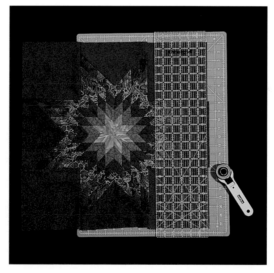

6. Insert the corner squares next. Mark one corner of a square, $\frac{1}{4}$" from the edges, on the wrong side of the fabric. Pin the marked corner of the square to the inside corner between the two diamonds. Align the raw edges of the square and the diamond. Sew from the outer edge to $\frac{1}{4}$" from the inside corner.

8. After inserting the slightly oversized triangles and squares, you will notice that the edges of the quilt top are uneven. Use a long cutting ruler and rotary cutter to trim the edges before adding the borders. Align the edge of the ruler with the raw edges of the squares on one side; be sure the corners are square; trim. Repeat for the remaining sides of the quilt top.

Garden Trellis

By Mary Hickey, 1993, Seattle, Washington, 56$\frac{1}{2}$" x 56$\frac{1}{2}$". Simple blocks create an enchanting illusion. Quilted by Hazel Montague. Directions begin on page 196.

Glowing Star

By Mary Hickey, 1993, Seattle, Washington, 31" x 31". A gradation of two lovely colors creates the soft glowing illusion. Quilted by Mary Hickey. Directions begin on page 203.

Garden Trellis

Quilt Plan

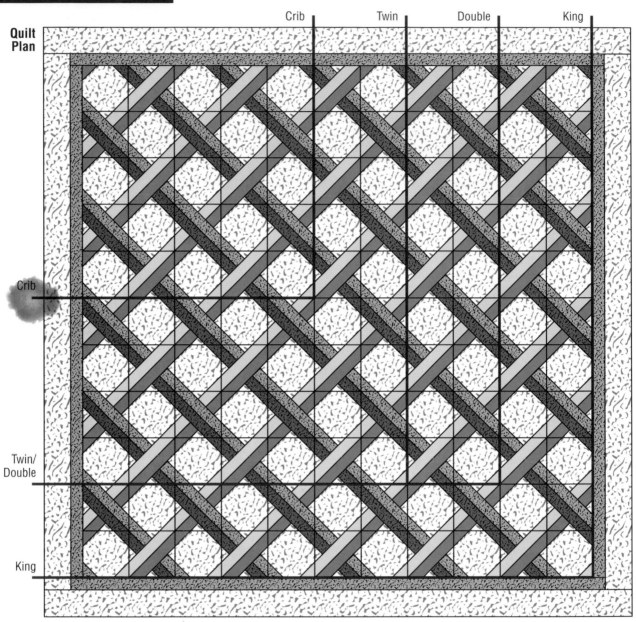

Crib

Twin/ Double

King

Color photo on page 194.

Color Key

- Light Green
- Dark Green
- Light Blue
- Dark Blue
- Floral Background

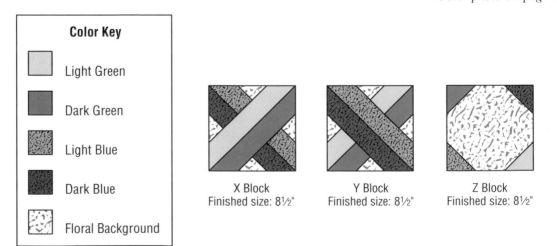

X Block
Finished size: 8½"

Y Block
Finished size: 8½"

Z Block
Finished size: 8½"

GETTING STARTED

*B*ouquets of violets peeking through a sun-dappled trellis give this quilt a lovely, nostalgic mood. A simple **X** shape forms the easy main block. Blues span the length of the main blocks in half the rows, and greens dominate in the other half. By alternating the **X** blocks with Snowball blocks, the **X**s are linked in a woven pattern similar to a garden trellis.

Color Scheme: Blue, green, and white. The floral chintz fabric inspired the colors chosen for the trellis blocks. Using a light and a medium shade of the blues and the greens creates the illusion of light and shadow. Placing the lighter-colored blocks in the upper left corner further enhances the sunny feeling of the quilt.

Setting: Side by Side. The blocks are sewn into a simple side-by-side setting. Careful placement of the colors in the Snowball blocks adds to the illusion of a continuous pattern weaving across the quilt top.

Quilt Vital Statistics

Measurements given are for finished sizes.

	Crib	Twin	Double	King
Quilt Size	56$\frac{1}{2}$" x 56$\frac{1}{2}$"	73$\frac{1}{2}$" x 90$\frac{1}{2}$"	90$\frac{1}{2}$" x 90$\frac{1}{2}$"	107$\frac{1}{2}$" x 107$\frac{1}{2}$"
Block Layout	5 x 5	7 x 9	9 x 9	11 x 11
No. of X Blocks	6	15	20	30
No. of Y Blocks	6	16	20	30
No. of Z Blocks	13	32	41	61
Inner Border Width	2"	2"	2"	2"
Outer Border Width	5"	5"	5"	5"

Materials: 44"-wide fabric

Purchase the required yardage for the quilt size you are making. Fabric requirements are in yards and are based on 42" of usable fabric width after preshrinking.
Purchase a variety of light blues, dark blues, light greens, and dark greens totaling the amounts given below.

	Crib	Twin	Double	King
Background	1$\frac{1}{2}$	2$\frac{3}{4}$	3$\frac{1}{2}$	5
Light Blues	$\frac{7}{8}$	1$\frac{3}{4}$	2	3
Dark Blues	$\frac{7}{8}$	1$\frac{3}{4}$	2	3
Light Greens	$\frac{7}{8}$	1$\frac{3}{4}$	2	3
Dark Greens	$\frac{7}{8}$	1$\frac{3}{4}$	2	3
Inner Border	$\frac{1}{2}$	$\frac{3}{4}$	$\frac{3}{4}$	$\frac{7}{8}$
Outer Border	1	1$\frac{1}{2}$	1$\frac{1}{2}$	1$\frac{3}{4}$
Binding	$\frac{5}{8}$	$\frac{3}{4}$	$\frac{7}{8}$	1
Backing	3$\frac{5}{8}$	5$\frac{1}{2}$	8$\frac{1}{8}$	9$\frac{3}{8}$
Piecing for Backing				

Rotary-Cutting Chart

Cut all strips across the fabric width. Measurements include ¼" seam allowances.

	Crib	Twin	Double	King
Background				
9" x 42" strips	4	8	11	16
Crosscut into 9" x 9" squares	13	32	41	61
4" x 42" strips	1	3	4	6
Crosscut into 4" x 4" squares	12*	31*	40	60
*Cut additional squares from leftovers.				
Light Blues, Dark Blues, Light Greens, and Dark Greens Cut the following number of pieces from each of the 4 colors.				
12" x 42" strips	2 each	4 each	5 each	8 each
3⅜" x 3⅜" squares (See Tip Box below.)	13 each	32 each	41 each	61 each

Cutting Tip

Some squares can be cut from the triangles left over after cutting bias strips. (See illustration following step 1 on page 199.) Cut 3⅜" strips as shown. Then crosscut into 3⅜" squares. You will get a minimum of 3 squares from each triangle.

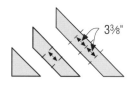

Block Assembly

Notice that some of the trellis pieces look as if they are woven over the others. We'll call these "over-trellis" pieces; they look like elongated diamonds. The ones that look like they go behind the others are "under-trellis" pieces. These will be joined to form the X and Y blocks.

"Over-Trellis" Pieces

"Under-Trellis" Pieces

"Over-Trellis" Pieces

1. Using the 12" x 42" pieces, layer the light blues and dark blues with right sides together, and the light greens and dark greens also with right sides together. Cut $2\frac{1}{2}$" bias strips from each pair of layered fabrics as shown.

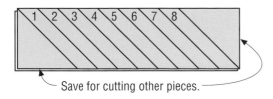

Save for cutting other pieces.

2. Sew each pair of bias strips together along the long edge as shown. Do this for all the pairs of strips. If you layered your fabrics correctly, you should be sewing a light blue strip to a dark blue strip, and a light green strip to a dark green strip. Press the seams open.

3. Place the diagonal line of the Bias Square ruler on the seam line as shown and trim the point to a perfect right angle.

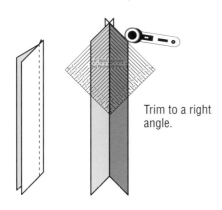

Trim to a right angle.

4. Measure from the point you just cut and make a mark $12\frac{3}{4}$" from the point as shown. Mark only the number of pieces required for the size quilt you are making. The rest will be used for the "Under-Trellis" pieces (page 200).

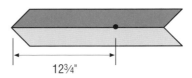

$12\frac{3}{4}$"

	Crib	Twin	Double	King
No. of Green Units to Mark	6	15	20	30
No. of Blue Units to Mark	6	16	20	30

5. Place the diagonal line of the Bias Square ruler on the seam line and the corner of the ruler on the $12\frac{3}{4}$" mark as shown. Trim around the corner of the ruler to make a point. The piece should measure $12\frac{3}{4}$" from point to point.

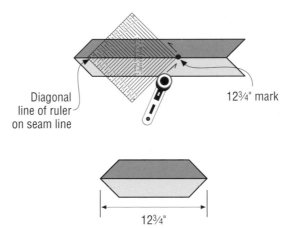

Diagonal line of ruler on seam line

$12\frac{3}{4}$" mark

$12\frac{3}{4}$"

"Under-Trellis" Pieces

1. Fold the remaining bias-strip pairs in half as shown below.
2. Cut a rectangle $4\frac{5}{8}$" wide from the folded bias-strip pair as shown.

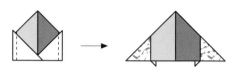

$4\frac{5}{8}$"

	Crib	Twin	Double	King
No. of Green Units to Cut	12	30	40	60
No. of Blue Units to Cut	12	32	40	60

3. Place a corner of the Bias Square ruler at one end of the rectangle and the diagonal line of the ruler on the seam line; trim around the corner of the ruler to make a point. The piece should measure $4\frac{5}{8}$" from the point to the straight edge. Repeat for all rectangles.

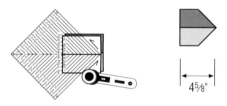

$4\frac{5}{8}$"

4. Cut the 4" background squares twice diagonally to yield quarter-square triangles. Sew the triangles to opposite sides of the under-trellis pieces, lining up the bottom of the triangles with the straight edge of the piece as shown. Press the seams toward the darker color.

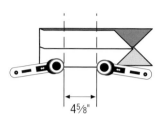

5. Join the over-trellis and under-trellis pieces as shown to make the X and Y blocks. Pay attention to the placement of the colors in each block. Keep each color pair pointing in the same direction and always sew the lighter colors toward the upper edge of the block.

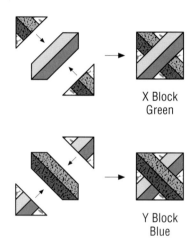

X Block
Green

Y Block
Blue

Z Block (Snowball)

1. Fold the 3 3/8" blue and green squares in half diagonally and gently press a crease.
2. Arrange 2 X blocks and 2 Y blocks on your floor or design wall with the colors pointing in the direction you want them to appear in the quilt, or as in our quilt, the greens to the right and the blues to the left. Pin a 9" background square in between the blocks. Pin a creased square of each trellis color on the corners of the squares to match the adjacent colors in the X and Y blocks.

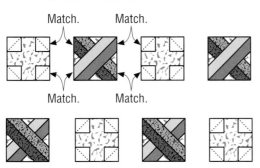

Note: If you used an assortment of blues and greens for your trellis, the Z blocks will have different fabrics placed in different corners, depending on where they are positioned in the quilt. To figure this out easily, lay out all of your X and Y blocks and place the background squares in between the blocks. Place the different squares of fabric on the background squares to match the adjacent X and Y blocks. To keep track of the Z blocks as you are sewing, sew the small squares to the background square and put the square back in its place before doing another one.

3. Sew on the crease line from corner to corner. Trim the excess fabric 1/4" from the seam. Fold the triangles toward the outer edges of the block and press the seams toward the center of the block.

Quilt Top Assembly and Finishing

1. Arrange the blocks, referring to the quilt plan on page 196. Keep each color pointing in the same direction and the lighter colors positioned at the top of the blocks.
2. Sew the blocks together into horizontal rows, carefully matching and pinning the Z blocks to the X and Y blocks. Press the seams toward the X and Y blocks.
3. Sew the rows together, making sure to match the seams between each block.
4. Cut the required number of inner border strips as shown on page 202. Join strips as necessary to make borders long enough for your quilt. Measure, cut, and sew borders to the sides first, then to the top and bottom edges of the quilt top, following directions on pages 23–24 for straight-cut borders. Repeat with outer borders.
5. Layer the quilt top with batting and backing; baste. Quilt as desired and bind the edges. Refer to the general directions for quilt finishing, beginning on page 238.

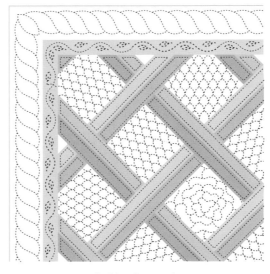

Quilting Suggestion

Border Cutting Chart

	Strip Size	Crib	Twin	Double	King
		No. of Strips			
Inner Border	2½" x 42"	5	8	8	10
Outer Border	5¼" x 42"	6	9	9	11

Template Cutting Chart

Templates begin on page 254.

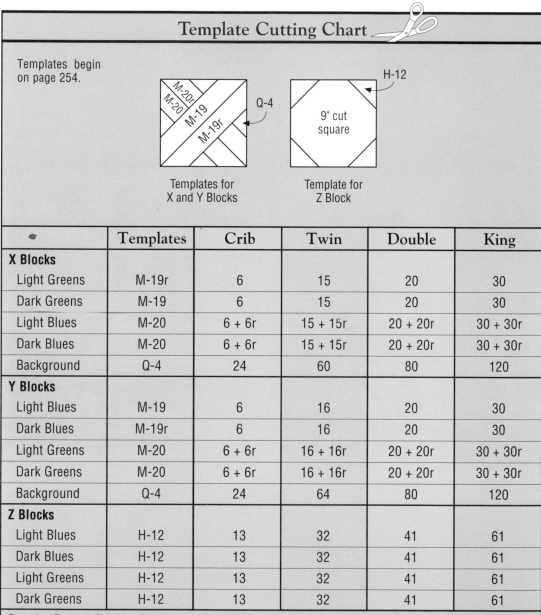

Templates for X and Y Blocks

Template for Z Block

	Templates	Crib	Twin	Double	King
X Blocks					
Light Greens	M-19r	6	15	20	30
Dark Greens	M-19	6	15	20	30
Light Blues	M-20	6 + 6r	15 + 15r	20 + 20r	30 + 30r
Dark Blues	M-20	6 + 6r	15 + 15r	20 + 20r	30 + 30r
Background	Q-4	24	60	80	120
Y Blocks					
Light Blues	M-19	6	16	20	30
Dark Blues	M-19r	6	16	20	30
Light Greens	M-20	6 + 6r	16 + 16r	20 + 20r	30 + 30r
Dark Greens	M-20	6 + 6r	16 + 16r	20 + 20r	30 + 30r
Background	Q-4	24	64	80	120
Z Blocks					
Light Blues	H-12	13	32	41	61
Dark Blues	H-12	13	32	41	61
Light Greens	H-12	13	32	41	61
Dark Greens	H-12	13	32	41	61

See the Rotary-Cutting Chart on page 198 for the number of 9" squares needed for the quilt size you are making. Use cut-off template C-4 on page 256 to remove the corners from the squares. See page 28 for using cut-off templates. Sew appropriate color H-12 to each corner to make the Z Block.

Quilt Plan

Wall

Color photo on page 195.

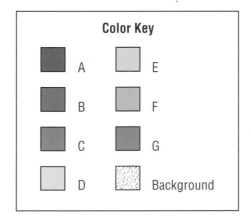

Color Key

A   E

B   F

C   G

D   Background

*T*he Traditional Lone Star, with its radiating rows of diamonds, has long been a favorite of quiltmakers. The energy, the sparkle, and the spectacular effect of a single glorious star make it one of the most satisfying quilts to create. Although the assembly is quite different from the other quilts in this book, the cutting techniques are similar to those used in many strip-pieced quilts.

Color Scheme: Complementary with dark to light and light to dark gradations. While the basic color scheme is complementary, the extraordinary glowing effect is the result of the graduation from dark to light in one color, and then the graduation from light to dark in a second color. The colors change from green to rose at the place where the two colors are at their lightest. The soft, almost imperceptible change in colors creates the luminous effect.

Setting: Medallion. To enlarge most quilts, you simply make more blocks. Since this is a single design quilt, you enlarge it by increasing the size and the number of the diamonds. Therefore, the charts for this quilt will look a bit different from the others in the book. Each chart gives the size of the finished star, the size of the diamonds, and the number of strips for the different-size stars.

Quilt Vital Statistics

Measurements given are for finished sizes.

	Wall	Crib	Dbl/Qn	King
Quilt Size	31" x 31"	$63^1/_2$" x $63^1/_2$"	$88^1/_2$" x $88^1/_2$"	$103^1/_2$" x $103^1/_2$"
Size of Star	20"	$51^1/_2$"	$73^1/_2$"	$73^1/_2$"
Size of Diamond	1"	2"	$2^1/_2$"	$2^1/_2$"
Inner Border Width	1"	$1^1/_2$"	$1^1/_2$"	3"
Outer Border Width	$4^1/_2$"	$4^1/_2$"	6"	12"

Materials: 44"-wide fabric

Purchase the required yardage for the quilt size you are making. Fabric requirements are in yards and are based on 42" of usable fabric width after preshrinking.

	Wall	Crib	Dbl/Qn	King
Background	$2/_3$	$1^3/_4$	$3^3/_4$	$3^3/_4$
Fabric A	$1/_8$	$1/_8$	$1/_8$	$1/_8$
Fabric B	$1/_8$	$1/_4$	$1/_3$	$1/_3$
Fabric C	$1/_4$	$1/_3$	$1/_3$	$1/_3$
Fabric D	$1/_3$	$3/_8$	$1/_2$	$1/_2$
Fabric E	$1/_4$	$1/_2$	$5/_8$	$5/_8$
Fabric F	$1/_4$	$3/_8$	$5/_8$	$5/_8$
Fabric G	$1/_8$	$1/_3$	$5/_8$	$5/_8$
Fabric H	—	$1/_4$	$1/_2$	$1/_2$
Fabric I	—	$1/_8$	$1/_3$	$1/_3$
Fabric J	—	—	$1/_4$	$1/_4$
Fabric K	—	—	$1/_8$	$1/_8$

Materials (cont.)

	Wall	Crib	Dbl/Qn	King
Inner Border	$1/4$	$3/8$	$5/8$	1
Outer Border	$3/4$	1	$1^7/8$	4
Binding	$3/8$	$5/8$	$3/4$	1
Backing	1	4	8	$9^1/8$
Piecing for Backing				

Rotary-Cutting Chart

Cut all strips across the fabric width. Measurements include $1/4$"-wide seam allowances.

Arrange your fabrics in the order you want them to appear in the quilt. Letter the fabrics according to their position in the star; start with the center as A, then B for the second fabric from the center, then C, and so on to the tip of the star.

	Wall $1^1/2$" Strips	Crib $2^1/2$" Strips	Dbl/Qn 3" Strips	King 3" Strips
Fabric A	1	1	1	1
Fabric B	2	2	2	2
Fabric C	3	3	3	3
Fabric D	4	4	4	4
Fabric E	3	5	5	5
Fabric F	2	4	6	6
Fabric G	1	3	5	5
Fabric H	—	2	4	4
Fabric I	—	1	3	3
Fabric J	—	—	2	2
Fabric K	—	—	1	1
Background for Corner Squares Cut 4 squares	$7^1/4$"	16"	23"	23"
Background for Side Triangles Cut 1 square	$11^1/4$"	24"	$33^3/4$"	$33^3/4$"

Star Assembly

Refer to pages 190–93 for Devising Diamonds. Cut strips in the widths indicated for the quilt size you are making. Follow the piecing diagrams below to make the strip units and assemble the segments.

1. Sew the strips together to make 1 of each strip unit as shown below for the quilt size you are making. Letters indicate the color placement. As you sew the strips together, offset them about the same distance as the width of the strips. Press the seams toward the strip with the highest letter.

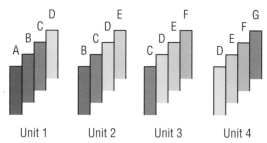

Strip Units for Wall
Offset strips 1½", cut segments 1½" wide.

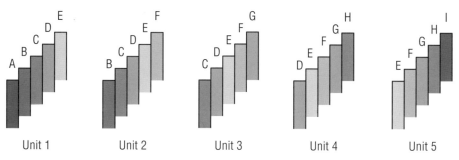

Strip Units for Crib
Offset strips 2½", cut segments 2½" wide.

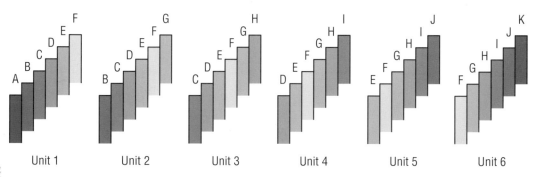

Strip Units for Double/Queen and King
Offset strips 3", cut segments 3" wide.

2. Cut 8 segments from each strip unit at a 45° angle, the same width as the strips were cut. Remember to trim the edge after every third or fourth cut to maintain accuracy.

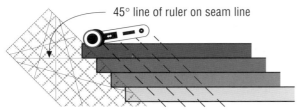

Make cuts parallel to the first cut.

3. Arrange the segments into large diamonds, using 1 segment from each strip unit. Handle the diamond segments carefully to avoid stretching the bias edges.

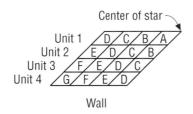

Wall

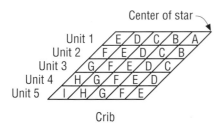

Crib

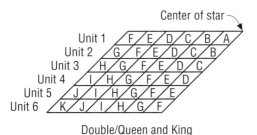

Double/Queen and King

4. Sew the segments together in pairs, matching and pinning at each seam intersection. Perfectly matched diamond tips are the hallmark of a good Lone Star, so pin each seam carefully. Leave all pins in place until just before the needle strikes them.

5. Sew the pairs to each other to make the large diamonds.

6. Sew the large diamonds into pairs. Match and pin all the seams. Sew from the center of the star to within 1/4" of the outer edge; backstitch. Sew 2 pairs together to form half of a star. Baste the two halves together, matching all points. Sew this seam from one side of the star to the other, starting and stopping 1/4" from the inside corners.

Quilt Top Assembly and Finishing

1. Cut the large background square for side triangles twice diagonally. (Wall–11 1/4"; Crib–24"; Dbl/Qn and King–33 3/4")

2. Arrange the star, side triangles, and corner squares on your work surface. The pieces are slightly oversized to give the effect that the star is floating on the background.

3. Insert the side triangles, then the corner squares, following directions on pages 192–93.

4. Use your long cutting ruler and rotary cutter to trim the sides so that they are straight and the corners are square. See page 193.

5. Cut the required number of inner border strips as shown in the cutting chart on page 208. Join strips as necessary to make borders long enough for your quilt. Measure, cut, and sew borders to the sides first, then to the top and bottom edges of the quilt top, following directions on pages 23–24 for straight-cut borders. Repeat with outer borders.

6. Layer the quilt top with batting and backing; baste. Quilt as desired and bind the edges. Refer to the general directions for quilt finishing, beginning on page 238.

Border Cutting Chart

	Strip Size	Wall	Crib	Dbl/Qn	King
		No. of Strips			
Inner Border	$1\frac{1}{2}$" x 42"	4	—	—	—
	2" x 42"	—	6	8	—
	$3\frac{1}{2}$" x 42"	—	—	—	8
Outer Border	$4\frac{3}{4}$" x 42"	4	6	—	—
	$6\frac{1}{4}$" x 42"	—	—	9	—
	$12\frac{1}{4}$" x 42"	—	—	—	10

Template Cutting Chart

Templates begin on page 254.	Wall	Crib	Dbl/Qn	King
	Template D-1	Template D-2	Template D-3	Template D-3
Fabric A	8	8	8	8
Fabric B	16	16	16	16
Fabric C	24	24	24	24
Fabric D	32	32	32	32
Fabric E	24	40	40	40
Fabric F	16	32	48	48
Fabric G	8	24	40	40
Fabric H	—	16	32	32
Fabric I	—	8	24	24
Fabric J	—	—	16	16
Fabric K	—	—	8	8

Refer to Rotary-Cutting Chart on page 205 for cutting side and corner triangles.

Note: Sew template-cut diamond shapes together as shown.

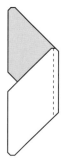

Quilting Suggestion

LESSON 11—
Creating with Templates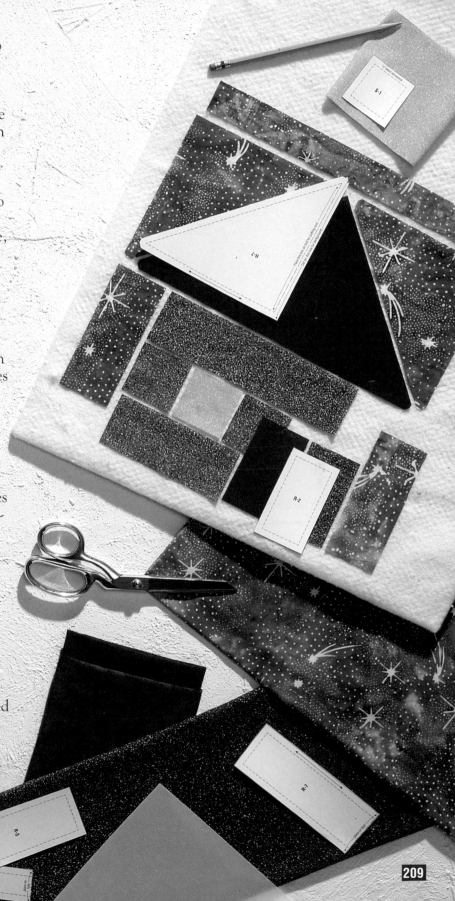

Many gorgeous quilts simply refuse to fit into any category. They will not permit their shapes to be strip-pieced but are too wonderful to be ignored. Sometimes, the shapes are quite easy to piece, such as the large pieces in "Winter in the Woods" on page 212. Occasionally, they are a bit harder to sew, as in the Lone Star. And, once in a while, you come across a few quilts that are not particularly difficult to sew but would really look best if the fabrics were selected and sewn one at a time, such as the "Good Neighbors" quilt on page 214 and the remarkable "Nesting Birds" quilt on page 215. For these types of quilts, we recommend cutting the shapes with templates.

Often, these quilts require you to work less as a production stitcher and more as an artist. Think of the shapes as colorful pieces of paint. You can compose with color, value, and pattern, moving the pieces around until you strike the right combination. The beauty of fabric is that you can move the shapes around several times before you sew them.

As you are trying to decide what pleases you, audition your colored pieces on a flannel board or on a clean floor, then look at the design from a distance or through a reducing glass or the wrong end of binoculars. Distancing yourself from the project gives you a better sense of how the design will appear as a whole. Don't anguish as you play with the patches, but just enjoy the process. It's your quilt, and if it pleases you, it is a successful quilt!

Templates for the shapes used in all of the quilts in *The Joy of Quilting* are included in the back of the book. When rotary-cutting a square, rectangle, triangle, or an unusual shape, you can check for accuracy by placing the cut shape over the template.

"Reading" a Template

The templates in *The Joy of Quilting* are grouped by shape. Each is given a letter designation to give you a clue as to what the shape is and a number designation to help you find the right one. For example, a template marked "S-4" tells you that you should look for a square template with the number 4.

Use the following key to read the templates:

A   Appliqué
B   Half-rectangle triangle
C   Corner cut-off template
D   Diamond
H   Half-square triangle
M   Miscellaneous
      (odd-shaped pieces)
Q   Quarter-square triangle
R   Rectangle
S   Square

Properly made templates include important information in an abbreviated form:

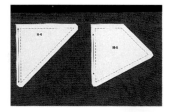

- The arrow on a triangle or on odd-shaped templates indicates the direction of the grain line and can be placed either on the lengthwise or crosswise grain of the fabric.

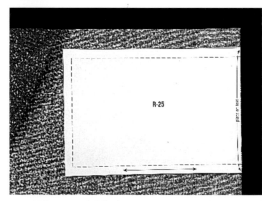

- "Place on fold" designations can be treated in two ways. You can fold the fabric in half as shown and place the line of the template on the fold of the fabric before you cut; or you can cut the template by placing it on a folded piece of paper to make the full-size template, and then cut the shape from a single layer of fabric.

- "r" means to reverse the template (flip it over) and cut additional pieces. You can accomplish the same thing by folding the fabrics so that part of the fabric is facing up and part is facing down.

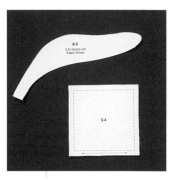

- Piecing templates include ¼"-wide seam allowances, while appliqué templates do not.

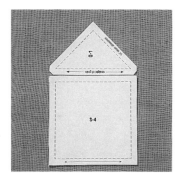

- The points of triangles and odd-shaped templates are nipped off and look blunt. As you cut the fabric pieces, be sure to nip off these points exactly as they appear on the template. This will allow you to match the fabric pieces edge to edge and corner to corner, thereby simplifying your job when sewing triangles to squares and matching long, skinny points.

Cutting with Templates

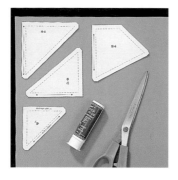

1. Reinforce your templates by gluing them to template plastic or lightweight cardboard. (Cereal boxes are a good weight.) Use your paper scissors, not your fabric scissors, to cut out the reinforced templates. Be sure to leave a seam allowance on piecing templates.

2. Fold and press the fabric you are cutting so that you can cut two or four layers at a time. Place your reinforced template on the fabric with the arrows parallel to the grain lines of the fabric. Carefully draw around the template. Use a sharp pencil to draw on light-colored fabrics and a white pencil on dark fabrics.

3. As you cut out the shapes, cut on the pencil line or just barely inside the pencil line.

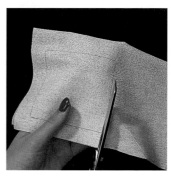

Sewing with Template Shapes

Using the piecing diagram as a guide, match the raw edges of the fabric patches and sew the shapes with an exact ¹/₄"-wide seam allowance. See page 32 for instructions on positioning a seam guide. If you sew accurate ¹/₄" seams, you will not have to mark a stitching line on the fabrics.

As you sew the shapes together, remember that you nipped off the points of the triangles at the exact spot where they should meet the edge of the next patch. Therefore, you should be able to pick up the two pieces to be sewn, lay them together, and sew them.

Winter in the Woods

By Mary Hickey, 1993, Seattle, Washington, 94½" x 94½". When Mary's father died in 1992, she took some of the old wool shirts that he wore and included them in this cherished quilt. Quilted by Mary Hickey. Directions begin on page 216.

Shining Stars

By Tricia Lund, 1987, Seattle, Washington, 87" x 115". The hand of a master artist shines in this stunning quilt. Quilted by Mrs. Neal C. Miller. Directions begin on page 224.

Good Neighbors

By Tricia Lund, 1992, Seattle, Washington, 108" x 80". Look carefully at this quilt. Can you find the only two identical houses? Quilted by Amanda Schlabach. Directions begin on page 228.

Nesting Birds

By Tricia Lund, 1990, Seattle, Washington, 60" x 87". Cozy families of birds, inspired by Joan Colvin's quilts in *Quilts from Nature*, show Tricia's remarkable skill at combining fabrics. From the collection of Liesel Lund. Quilted by Mrs. Henry Mast. Directions begin on page 232.

Winter in the Woods

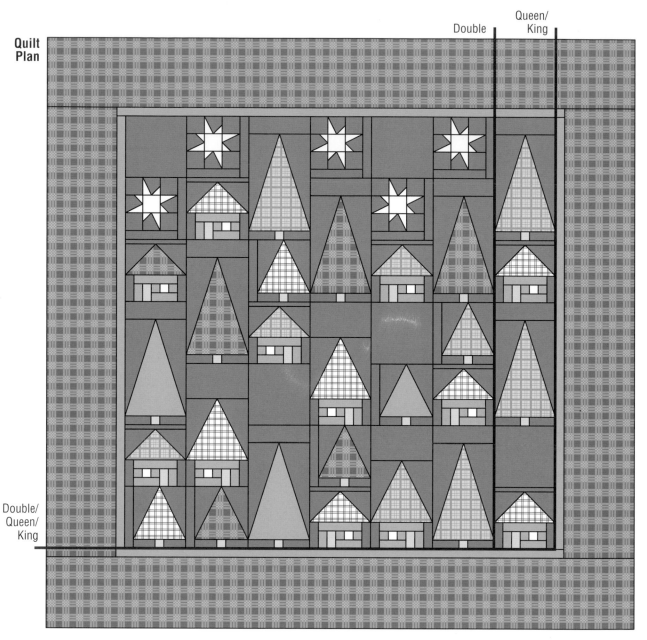

Double

Queen/ King

Double/ Queen/ King

Color photo on page 212.

Color Key

Plaids

Solids

Yellow or White

Background

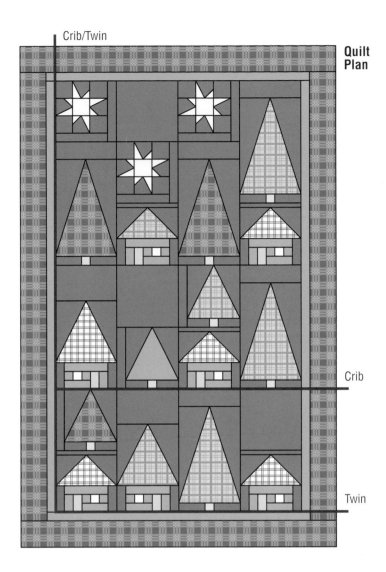

Crib/Twin

Quilt Plan

Crib

Twin

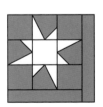

Star Block
Finished size: 10½"

Small House Block
Finished size: 10½"

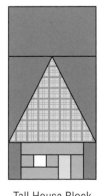

Tall House Block
Finished size: 10½" x 21"

Small Tree Block
Finished size: 10½"

Tall Tree Block
Finished size: 10½" x 21"

11
LESSON

GETTING STARTED

*T*hree generations of family memories are patched into this striking example of a scrap quilt. Life in the Northwest requires warm shirts, skirts, and robes. The lovely plaids of these garments are apt to work their way into our minds, adding to the fun of skiing and sledding and warming us through our raw winters. Often, the fronts and sleeves of the shirts and robes deteriorate long before the backs wear out, leaving us with boxes of guilt-producing wool scraps. You could, of course, make just as striking a quilt using shirting cottons or cotton flannel.

Color Scheme: Red, yellow, green, and blue, with tan and plaid accents. Managing the large-scale and strong colors of these fabrics takes some thought. Audition the fabrics for the blocks until you find a color combination for each individual block that is pleasing to you. Then, arrange the blocks, paying particular attention to the reds and yellows. Notice that, in our sample, the yellows appear along the top of the quilt, so an effort was made to balance the impact of the yellows by using some light tans in the lower rows of the quilt. Next, the reds were placed in pleasing, yet not entirely predictable places. The greens and blues fill in the forest and color a few more houses. Last of all, the North Forties (unpieced squares of plaid) were added.

Setting: Side by Side. Notice that some of the blocks are twice as tall as others. By simply sewing the rows in long columns, the pieces of the composition all fit perfectly.

Quilt Vital Statistics

Measurements given are for finished sizes.

	Crib	Twin	Double	Queen	King
Quilt Size	51" x 61½"	54" x 85½"	84" x 94½"	94½" x 94½"	103½" x 103½"
No. of Star Blocks	3	3	5	5	5
No. of Small Tree Blocks	2	3	6	6	6
No. of Tall Tree Blocks	4	5	7	9	9
No. of Small House Blocks	3	5	7	9	9
No. of Tall House Blocks	1	2	3	3	3
No. of Solid Blocks	2	3	4	5	5
Inner Border Width	1½"	1½"	1½"	1½"	3"
Outer Border Width	3"	4½"	9"	9"	12"

Note: Wool fabric is usually woven on wider looms than cotton. If you are purchasing wool, you will not need as much yardage as indicated in the chart. Our wools came from two unfinished projects, the backs of old shirts, robes, skirts, jumpers, walking shorts, kilts, and marching-band uniforms. It was somewhat alarming to realize that making a quilt as large as our sample did not even make a dent in our wool scrap boxes!

Materials: 44"-wide fabric

Purchase the required yardage for the quilt size you are making. Fabric requirements are in yards and are based on 42" of usable fabric width after preshrinking.

	Crib	Twin	Double	Queen	King
Background	$1\frac{1}{2}$	2	$3\frac{1}{2}$	5	5
Yellow for Stars	$\frac{1}{4}$	$\frac{1}{4}$	$\frac{1}{3}$	$\frac{1}{3}$	$\frac{1}{3}$
Tree Plaids	$\frac{1}{2}$	$\frac{3}{4}$	$\frac{3}{4}$	1	1
Roof Plaids	$\frac{1}{4}$	$\frac{1}{3}$	$\frac{1}{2}$	$\frac{3}{4}$	$\frac{3}{4}$
House Solids	$\frac{1}{4}$	$\frac{1}{3}$	$\frac{1}{2}$	$\frac{3}{4}$	$\frac{3}{4}$
Tree Trunks	$\frac{1}{8}$	$\frac{1}{8}$	$\frac{1}{8}$	$\frac{1}{8}$	$\frac{1}{8}$
Inner Border	$\frac{1}{2}$	$\frac{5}{8}$	$\frac{5}{8}$	$\frac{2}{3}$	1
Outer Border	$\frac{3}{4}$	$1\frac{1}{8}$	$2\frac{3}{8}$	$2\frac{5}{8}$	$3\frac{5}{8}$
Binding	$\frac{5}{8}$	$\frac{3}{4}$	$\frac{3}{4}$	$\frac{7}{8}$	1
Backing	$3\frac{1}{4}$	$5\frac{1}{8}$	$5\frac{5}{8}$	$8\frac{3}{8}$	$9\frac{1}{8}$
Piecing for Backing	⊟	⊓	⊓	⫼	⫼

Use scraps from star fabric for windows and scraps from roof fabric for doors.

Block Assembly

Templates begin on page 254.

1. Make plastic or cardboard templates. Be sure to mark the template number and grain line on each template.
2. Cut required pieces for each block as indicated in the Template Cutting Charts.
3. Arrange the pieces, right side up, and assemble, following the piecing diagrams for each block.

Quilt Top Assembly and Finishing

1. Arrange and rearrange the blocks until you find a composition that pleases you, or follow the quilt plan on pages 216–17.

2. Sew the blocks together into vertical rows. Press the seams in opposite directions from row to row. Sew the rows together.
3. Cut the required number of inner border strips as shown on page 220. Cut the borders in the width required for the quilt size you are making. Join strips as necessary to make borders long enough for your quilt.
4. Measure, cut, and sew the inner borders to the sides first, then to the top and bottom edges of the quilt top, following directions on pages 23–24 for straight-cut borders. Repeat with outer border.
5. Layer quilt top with batting and backing; baste. Quilt as desired and bind the edges. Refer to general directions for quilt finishing, beginning on page 238.

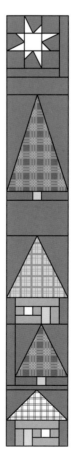
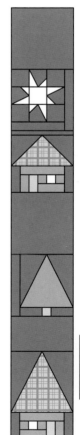

Border Cutting Chart

	Strip Size	Crib	Twin	Double	Queen	King
				No. of Strips		
Inner Border	2" x 42"	5	7	7	8	—
	3½" x 42"	—	—	—	—	8
Outer Border	3¼" x 42"	6	—	—	—	—
	4¾" x 42"	—	7	—	—	—
	9¼" x 42"	—	—	8	9	—
	12¼" x 42"	—	—	—	—	10

Template Cutting Chart

Star Blocks

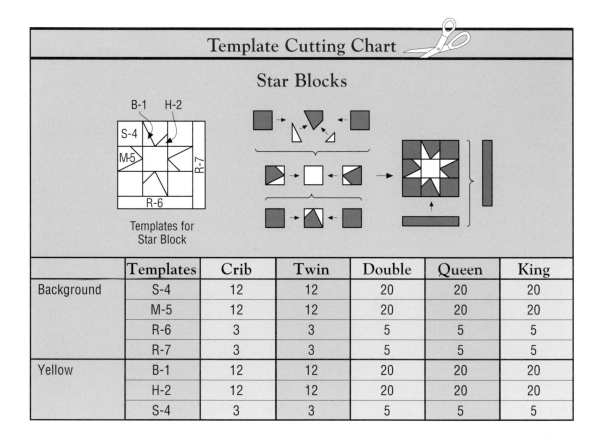

Templates for
Star Block

	Templates	Crib	Twin	Double	Queen	King
Background	S-4	12	12	20	20	20
	M-5	12	12	20	20	20
	R-6	3	3	5	5	5
	R-7	3	3	5	5	5
Yellow	B-1	12	12	20	20	20
	H-2	12	12	20	20	20
	S-4	3	3	5	5	5

Small Tree Blocks

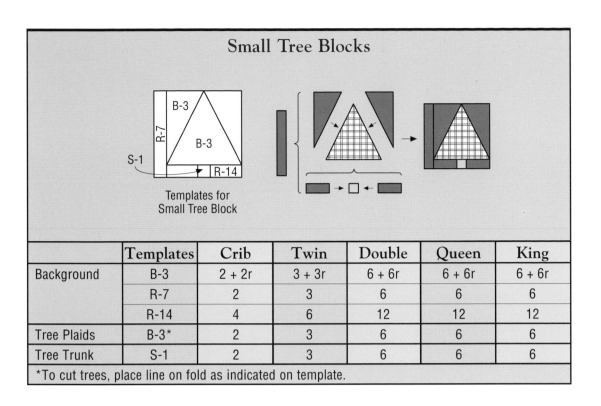

Templates for
Small Tree Block

	Templates	Crib	Twin	Double	Queen	King
Background	B-3	2 + 2r	3 + 3r	6 + 6r	6 + 6r	6 + 6r
	R-7	2	3	6	6	6
	R-14	4	6	12	12	12
Tree Plaids	B-3*	2	3	6	6	6
Tree Trunk	S-1	2	3	6	6	6
*To cut trees, place line on fold as indicated on template.						

Tall Tree Blocks

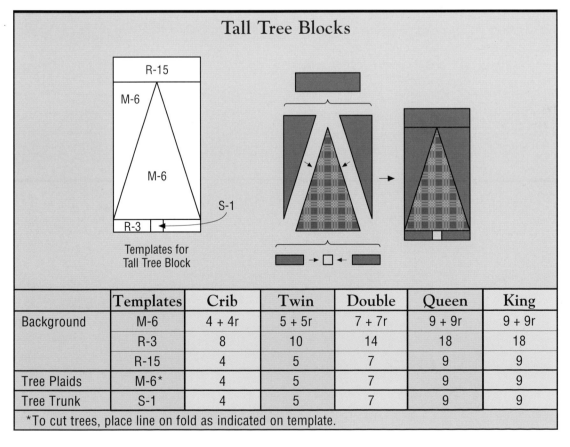

Templates for
Tall Tree Block

	Templates	Crib	Twin	Double	Queen	King
Background	M-6	4 + 4r	5 + 5r	7 + 7r	9 + 9r	9 + 9r
	R-3	8	10	14	18	18
	R-15	4	5	7	9	9
Tree Plaids	M-6*	4	5	7	9	9
Tree Trunk	S-1	4	5	7	9	9
*To cut trees, place line on fold as indicated on template.						

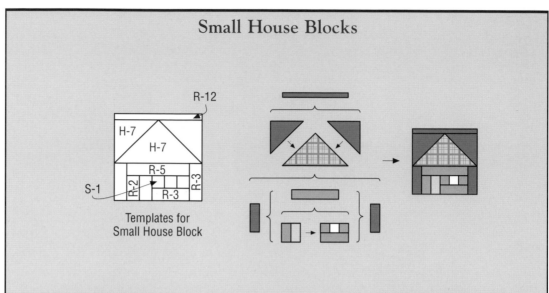

Small House Blocks

Templates for Small House Block

	Templates	Crib	Twin	Double	Queen	King
Background	R-3	6	10	14	18	18
	R-12	3	5	7	9	9
	H-7	3 + 3r	5 + 5r	7 + 7r	9 + 9r	9 + 9r
House Solids	S-1	6	10	14	18	18
	R-2	3	5	7	9	9
	R-3	3	5	7	9	9
	R-5	3	5	7	9	9
Door Fabric	R-2	3	5	7	9	9
Window Fabric	S-1	3	5	7	9	9
Roof Fabric	H-7*	3	5	7	9	9

*To cut roof, place line on fold as indicated on template.

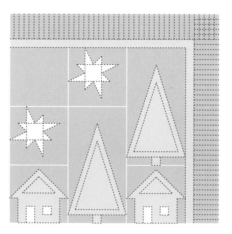

Quilting Suggestion

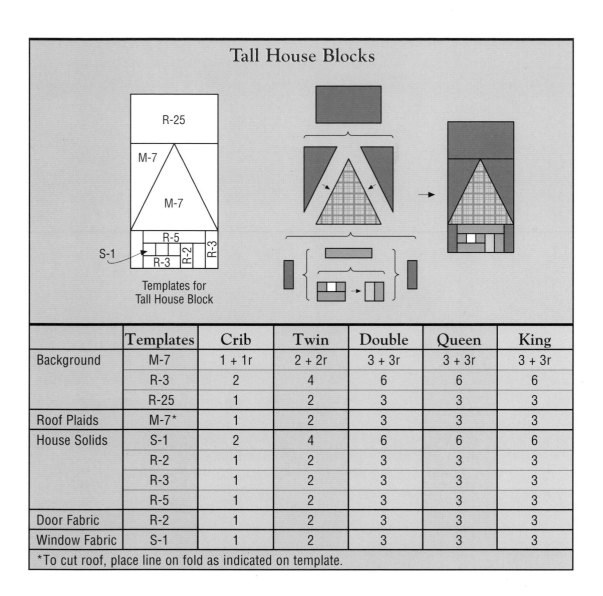

Tall House Blocks

Templates for
Tall House Block

	Templates	Crib	Twin	Double	Queen	King
Background	M-7	1 + 1r	2 + 2r	3 + 3r	3 + 3r	3 + 3r
	R-3	2	4	6	6	6
	R-25	1	2	3	3	3
Roof Plaids	M-7*	1	2	3	3	3
House Solids	S-1	2	4	6	6	6
	R-2	1	2	3	3	3
	R-3	1	2	3	3	3
	R-5	1	2	3	3	3
Door Fabric	R-2	1	2	3	3	3
Window Fabric	S-1	1	2	3	3	3
*To cut roof, place line on fold as indicated on template.						

North-Forty Plaid Blocks					
	Crib	Twin	Double	Queen	King
From plaids, cut: 11" x 11" squares	2	3	4	5	5

Shining Stars

Quilt Plan

Crib

Twin/ Double

Queen/ King

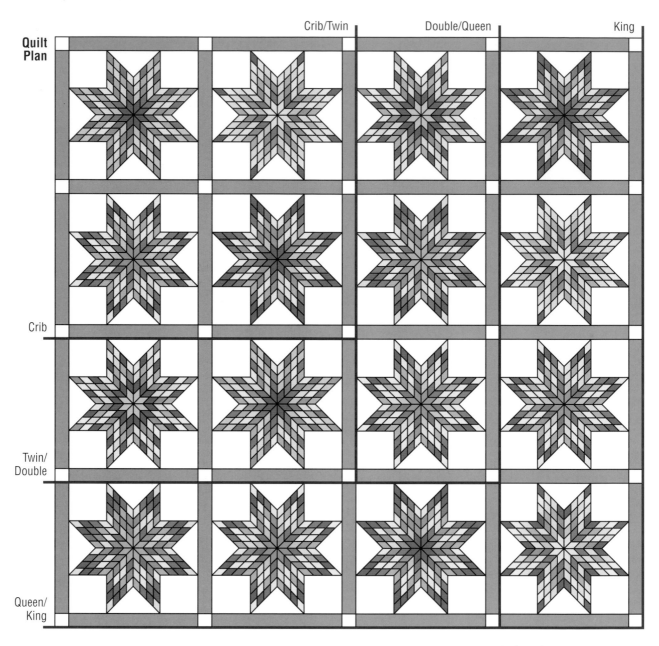

Color photo on page 213.

Color Key

Scrappy Diamonds

Sashing

Background

Diamond Star Block
Finished size: 24"

GETTING STARTED

The old and often-used Lone Star pattern abounds with possibilities. Many quilts contain only one star with numerous rings of diamonds, others have many stars with only three rings. This quilt tries to do it all—twelve stars in which to try different color variations, and seven rings of diamonds within each star for color variations.

Color Scheme: Red, green, gold, brown, and black. Only two blocks in this quilt contain all five colors. In contrast, two other blocks use only two colors. These two are of particular interest, because the two colors are brown and black. While one might not be initially drawn to a brown and black block, notice the contribution these blocks make to the quilt. Not only do the shadings make them rich and glowing in their own right, but they also serve as a comparison against which the more colorful blocks stand out. All these subtle changes in value are made possible by the variety of fabrics used in each ring of diamonds, which can be achieved only by sewing the diamonds together individually, rather than strip-piecing them. In this case, speed is the enemy of art.

Setting: Sashing and Cornerstones. The stars are set with wide red sashing strips and cornerstones cut from the background fabric, an effect often seen in antique quilts.

Quilt Vital Statistics

Measurements given are for finished sizes.

	Crib	Twin	Double	Queen	King
Quilt Size	57" x 57"	57" x 84"	84" x 84"	84" x 111"	111" x 111"
Block Layout	2 x 2	2 x 3	3 x 3	3 x 4	4 x 4
Total Blocks	4	6	9	12	16
Sashing Width	3"	3"	3"	3"	3"

Materials: 44"-wide fabric

Purchase the required yardage for the quilt size you are making. Fabric requirements are in yards and are based on 42" of usable fabric width after preshrinking.
Purchase a variety of fabrics for the diamonds totaling the amounts given below.

	Crib	Twin	Double	Queen	King
Total Assorted Fabrics for Diamonds	$2\frac{1}{4}$	$3\frac{1}{4}$	$4\frac{3}{4}$	$6\frac{3}{8}$	$8\frac{3}{8}$
Background	$1\frac{3}{4}$	2	3	$3\frac{7}{8}$	$5\frac{1}{8}$
Red Print for Sashing	$\frac{7}{8}$	$1\frac{5}{8}$	$1\frac{5}{8}$	$2\frac{1}{4}$	3
Binding	$\frac{5}{8}$	$\frac{2}{3}$	$\frac{3}{4}$	$\frac{7}{8}$	1
Backing	$3\frac{5}{8}$	$5\frac{1}{8}$	$7\frac{1}{2}$	$7\frac{1}{2}$	$9\frac{3}{4}$
Piecing for Backing					

Template Cutting Chart

Templates begin on page 254.

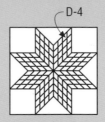

Templates for
Diamond Star Block

	Crib	Twin	Double	Queen	King
Assorted Fabric for Diamonds					
Template D-4	512	768	1152	1536	2048
Background					
$7^5/_8$" x $7^5/_8$" squares	16	24	36	48	64
$11^1/_4$" x $11^1/_4$" squares	4	6	9	12	16
$3^1/_2$" x $3^1/_2$" squares	9	12	16	20	25
Sashing*					
$24^1/_2$" x 42" pieces	1	2	2	3	4
Crosscut into $3^1/_2$" x $24^1/_2$" strips	12	17	24	31	40

*It's a good idea to wait until you've made all the blocks before cutting the sashing strips, just in case your blocks turn out to be a slightly different size.

Block Assembly

1. Pin a 30" square of flannel to your design wall.

2. Arrange a selection of diamonds on the flannel square. Try keeping one color in each ring of a star but use two or three shadings of the color. Add and subtract diamonds in rings of colors until you find a combination that pleases you. Each star is made using 128 diamonds.

3. When you have completed an arrangement of the star that you like, carefully remove the flannel from your wall and carry it to your sewing machine.

4. Sew the diamonds together in pairs aligning the edges and points of the diamond pieces as shown. Then sew the pairs together to make a row of 4 diamonds.

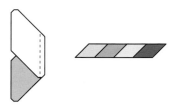

5. Sew 4 rows together as shown to make a large diamond, carefully matching and pinning the seam intersections. See page 191.

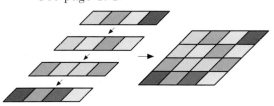

6. Cut the 11^1/$_4$" background squares twice diagonally for side triangles. Assemble the diamonds and insert the side triangles and 7^5/$_8$" corner squares, following the directions on pages 192–93.

7. Measure the blocks to make sure they are perfectly square. They should finish to 24" (24^1/$_2$" including seam allowances). If necessary, square up the sides and corners using a long ruler and a rotary cutter. Align the ^{1}/$_4$" mark on your ruler with the points of the stars and trim along the edge of the ruler.

Quilt Top Assembly and Finishing

1. Sew the blocks and sashing strips together, beginning and ending each row with a sashing strip.

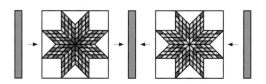

2. Sew the remaining sashing strips and cornerstones together, beginning and ending each row with a cornerstone.

3. Sew the rows together, alternating the rows of blocks and rows of sashing strips with cornerstones.

4. Layer the quilt top with batting and backing; baste. Quilt as desired and bind the edges. Refer to the general directions for quilt finishing, beginning on page 238.

Quilting Suggestion

Good Neighbors

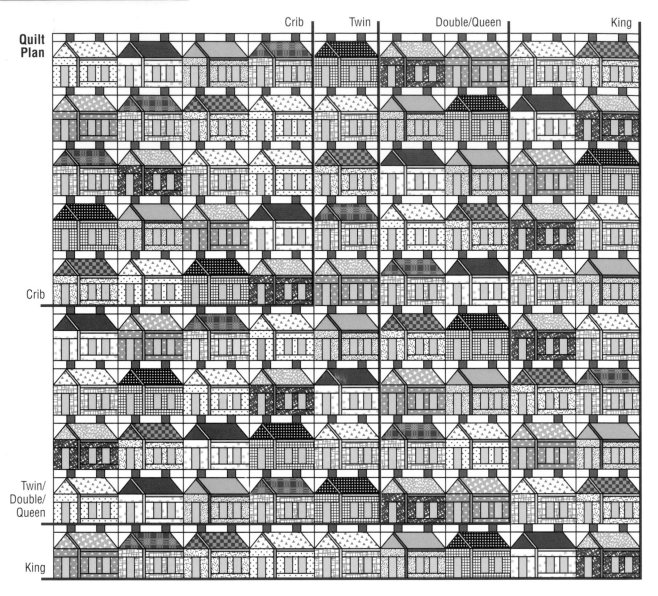

Color photo on page 214.

Color Key

Scrappy Fabrics

Chimney

Sky

Doors and Windows

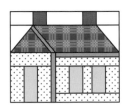

House Block
Finished size: 12" x 10"

GETTING STARTED

*O*nly *two houses are alike in this friendly village quilt. Can you spot which ones? Abundant use of plaids, stripes, and other geometric prints, with relatively few florals, emphasize the antique look of this quilt.*

Color Scheme: Red, blue, brown, and black. Although the reds and blues appear predominate, the number of houses that are done primarily in these two colors is actually less than half. The majority of the houses are shades of brown and black. Rather than appearing somber, though, these colors are more likely to make the reds and blues sparkle. Cohesiveness in a scrap quilt can be achieved by limiting the number of colors used, as well as by keeping a design element constant from block to block. In this quilt, the same sky and chimney fabrics are used throughout.

Setting: Side by Side. The rectangular houses snuggle up next to each other with no sashing or borders. The red binding forms a subtle frame.

Quilt Vital Statistics

Measurements given are for finished sizes.

	Crib	Twin	Dbl/Qn	King
Quilt Size	48" x 50"	60" x 90"	84" x 90"	108" x 100"
Block Layout	4 x 5	5 x 9	7 x 9	9 x 10
Total No. of Blocks	20	45	63	90

Materials: 44"-wide fabric

Purchase the required yardage for the quilt size you are making. Fabric requirements are in yards and are based on 42" of usable fabric width after preshrinking.

Choose an assortment of fabrics for the houses, purchasing at least 1/4-yard pieces. If you are a fabric collector, pull fabrics from your collection and fill in with colors you are missing. The more fabrics you have, the scrappier the look and the more fun you will have "painting" each house.

	Crib	Twin	Dbl/Qn	King
Assorted House Fabrics	$1^3/_4$	$3^3/_4$	$5^1/_4$	$7^1/_2$
Sky Fabric	$^3/_4$	$1^1/_2$	2	$2^1/_2$
Chimney	$^1/_4$	$^3/_8$	$^1/_2$	$^5/_8$
Binding	$^1/_2$	$^3/_4$	$^3/_4$	1
Backing	$3^1/_8$	$5^1/_2$	$7^5/_8$	$8^7/_8$
Piecing for Backing				

Cutting

Templates begin on page 254.

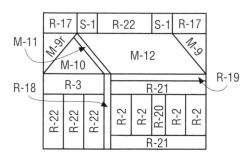

Templates for
House Block

Houses

Refer to the block template diagram above for placement of pieces before selecting and cutting fabrics. See directions below for quick-cutting and quick-piecing the sky and chimney instead of cutting individual templates.

Cut the following pieces for one House block. Make as many blocks as required for the quilt size you are making.

For sky, cut:
  1 and 1 reversed Template M-9
  2 Template R-17
  1 Template R-22
For chimney, cut 2 Template S-1
For house, cut:
  2 Template R-2
  1 Template R-3
  1 Template R-18
  1 Template R-19
  1 Template R-20
  2 Template R-21
  2 Template R-22
For roof, cut:
  1 Template M-10
  1 Template M-11
  1 Template M-12
For window, cut 2 Template R-2
For door, cut 1 Template R-22

Sky/Chimney Cutting

	Crib	Twin	Dbl/Qn	King
Sky Fabric				
3" x 42" strips	2	5	7	9
4¹/₂" x 42" strips	1	2¹/₂*	3¹/₂*	4¹/₂*
Chimney Fabric				
2" x 42" strips	2	5	7	9
*¹/₂ strip = 21" long.				

Block Assembly

1. Sew 3" sky strips, 4¹/₂" sky strip, and 2" chimney strips together to make a strip unit as shown. To make ¹/₂ of a strip unit, cut the 42" strips in half to yield 2 strips 21" long, then sew 21" long strips together to make the strip unit. Press the seams toward the chimney strips. Cut the strip unit into 2"-wide segments.

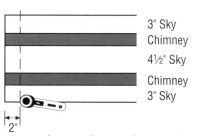

3" Sky
Chimney
4¹/₂" Sky
Chimney
3" Sky

	Crib	Twin	Dbl/Qn	King
No. of Strip Units to Make	1	2¹/₂	3¹/₂	4¹/₂
No. of Segments to Cut	20	45	63	90

2. Arrange the pieces for each house, right sides up, and assemble following the piecing diagram. Press the seams toward the darker fabrics as you go.

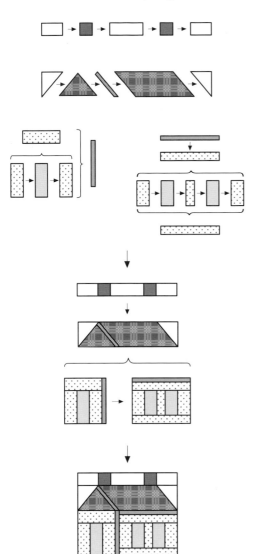

Quilt Top Assembly and Finishing

1. Arrange the houses into horizontal rows and sew them together. Press the seams in opposite directions from row to row.
2. Sew the rows together, making sure to match the seams between the blocks.
3. Layer the quilt top with batting and backing; baste. Quilt as desired and bind the edges. Refer to the general directions for quilt finishing, beginning on page 238.

Quilting Suggestion

Nesting Birds

Quilt Plan

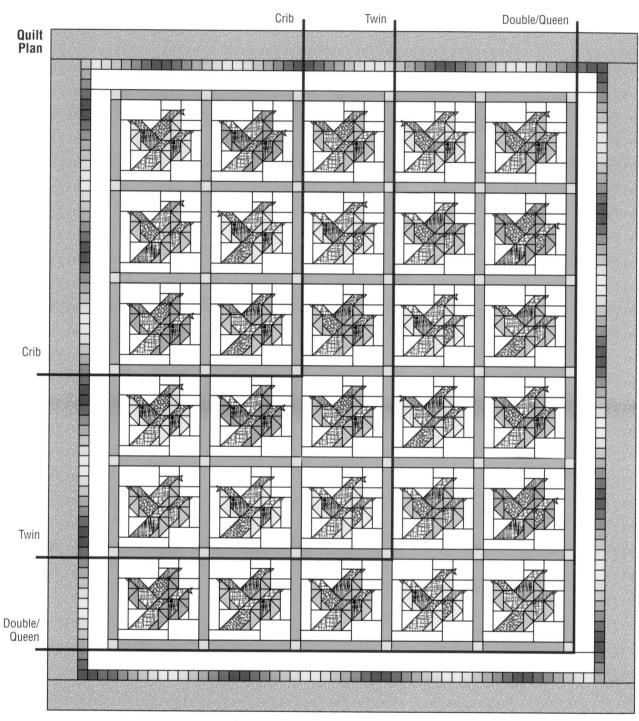

Crib · Twin · Double/Queen

Crib

Twin

Double/Queen

Color Key

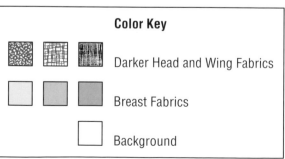

Darker Head and Wing Fabrics

Breast Fabrics

Background

Color photo on page 215.

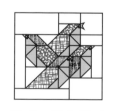

Nesting Birds Block
Finished size: 12"

GETTING STARTED

Nesting Birds exemplifies the interaction of ideas that has always been an important part of quilting. Tricia Lund's quilt is an adaptation of a wonderful, more contemporary quilt by Joan Colvin first shown at a quilt show in 1990 and later published in her book Quilts from Nature. In this quilt, Tricia gathers the individual birds from Joan's quilt into families, each in its own block. This design is for an advanced beginner.

Color Scheme: Controlled scrappy in black, rose, blue, brown, peach, and gold. The interplay of color in this quilt is challenging and fun. Seven shades of each of six colors, a total of forty-two, are intermingled in the blocks and arranged in the pieced border. The quilt could, of course, be made with fewer fabrics, perhaps by using only one for each bird breast, but the shadings of color add interest and richness to the piece. It is also important to use enough contrast so that the birds stand out, however subtly, from each other. Remember to view the blocks from a distance while designing them.

Setting: Sashing and Cornerstones. Simple sashing and cornerstones divide the blocks. Notice how the inner muslin border sets the design area apart, then a pieced border organizes the colors into a shaded sequence, and finally a wide dark border encloses the total design. To make a stunning wall quilt to hang over a sofa, rotate the blocks so the quilt has three blocks across and two blocks down.

Quilt Vital Statistics

Measurements given are for finished sizes.

	Crib	Twin	Dbl/Qn
Quilt Size	46^1/$_2$" x 60"	60" x 87"	87" x 100^1/$_2$"
Block Layout	2 x 3	3 x 5	5 x 6
Total No. of Blocks	6	15	30
Sashing Width	1^1/$_2$"	1^1/$_2$"	1^1/$_2$"
Inner Border Width	3"	3"	3"
Middle Pieced Border Width	1^1/$_2$"	1^1/$_2$"	1^1/$_2$"
Outer Border Width	4^1/$_2$"	4^1/$_2$"	4^1/$_2$"

Materials: 44"-wide fabric

Purchase the required yardage for the quilt size you are making. Fabric requirements are in yards and are based on 42" of usable fabric width after preshrinking.

	Crib	Twin	Dbl/Qn
Background	^{3}/$_4$	1^2/$_3$	3
Assorted Bird Fabrics	1^1/$_2$	2	3
Sashing	^{1}/$_2$	^{7}/$_8$	1^1/$_2$
Cornerstones	^{1}/$_8$	^{1}/$_4$	^{1}/$_4$
Inner Border	^{2}/$_3$	^{7}/$_8$	1
Outer Border	^{7}/$_8$	1^1/$_8$	1^5/$_8$
Binding	^{5}/$_8$	^{3}/$_4$	^{7}/$_8$
Backing	3	5^1/$_4$	7^3/$_4$
Piecing for Backing			

Cutting Chart

Cut all strips across the fabric width. Measurements include ¼"-wide seam allowances.

	Crib	Twin	Dbl/Qn
Sashing 12½" x 42" strips*	1	2	4
Crosscut into 2" x 12½" strips	17	38	71
Cornerstones 2" x 42" strips	1	2	2
Crosscut into 2" x 2" squares	12	24	42

*It's a good idea to wait until you've made all the blocks before cutting the sashing strips, just in case your blocks turn out to be a slightly different size.

Cutting Templates

Templates begin on page 254.
Refer to the block template diagram below for placement of pieces before selecting and cutting pieces.

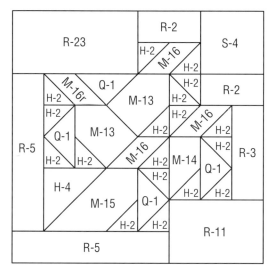

Templates for
Nesting Birds Block

Cut the following pieces for each block. Measurements for squares and rectangles are given in parentheses if you want to rotary-cut these pieces. Some triangles can also be quick-cut: cut the size of square indicated and cut diagonally.

From background, cut:
4 Template H-2 (or cut 2³⁄₈"
   square once diagonally)
1 Template H-4 (or cut 3⁷⁄₈"
   square once diagonally)
1 Template Q-1 (or cut 4¼"
   square twice diagonally)
2 Template R-2 (2" x 3½")
1 Template R-3 (2" x 5")
2 Template R-5 (2" x 8")
1 Template R-11 (3½" x 5")
1 Template R-23 (3½" x 6½")
1 Template S-4 (3½" x 3½")

Since the colors for each bird are chosen individually, you will need a variety of colored shapes to "paint" with on your design wall. Notice how the bird's head and wing are usually darker than the face and breast. Cut a variety of pieces, using the templates indicated in the appropriate color range. Happy painting!

From assorted bird fabrics, cut:
14 Template H-2
2 Template M-13
1 Template M-14
1 Template M-15
3 Template M-16
1 Template M-16r
3 Template Q-1
4 Template S-1 for bird beaks*

*You can use synthetic suede for the bird beaks, or use a 2" square of calico folded and stitched, following directions on page 252.

Block Assembly

1. Using the block drawing and color photo on page 215 as a guide, "paint" the patches together on your design wall to make the block. Stand back and squint, or use a reducing glass or the wrong end of a pair of binoculars to check the color placement.

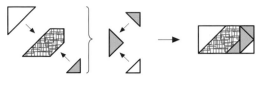

TIP TIP TIP TIP TIP TIP TIP

Shading Tip
The birds in Tricia's quilt have the breast (Temp. Q-1) divided into two triangles (Temp. H-2). To add richness to your quilt, add an additional color in the breasts of some or all of your birds.

2. When you are pleased with the block, assemble the pieces, following the piecing diagram. Press seams toward the dark fabric or press open to reduce the thickness of bulkier seams. Repeat for all blocks.

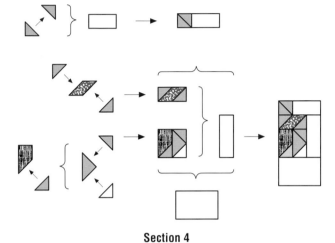

Section 3

Section 4

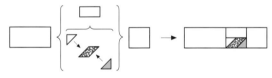

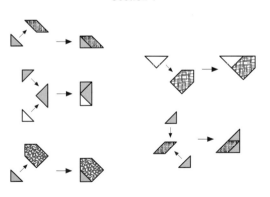

Section 1

Section 2

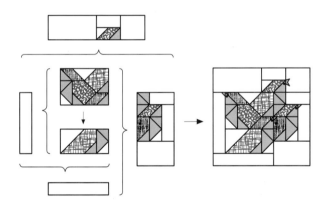

3. Embroider the eyes with a single strand of floss. Use a satin stitch for the center of the eye and an outline stitch around the outside.

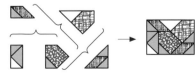

11
LESSON

Quilt Top Assembly and Finishing

1. Sew the blocks and sashing strips together, beginning and ending each row with a sashing strip.

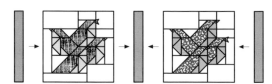

2. Sew the remaining sashing strips and cornerstones together, beginning and ending each row with a cornerstone.

3. Sew the rows together, alternating the rows of blocks and rows of sashing strips with cornerstones.

4. Cut the required number of inner border strips as shown in the chart on page 237. Join strips as necessary to make borders long enough for your quilt. Measure, cut, and sew borders to the sides first, then to the top and bottom edges of the quilt top, following directions on pages 23–24 for straight-cut borders.

5. For the pieced middle border, cut the required number of 2" strips from assorted bird fabrics as shown in the chart on page 237.

6. Sew the strips together, arranging them from light to dark to make one strip unit. Cut the strip unit into 2"-wide segments.

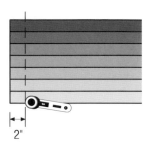

2"

7. Arrange the segments around the edges of the quilt, playing with the placement of the colors. Refer to the color photo on page 215. Sew the segments together end to end to make border strips that are long enough for the sides of your quilt. Sew the borders to the sides first, then to the top and bottom edges of the quilt.

8. Cut the required number of outer border strips as shown in the chart on page 237. Join strips as necessary to make borders long enough for your quilt. Measure, cut, and sew borders to the sides first, then to the top and bottom edges of the quilt top, following directions on pages 23–24 for straight-cut borders.

9. Layer the quilt top with batting and backing; baste. Quilt as desired and bind the edges. Refer to the general directions for quilt finishing, beginning on page 238.

Border Cutting Chart

	Strip Size	Crib	Twin	Dbl/Qn
		No. of Strips		
Inner Border	3½" x 42"	5	7	9
Asst. Bird Fabrics	2" x 42"	6	9	11
Outer Border	4¾" x 42"	5	7	10

Quilting Suggestion

LESSON 12—
Finishing with a Flourish

Quilting is an extraordinary art form. It combines a flat visual image; bold, abstract graphics; and the soft sculptural qualities obtained when the layers of the quilt are sandwiched together and stitched. The stitching that holds the layers and forms the sculpted designs is called "quilting" and it is from these stitches that we get the name "quilts." The quilting stitches can be simple outlines of the patches, generous echoes of the shapes, or elaborate patterns that add a new dimension of design to the surface.

Early quilters did both the piecing and quilting by hand as well as all of the sewing of garments and household linens. The minute the sewing machine became available, these same early homemakers scrimped and saved to purchase the wonderful machine that would free them from these time-consuming tasks. However, the size of the machines limited the size of the project, so quilting, the sculpturing of the three layers, remained a hand-sewing task. Women on isolated farms and homesteads or in busy towns and cities loved to gather and visit as they worked in neighborly groups to baste the layers together and quilt them. These women took great delight and pride in working to complete a practical object of lasting beauty.

Recent improvements in home sewing machines have solved some of the difficulties of machine quilting. For many busy quilters, stitching the designs by machine has become a satisfying alternative to hand quilting. Pick whatever method suits your personality and lifestyle and enjoy the magical process of quilting.

Preparing the Layers

Marking the Quilting Lines

Elaborate quilting designs must be marked before you sandwich the quilt, when it is easier to trace the quilting design accurately. Straight quilting lines can be marked as you go, and in-the-ditch quilting need not be marked at all. As you plan your quilting designs, keep in mind that the layers of fabric in a seam allowance are difficult to hand quilt, so plan your design to avoid stitching across too many seams.

1. Carefully press the quilt top and trace the quilting designs onto it. Draw the design lightly with a sharp pencil; a mechanical pencil marks nicely. Powdered chalk dispensers, white pencils, and soap slivers are all useful for marking quilting lines on dark fabrics. Test your marking tool on your fabrics to be sure the marks can be removed easily. A quilt top may also be marked for straight-line quilting with $1/4$" masking tape after the quilt is basted.

Note: Tape only small sections at a time and remove the tape as soon as you are finished with the section; the sticky residue can be difficult to remove if the tape is left on for longer periods.

2. If you mark the quilting design before you baste, you can trace your design onto all but the darkest fabrics. To mark your quilt top, either tape the quilting design to a window and tape your quilt over it, or create a light table by supporting a piece of glass or Plexiglas over a small lamp. Do this by taking the leaf out of your dining room table and putting the glass or Plexiglas on top of the table and a light on a chair below or on the floor. For dark fabrics, you may need to use a stencil and draw your quilting design with chalk or soap.

Backing

Make a quilt backing that extends 2"– 4" beyond the outer edges of the quilt top. For most of the quilts, you will have to sew two or three lengths of fabric together. Press the backing seams open to make quilting easier. The following illustrations are provided in "Piecing for Backing" at the bottom of the materials list for each quilt. Yardage requirements for the backing are based on sewing your backing as illustrated for the quilt size you are making.

Many quilters enjoy piecing extra units or blocks not used in the quilt top or large scraps left over from the quilt top into the back of the quilt. This is an area in which you can be very free and whimsical. Keep in mind, however, that a large number of seams make hand quilting more difficult.

Batting

Batting is the layer between the quilt top and the backing. It can be purchased in standard bed sizes or by the yard. There are also many types of batting to choose from: 100% cotton, 100% polyester, various combinations of cotton and polyester, and 100% wool batting. Consider how much quilting you want to do and how you want the quilt to look. Cotton and wool battings must be quilted every 2"–3", while polyester batting can be quilted every 4"–6". A thin batting works well for hand quilting as well as machine quilting and is preferable for wall hangings. For a puffier look, choose one of the high-loft polyester battings.

Basting for Hand Quilting

We recommend basting the quilt layers together with a needle and thread for hand quilting.

1. Spread the backing wrong side up on a clean, flat surface. Use masking tape or binder clamps to anchor the backing to the surface without stretching it.

2. Spread the quilt batting on the backing, making sure it covers the entire backing and is smooth. Center the pressed and marked top on the batting and backing right side up. Align borders and straight lines with edges of the backing.

3. Pin the layers in place with large straight pins to hold the layers smooth. Hand baste the three layers together, using a long needle and light-colored quilting thread. If you thread your needle without cutting the thread off the spool, you will be able to baste the entire quilt without rethreading your needle. Starting at the center of the quilt, use large stitches to baste a "snail's trail" on the quilt. Continue basting, creating a series of parallel lines 6"–8" apart. Complete the basting with a line of stitches around the outside edges. After the basting is complete, remove the pins.

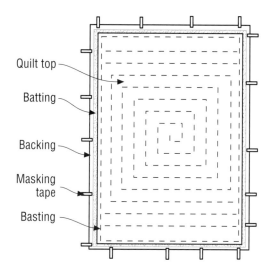

Quilt top

Batting

Backing

Masking tape

Basting

Basting for Machine Quilting

The smooth layering and careful pinning of your quilt top will prevent endless frustration as you quilt on the machine and will help ensure the success of your project. Follow steps 1 and 2 on page 240 for layering the backing, batting, and quilt top. Use #1 safety pins to pin baste for machine quilting.

1. Start pinning in the center and work toward the outer edges of the quilt, spacing the pins about 4"– 6" apart. Avoid pinning over seam lines where you intend to stitch in-the-ditch and avoid pinning your design lines. Use a needle and thread to baste a line of stitches around the outside edges.

Pinning Tip
Insert all the safety pins like straight pins. Close the safety pin later, using the serrated edge of a grapefruit spoon to push the point toward the clasp. This will prevent sore fingertips from closing all those pins by hand.

Pins
Quilt top
Batting
Backing
Masking tape
Thread basting

2. Sew a row of basting stitches around the outside of the quilt about $1/4$" from the raw edges. This will keep the edges from fraying while you machine quilt and also keep the edges aligned when you stitch the binding to the quilt.
3. Trim off excess batting and backing, leaving about 1" all around.

Hand Quilting

Quilting is simply a short running stitch that goes through all three layers of the quilt. While hand quilting is traditional, beautiful, and pleasant to do, it is time-consuming.

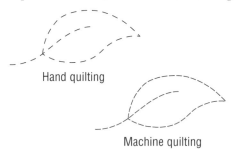

Hand quilting

Machine quilting

You can hand quilt on a frame, on a hoop, on a tabletop, or on your lap. Use 100%

cotton thread marked "Quilting" on the top of the spool. It is thicker and less likely to tangle. Beginners usually prefer to use a #7 or larger needle. As you become more familiar with hand quilting, you will find that a smaller (#8, #10, or #12) needle will enable you to take smaller stitches. Use a thimble with a rim around the top to help push the needle through the layers. For a more comfortably fitting thimble, gently bend the opening to form it into an oval so it will match the shape of your finger.

12

1. Cut the thread 24" long and tie a small knot. Starting about 1" from where you want the quilting to begin, insert the needle through the top and batting only. Gently tug on the knot until it pops through the quilt top and is caught in the batting.

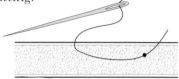

Gently pop knot into batting.

2. Insert the needle and push it straight down through all the layers. Then rock the needle up and down through all layers, "loading" three or four stitches on the needle. Push the needle with a thimble on your middle finger, then pull the needle through, aiming toward yourself as you work. Place your other hand under the quilt and use your thumbnail to make sure the needle has penetrated all three layers with each stitch.

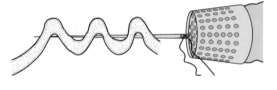

3. To end a line of quilting, make a small knot close to the quilt top and then take one stitch through the top and batting only. Pull the knot through the fabric into the batting. Clip the thread near the surface of the quilt.

When hand quilting thicker fabrics, such as wool or shirting flannel, be kind to yourself and plan to sew with the large stitches called utility quilting. A thicker thread will give a decorative appearance to the quilting. Try using a pearl cotton or rayon. See the "Winter in the Woods" quilt on page 212 for a fine example of utility quilting.

Machine Quilting

As quilters find that they are able to piece more quilt tops than they can quilt by hand, they realize that machine quilting is a practical alternative to hand quilting. Choose a small quilt for your first foray into machine quilting. Plan a quilting design that involves continuous long straight lines, gentle curves, and few switchbacks or direction changes. The "Ladybug's Luncheon" on page 40 is a good example of a quilt that lends itself to this type of machine quilting. In-the-ditch and outline quilting can also be adapted to machine work. Keep the spacing between quilting lines consistent over the entire quilt. Avoid tight, complex little designs and don't leave large spaces unquilted.

Quilting in-the-ditch   Outline quilting

Use either a fine 100% cotton silk-finish thread or a very fine, high-quality, .004m nylon thread made specifically for machine quilting. Thread your bobbin with fine 100% cotton thread. There are many excellent battings (including lovely cotton and wool ones) that can be quilted with lines 3"– 4" apart. Read and follow the instructions that come with the batting you choose.

A walking foot or even-feed foot for your sewing machine allows the fabrics to move through the machine without shifting. This type of foot is necessary for straight-line and grid quilting and for large, simple curves. Read the machine instruction manual for the special tension settings used to sew through several thicknesses.

Walking foot

If you wish to do curved quilting designs with your machine, you will need to use a darning foot or a special machine quilting foot, and you must be able to lower the feed dogs on your machine. Curved designs require free fabric movement under the foot of the sewing machine. This is called free-motion quilting and, with practice, you can use it to reproduce beautiful hand quilting designs quickly.

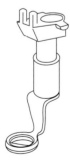

Darning foot

With free-motion quilting, you do not turn the fabric under the needle. You guide the fabric as if it were under a stationary pencil. When the feed dogs are lowered, the stitch length is determined by the speed with which you run the machine and feed the

fabric under the foot. Practice running the machine fairly fast since this enables you to sew smoother lines of quilting.

Practice first with layers of scrap batting and fabrics until you get the feel of controlling the motion of the fabric with your hands. Stitch some scribbles, zigzags, and curves. Try a heart or a star. Make sure your chair is adjusted to a comfortable height. Be patient with yourself. The difference between hand and machine quilting is like the difference between walking and jogging. You can go faster on the machine but it does require some skill and practice. With a little determination and patience, you will be able to do beautiful machine quilting.

Start quilting in the center, stitch all the lines in one direction, then repeat for the other direction. Do not try to quilt all at one sitting. Break the work up into short periods and be sure to stretch and rest your muscles regularly. To handle the bulk of a large quilt under the sewing-machine arm, roll the outer edges of your quilt like a scroll. Start in the center and quilt in one direction, then reroll and quilt in the other direction.

When all the quilting is completed, remove the pins but do not remove the basting stitches around the edges. What a wonderful moment this is!

Making a Sleeve

If you are going to hang your quilt, attach a sleeve or rod pocket to the back before you bind the quilt.

1. From the leftover backing fabric, cut a piece 8" wide to match the width of your quilt. On each end, fold over a $\frac{1}{2}$" hem and then fold over again. Press and stitch.

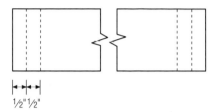

1/2" 1/2"

2. Fold the strip in half lengthwise, wrong sides together, and machine baste the raw edges to the top edge of your quilt. Your quilt should be about 1" wider on both sides.

3. Make a little pleat in the sleeve to accommodate the thickness of the rod, then slipstitch the bottom edge of the sleeve edge to the backing fabric.

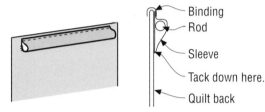

Binding
Rod
Sleeve
Tack down here.
Quilt back

Binding

A double-fold bias binding is easy to make and gives the quilt a neat and durable finish.

1. Trim the batting and backing even with the quilt top. Make sure the corners are square.

2. Using the 45°-angle line on your large cutting ruler as a guide, cut bias strips 2$\frac{1}{2}$" wide. Cut enough strips to go around the perimeter of the quilt plus 10" for joining the strips.

3. Seam the bias strips end to end to make one long piece of binding.

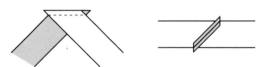

4. Turn the end under $\frac{1}{4}$" at a 45° angle and press. Fold the strip in half lengthwise, wrong sides together, and press.

Fold line

5. Place the binding just to the right of the center on one side of the front of the quilt, with the raw edges of the binding on the edge of the quilt. Sew the binding to the quilt on the front, using a $\frac{1}{4}$"-wide seam. Do not pin the binding to the quilt but work with it, smoothing it in place about 3" at a time without stretching it. Stop your stitching $\frac{1}{4}$" from the corner of the quilt and backstitch.

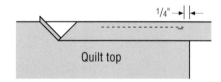

1/4"

Quilt top

6. Remove the quilt from the sewing machine. Fold the binding back at a 45° angle as shown.

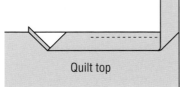

Quilt top

7. Hold the fold down with your finger and fold the rest of the binding back over itself to the second edge to be sewn. Start sewing ¼" from the corner.

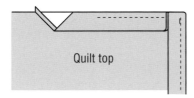

Quilt top

8. Continue around all four sides and corners of your quilt. When you reach the beginning of the binding, overlap the beginning stitches by about 1" and cut away any excess binding. Trim the end at a 45° angle and tuck the end of the binding into the fold; finish the seam.

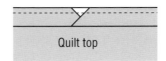

Quilt top

9. At each corner, place your finger under one of the corners and push the fold toward the point. Fold the fabric back around to the back of the quilt and fold a miter on the back of the corner. Complete all four corners this way. Blindstitch the binding on the back of the quilt by hand, covering the machine stitching.

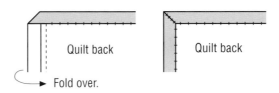

Quilt back   Quilt back

Fold over.

Labeling

Labeling your quilt is an important finishing touch. Embroider or cross-stitch your name, city, and the date on the back of your quilt. If you have too much information to stitch, you can write it on a label with a permanent pen on muslin or even type it on muslin and stitch it to the back.

MARY HICKEY
SEATTLE WASHINGTON
1992

Putting It All Together– Exampler Quilt

When a toddler learns to walk, the first tentative steps take courage, but with a little practice and encouragement, the initial, unsteady steps turn into walking and then running, skipping, and jumping. Learning to make quilts feels much the same way. We designed our Exampler to allow you to advance through many quiltmaking skills. As you take your first steps, cutting and piecing the outer border, you will become acquainted with rotary-cutting and strip-piecing squares and rectangles. By the time you sew the center block, you will be running, skipping, and jumping since you will have mastered accurate methods of cutting and piecing half-square units, quarter-square units, half-rectangle units, unusual shapes, and appliqué.

We hope you will learn many useful piecing skills and concepts that will enable you to create stunning quilts. This is an interesting and enjoyable process, especially if you allow yourself to trip and fall down once in a while, laugh about it, and try again. When learning a new skill, no one does it perfectly the first time. Don't expect perfection from yourself; but instead, enjoy the experience.

Spring Exampler

By Mary Hickey, 1993, Seattle, Washington, 45" x 45". Joan Colvin's pieced birds inspired Tricia Lund's Nesting Bird quilt (page 215), which in turn, inspired our singing bird for the center of this lively quilt. Quilted by Hazel Montague.

Christmas Exampler

By Joan Hanson, 1993, Seattle, Washington, 45" x 45". The partridge sings from his perch on the Christmas pear tree. Quilted by Joan Hanson.

Autumn Exampler

By Pat Thompson, 1993, Mequon, Wisconsin, 45" x 45". Pat's rich, warm palette recalls for us the glorious colors bestowed on the earth in autumn. Quilted by Pat Thompson.

12
LESSON

Exampler Quilt

Quilt Plan

GETTING STARTED

Color Scheme: Theme fabric with coordinating colors. The colors are organized around a theme fabric and two to four coordinating colors. Since the theme fabric is used in large, prominent spaces of the design, this is a good place to use a fabric with a large-scale print or other distinguishing feature that you like.

Setting: Medallion. Since the intent of a good sampler quilt is to give you practice in several different types of piecing, this quilt has blocks and rows that are made with different techniques, all organized around a central block. We have used a pieced bird in the center of our quilts, but you could use any 9" block in the middle.

Materials: 44"-wide fabric

Fabric requirements are based on 42" of usable fabric width after preshrinking.

Look for fabrics with a variety of scales and textures, such as allover florals, geometrics, and plaids.

$^3/_4$ yd. theme fabric
$^3/_4$ yd. each of 4 darks
$^3/_4$ yd. each of 4 lights
$^3/_8$ yd. medium
$^3/_4$ yd. background fabric
$^1/_2$ yd. binding
$2^7/_8$ yds. backing

Cutting

Templates begin on page 254.

You will be cutting and setting aside large pieces of fabrics to be used for half-square units, quarter-square units, half-rectangle units, the large Star Point blocks, and the Bird block. The remainder of the fabric will be used for the outer border. (Even though it will be sewn first, it will be cut last.) Use the block drawings as a guide to decide where you will place each fabric in the quilt, then cut your pieces as follows.

Quarter-Square Units

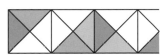

Quarter-Square Border

From each of 4 lights and 4 darks, cut:
1 square, 14" x 14"

Half-Square Units

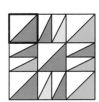

Give-and-Take Block
Finished size: 9"

From 1 light and 1 dark, cut:
1 piece, 14" x 20"

Large Star Point Blocks

Star Point Block
Finished size: 9"

From 1 light and 1 medium, cut:
1 square, $10^1/_4$" x $10^1/_4$"
From the theme fabric, cut:
2 squares, each $10^1/_4$" x $10^1/_4$"

Half-Rectangle Units

Give-and-Take Block
Finished size: 9"

From the theme fabric and 1 light fabric, cut:
1 piece, 18" x 20"

Bird Block

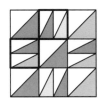 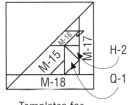

Bird Block
Finished size: 9"

Templates for
Bird Block

From the background fabric, cut:
1 square, $9^7/_8$" x $9^7/_8$"
2 Template H-2
1 Template M-17
1 Template M-18

From assorted lights and darks, cut:
4 Template H-2
1 Template Q-1
1 Template M-15
1 Template M-16

Rectangle and Square Border

Rectangles
and Squares

From each of 3 darks, cut:
1 strip, 2" x 42"
From the 4th dark, cut:
2 strips, each 2" x 42"
From each of 3 lights, cut:
1 strip, $3\frac{1}{2}$" x 42"
From the 4th light, cut:
2 strips, each $3\frac{1}{2}$" x 42"

Note: The lights and darks can be reversed if you want the darks to be the rectangles and the lights to be the squares.

Ninepatch Corners

Ninepatch
Corners

From the theme fabric, cut:
2 strips, each 2" x 20"
1 strip, 2" x 10"
From 1 light fabric, cut:
1 strip, 2" x 20"
2 strips, each 2" x 10"

Block Assembly

Lesson 5 —
Sewing Squares and Rectangles

1. Sew the 2" dark strips and $3\frac{1}{2}$" dark strips in pairs. Press the seams toward the light strips. Cut the strip unit into 2"-wide segments.

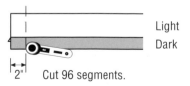

Light

Dark

2"   Cut 96 segments.

2. Alternating the colors and rotating every other unit, sew the segments into 4 border sections, each with 24 units.

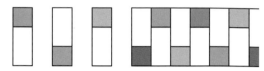

Join 24 segments.
Make 4 pieced borders.

3. Sew the 2" theme strips and 2" background strips as shown to make 2 different strip units. Press the seams toward the theme strips. Cut the strip units into 2"-wide segments.

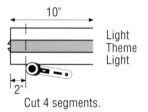

10"

Light
Theme
Light

2"

Cut 4 segments.

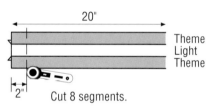

20"

Theme
Light
Theme

2"   Cut 8 segments.

4. Sew the segments together to make 4 Ninepatch corner blocks. Press the seams toward the outside of the block.

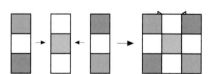

Lesson 7 —
Mastering Half-Square Units

1. Layer the two 14" x 20" pieces of fabric right sides up.
2. Follow the directions on pages 101–103 for cutting half-square units.

Cut bias strips $3\frac{1}{4}$" wide.
Cut segments $3\frac{1}{2}$" wide.
Cut 20 half-square units, each $3\frac{1}{2}$" x $3\frac{1}{2}$".

$3\frac{1}{2}$"

Lesson 8 —
Assembling Quarter-Square Units

1. Make 2 stacks of 14" squares; one of 4 lights and one of 4 darks. Place fabrics right side up in both stacks. Cut the 14" squares in half diagonally and then cut into 5"-wide bias strips as shown. Make cuts parallel to the center cut.

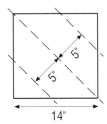

2. Working with the strips cut from the dark squares, sew strips together alternating the fabrics from different stacks to create pieced squares as shown. Press all seams in one direction. Follow directions on pages 101–103 to cut half-square units, each $5^3/8$" x $5^3/8$". Repeat with strips cut from light squares. Cut 14 squares from the dark fabrics, and 14 squares from the light fabrics.

Sew dark strips   Sew light strips
together.   together.

3. Cut the half-square units once diagonally perpendicular to the seam.

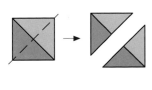
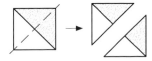

4. Sew the dark triangle pairs and the light triangle pairs together as shown to make quarter-square units. You should have 32 quarter-square units. You will need 28 for your quilt.

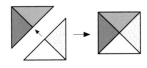

Lesson 9 —
Conquering Half-Rectangle Units

1. Layer the two 18" x 20" pieces of fabric with right sides up. Fold the layered fabrics in half lengthwise. Cut off the fold, leaving four 9" x 20" pieces, two facing down and two facing up.

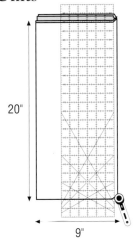

2. Keep the 9" x 20" fabrics layered but do not fold them in half before cutting the strips. Follow directions on pages 162–66 for making half-rectangle units. Sew the down-facing strips together first.
    Cut angled strips $2^1/2$" wide.
    Cut segments $3^1/2$" wide.
    Cut rectangles 2" x $3^1/2$".

TIP TIP TIP TIP TIP TIP TIP

Bias Strip Tip
Beware! The bias strips you cut to make the half-rectangle units are very sneaky. They will try and get mixed up with each other and trick you. Keep a close eye on them. Before you disturb your strips, remove the down-facing strips and put them in one pile, then take the up-facing strips and put them in the kitchen. At a glance, they may look the same, but they are backward from each other.

12
LESSON

Left   Right

3. Sew the up-facing strips (the ones in the kitchen) just as you did the first set. Cut the segments and squares from the wrong side of the fabric. (Turn the fabric over, not the BiRangle.) You will need 16 left-angled units and 16 right-angled units for your quilt.

Give-and-Take Blocks

1. Arrange the half-square units and half-rectangle units as shown below. Squint at the block to make sure the lights and darks are in the correct position.
2. Sew the units in rows, then join the rows together to complete the blocks. Press the seams toward the half-square units.

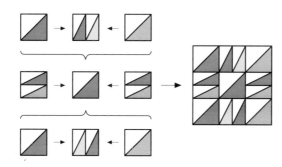

Large Star Point Block

Cut the 10¼" light, medium, and theme squares twice diagonally. Sew the triangles together as shown. Be careful not to stretch the bias seams out of shape. Press the seams toward the dark fabrics.

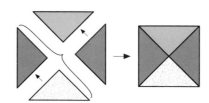

Lesson 11 — Creating with Templates

Bird Block

1. Cut the 9⅞" square once diagonally. Use cut-off template C-5 on page 256 to remove the corner of one of the triangles as shown. See page 28 for using cut-off templates. Sew the tail piece H-2 to the end of the large triangle.

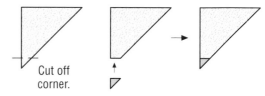

Cut off corner.

2. Piece the bird, following the piecing diagram below. For a beak, fold a 2" square of fabric, as shown below. Pin the beak in the seam and stitch. Press seams toward the dark fabrics. Sew the pieced triangle to the bird to complete the block.

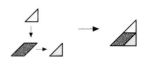

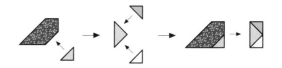

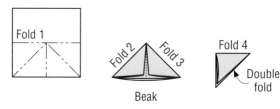

Fold 1

Fold 2   Fold 3

Beak

Fold 4

Double fold

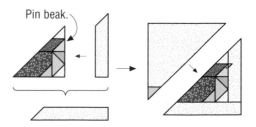

Pin beak.

Quilt Top Assembly and Finishing

1. Sew the Give-and-Take blocks, the large Star Point blocks, and the Bird block into a large ninepatch unit. Press the seams in each row toward the large Star Point blocks. Join the rows, making sure to match the seams between the blocks.

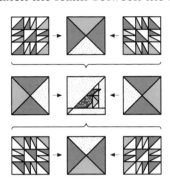

Lesson 6 — Stitching Appliqué

2. Referring to the color photos on pages 246–47, decide which appliqué design you would like to use for your quilt. Use Templates A-13 and A-14 for the Christmas Exampler and Template A-15 for the Spring and Autumn Exampler quilts. Or be creative and design your own leaves and flowers to embellish your quilt.

   For the branches, cut 4 bias strips, each $1\frac{1}{8}$" x 20", from fabrics that coordinate with the quilt you are making. Refer to page 74 for making bias stems.

   Choose one of the appliqué techniques on pages 71–75 and make leaves and pears as required for the design you have chosen.

3. Cut the bias stems as desired to create the branches. Arrange the branches, leaves, and pears around the Bird block and appliqué in place.

4. Arrange the quarter-square units around the center blocks, alternating the color combinations as shown. Sew 6 quarter-square units together for side borders; stitch to opposite sides of the quilt. Sew 8 quarter-square units together for each of the top and bottom borders; stitch to the top and bottom edges of the quilt top.

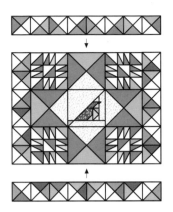

5. Sew the rectangle and square border units made on page 250 to opposite sides of the quilt. Sew a Ninepatch corner block to each end of the top and bottom border units and stitch to the top and bottom edges of the quilt top.

6. Layer your quilt top with batting and backing; baste. Quilt as desired and bind the edges. Refer to the general directions for quilt finishing, beginning on page 238.

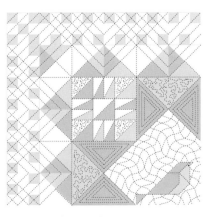

Quilting Suggestion

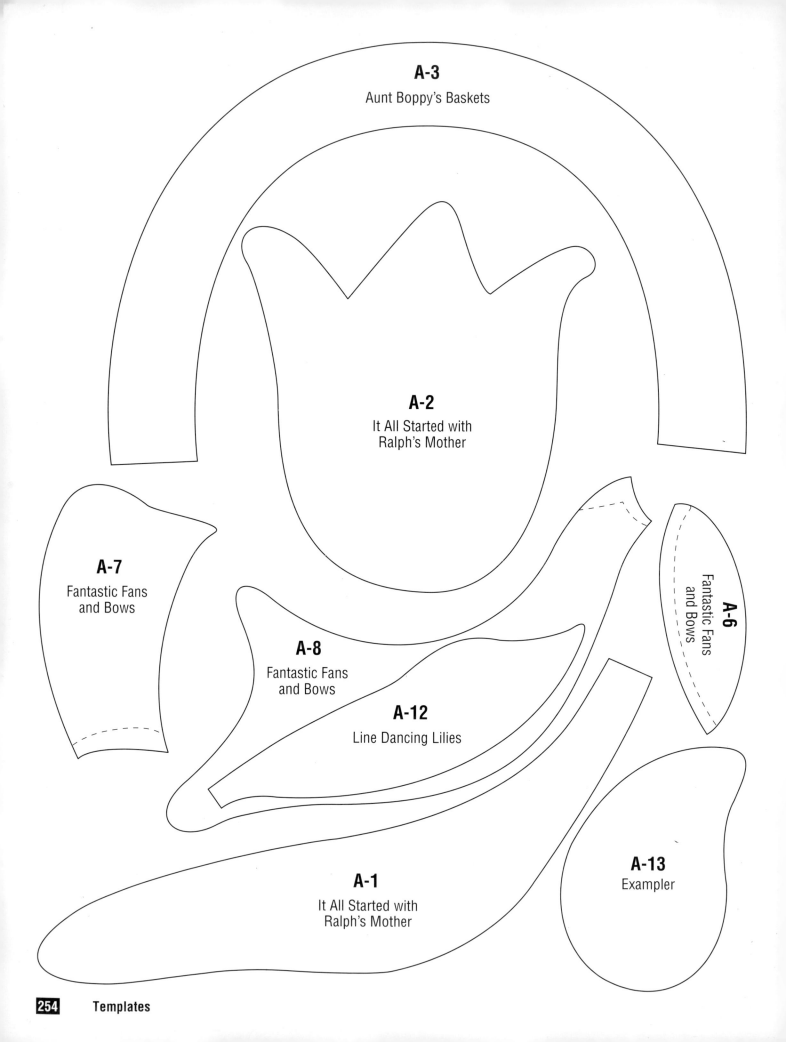

A-3

Aunt Boppy's Baskets

A-2

It All Started with
Ralph's Mother

A-7

Fantastic Fans
and Bows

A-6

Fantastic Fans
and Bows

A-8

Fantastic Fans
and Bows

A-12

Line Dancing Lilies

A-1

It All Started with
Ralph's Mother

A-13

Exampler

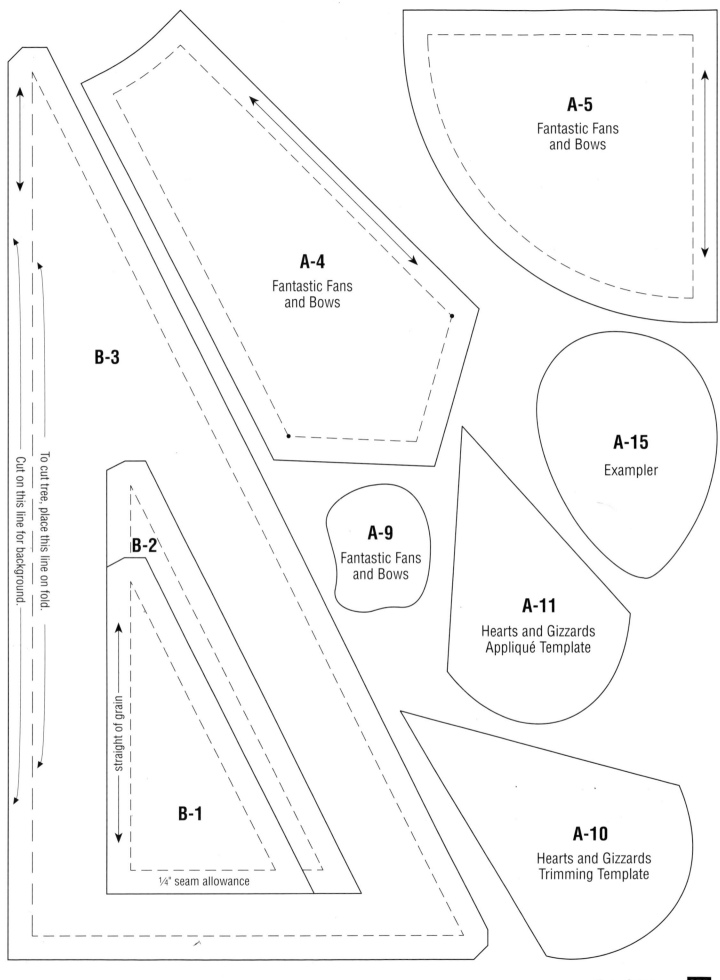

A-5
Fantastic Fans
and Bows

A-4
Fantastic Fans
and Bows

B-3

To cut tree, place this line on fold.

Cut on this line for background.

B-2

straight of grain

B-1

¼" seam allowance

A-9
Fantastic Fans
and Bows

A-15
Exampler

A-11
Hearts and Gizzards
Appliqué Template

A-10
Hearts and Gizzards
Trimming Template

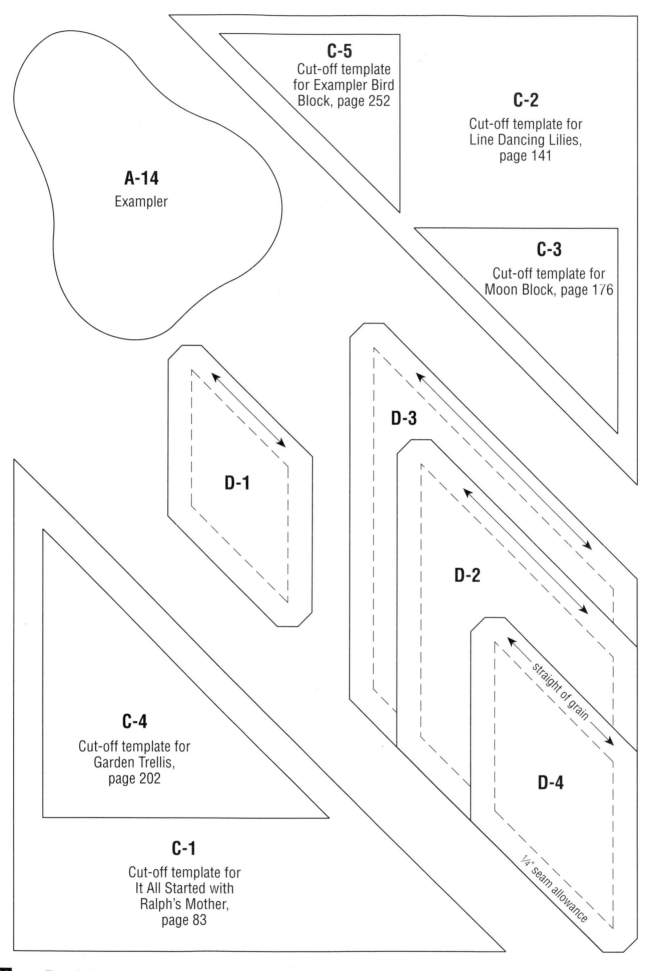

A-14
Exampler

C-5
Cut-off template
for Exampler Bird
Block, page 252

C-2
Cut-off template for
Line Dancing Lilies,
page 141

C-3
Cut-off template for
Moon Block, page 176

D-3

D-1

D-2

straight of grain

D-4

C-4
Cut-off template for
Garden Trellis,
page 202

C-1
Cut-off template for
It All Started with
Ralph's Mother,
page 83

¼" seam allowance

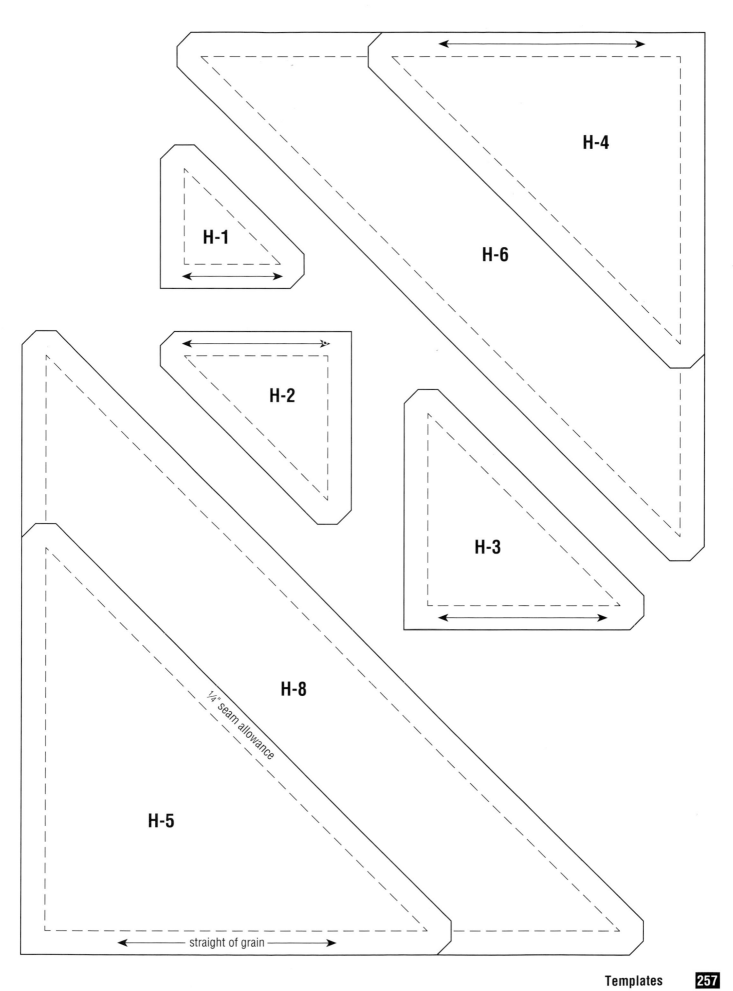

H-4

H-1

H-6

H-2

H-3

H-8

¼" seam allowance

H-5

← straight of grain →

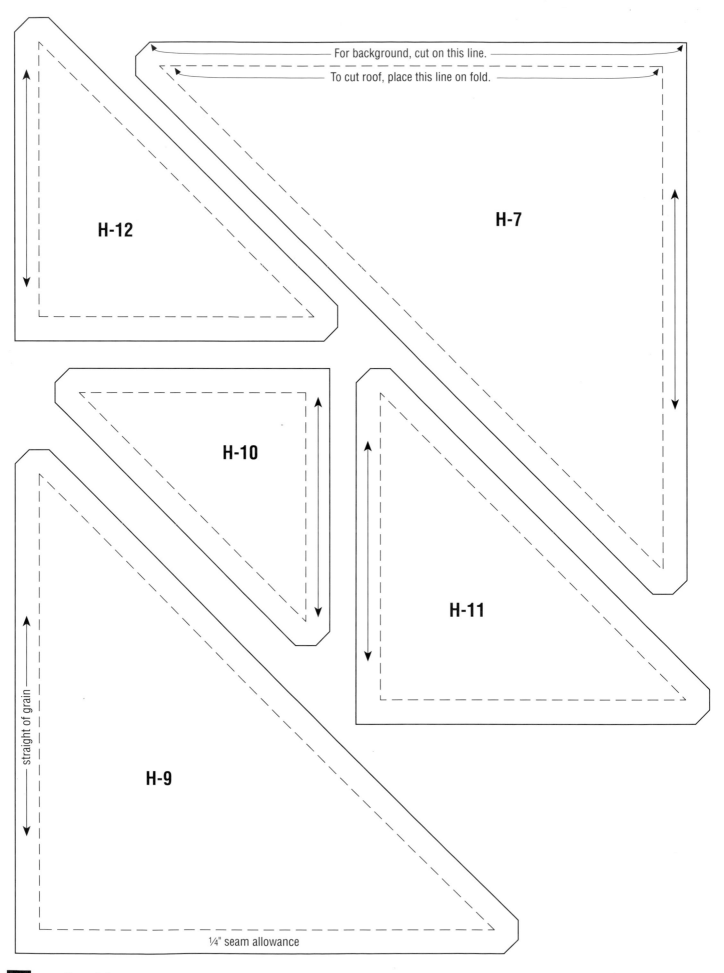

For background, cut on this line.

To cut roof, place this line on fold.

H-12

H-7

H-10

H-11

straight of grain

H-9

¼" seam allowance

Templates

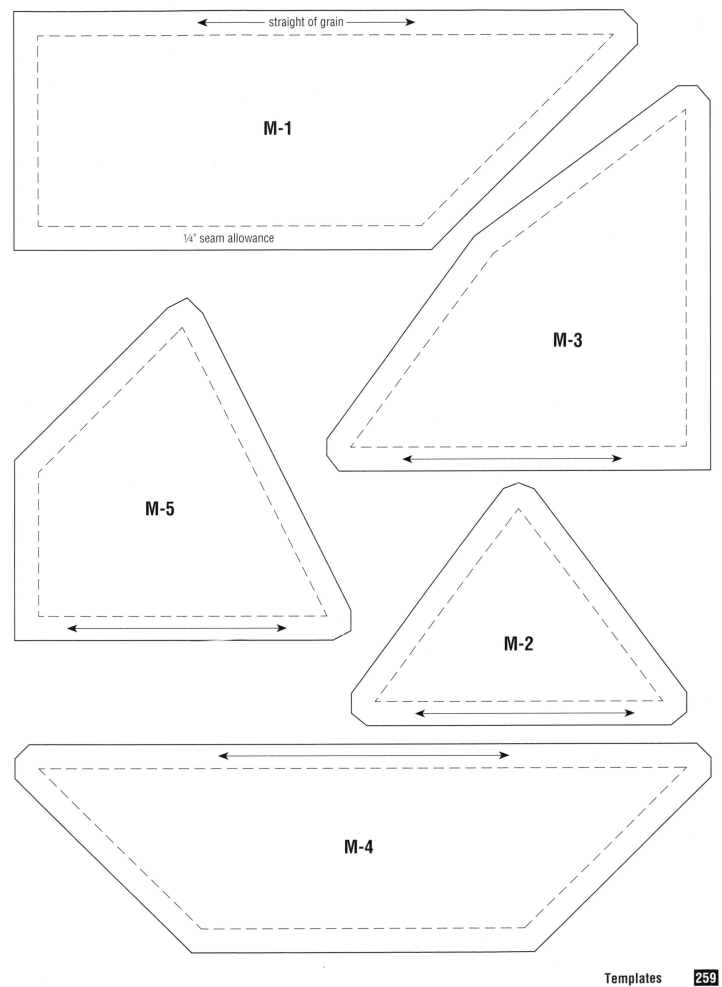

straight of grain

M-1

¼" seam allowance

M-3

M-5

M-2

M-4

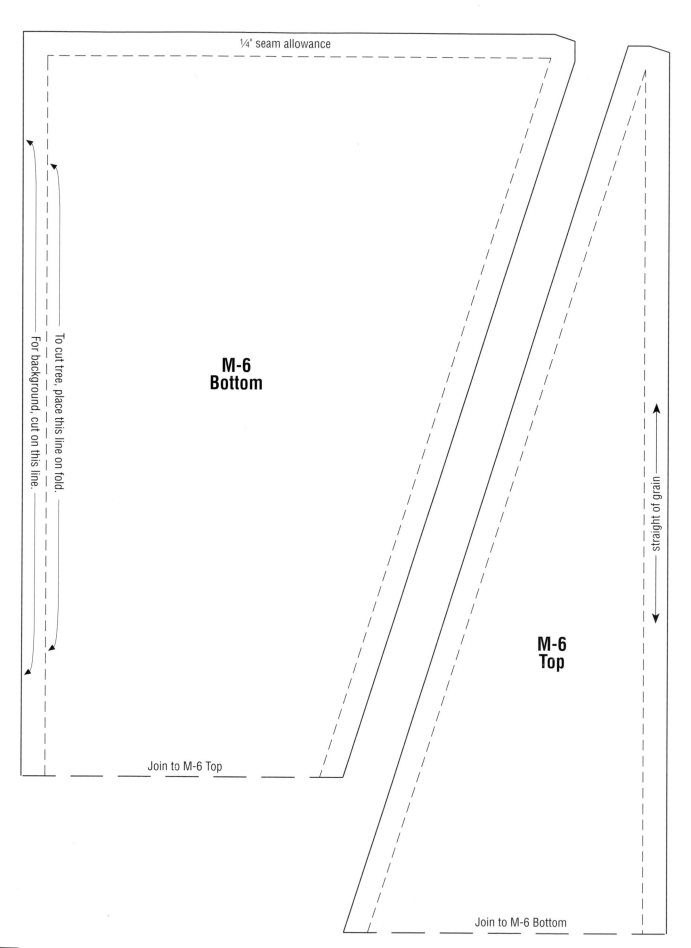

¼" seam allowance

M-6
Bottom

To cut tree, place this line on fold.

For background, cut on this line.

straight of grain

M-6
Top

Join to M-6 Top

Join to M-6 Bottom

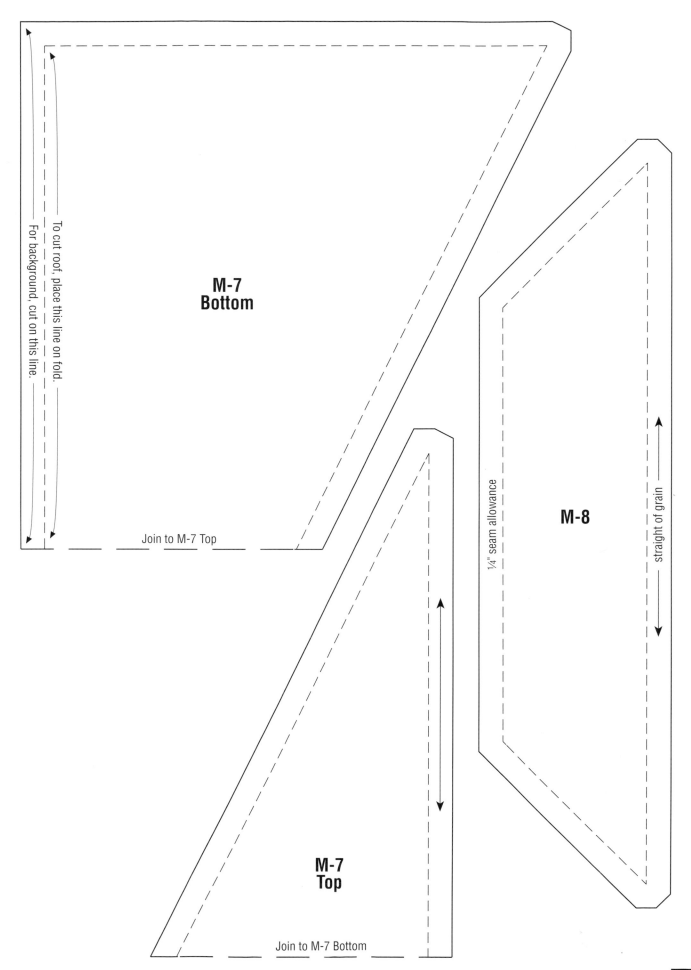

M-7 Bottom

To cut roof, place this line on fold.

For background, cut on this line.

Join to M-7 Top

M-7 Top

Join to M-7 Bottom

¼" seam allowance

M-8

straight of grain

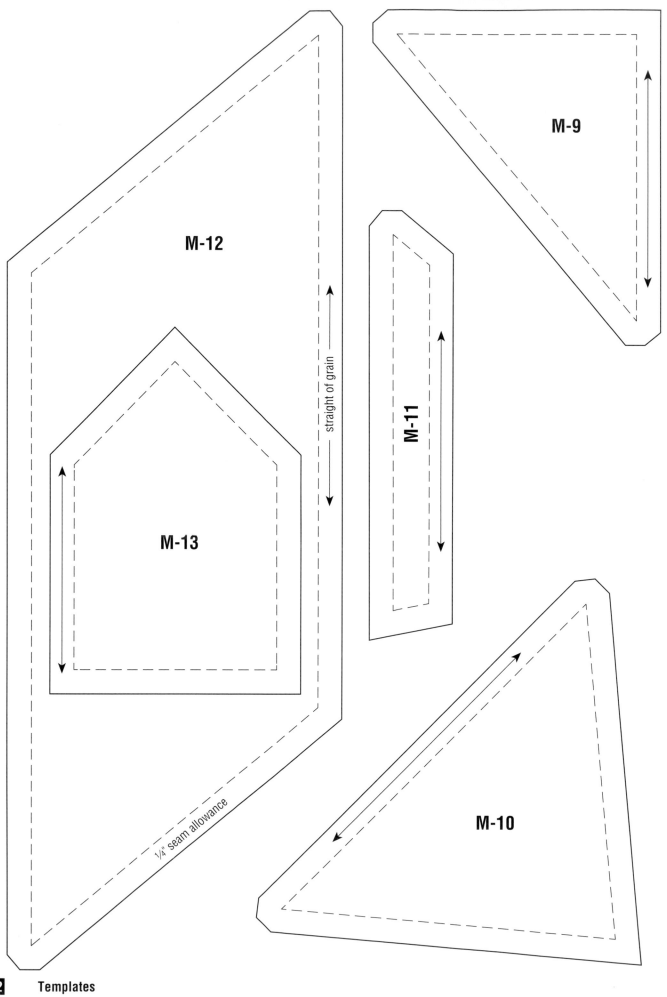

M-12

M-9

M-11

M-13

straight of grain

¼" seam allowance

M-10

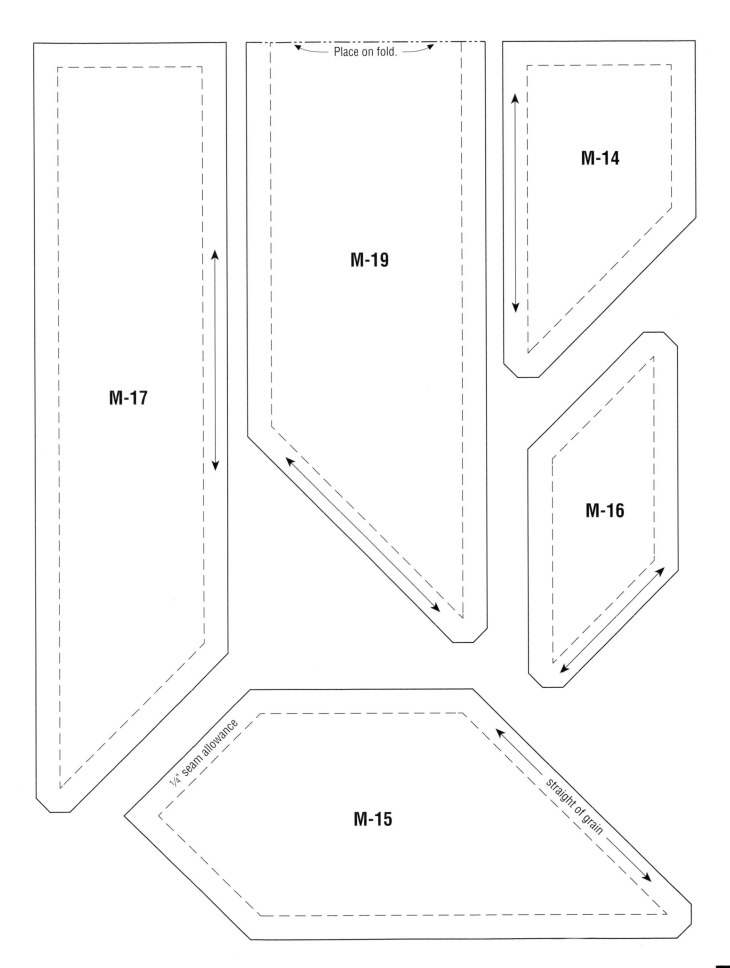

M-17

M-19

M-14

M-16

M-15

Place on fold.

¼" seam allowance

straight of grain

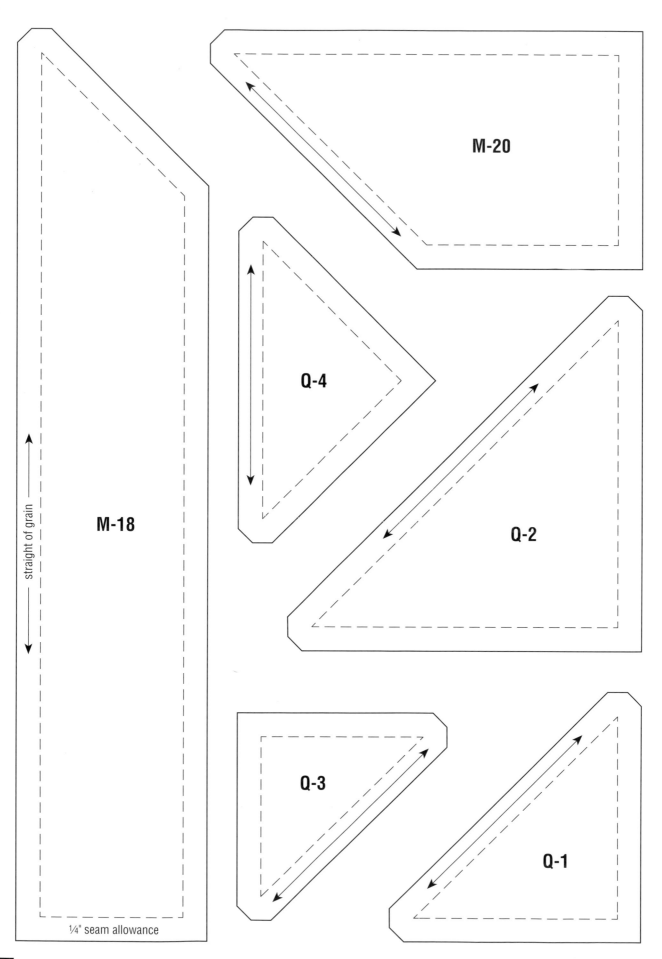

M-20

Q-4

Q-2

M-18

straight of grain

Q-3

Q-1

¼" seam allowance

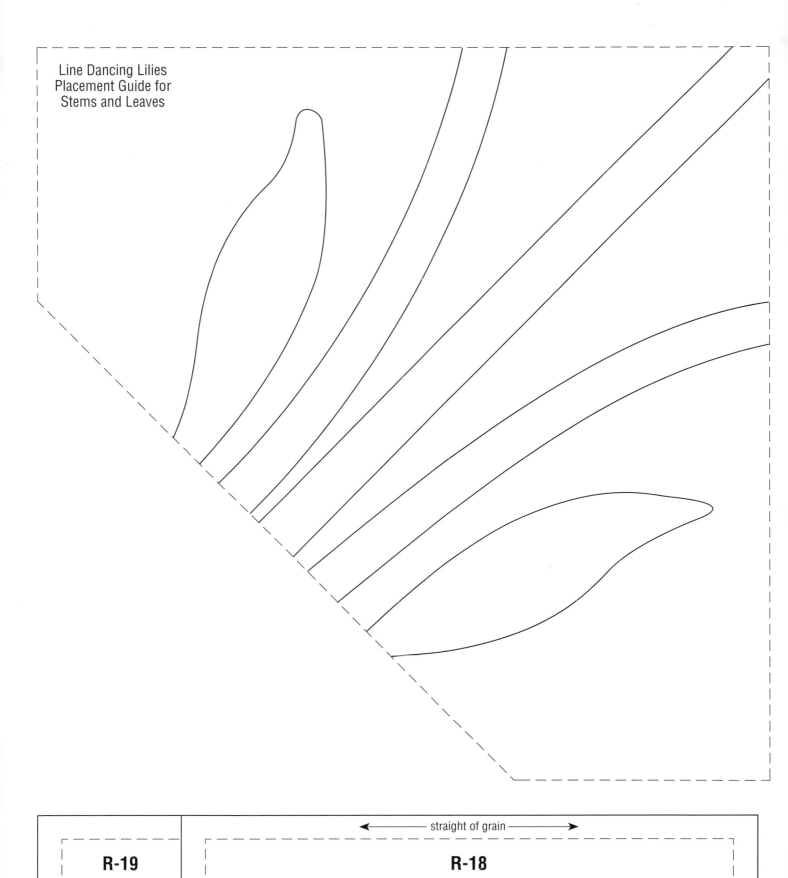

Line Dancing Lilies
Placement Guide for
Stems and Leaves

R-19

← straight of grain →

R-18

¼" seam allowance

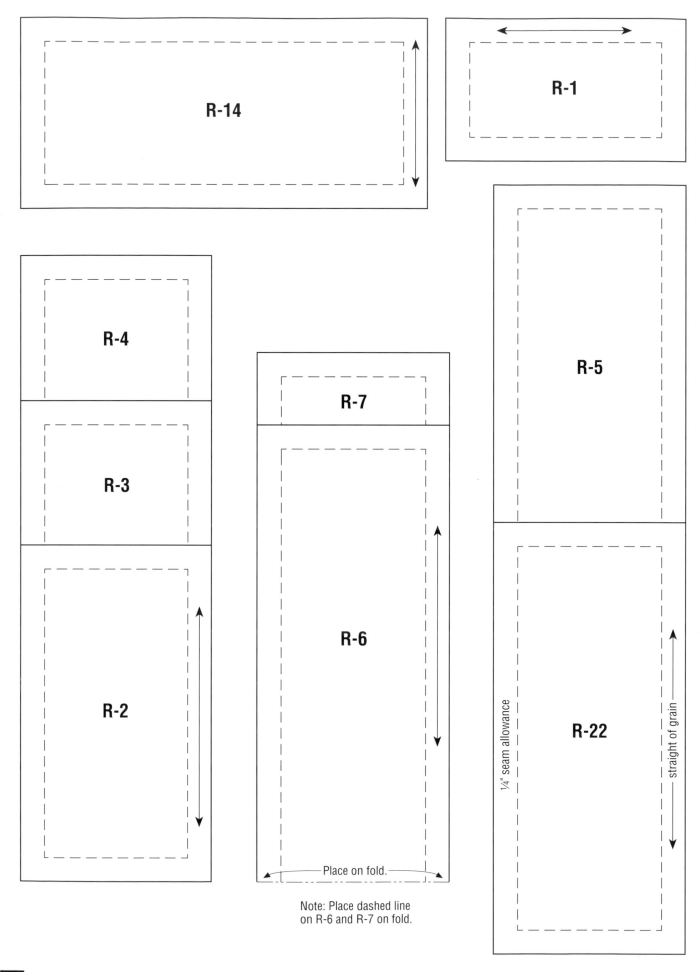

R-14

R-1

R-4

R-3

R-2

R-7

R-6

Place on fold.

Note: Place dashed line on R-6 and R-7 on fold.

R-5

¼" seam allowance

straight of grain

R-22

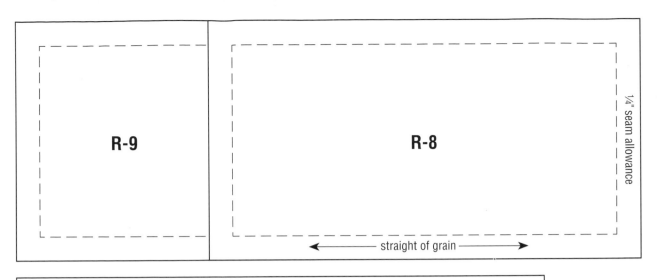

R-9

R-8

¼" seam allowance

straight of grain

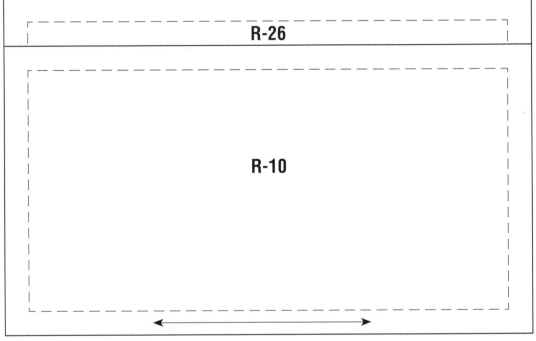

R-26

R-10

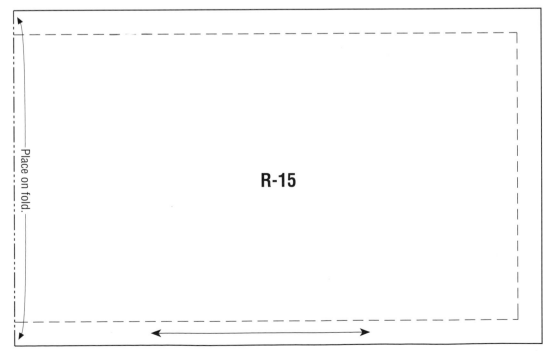

Place on fold.

R-15

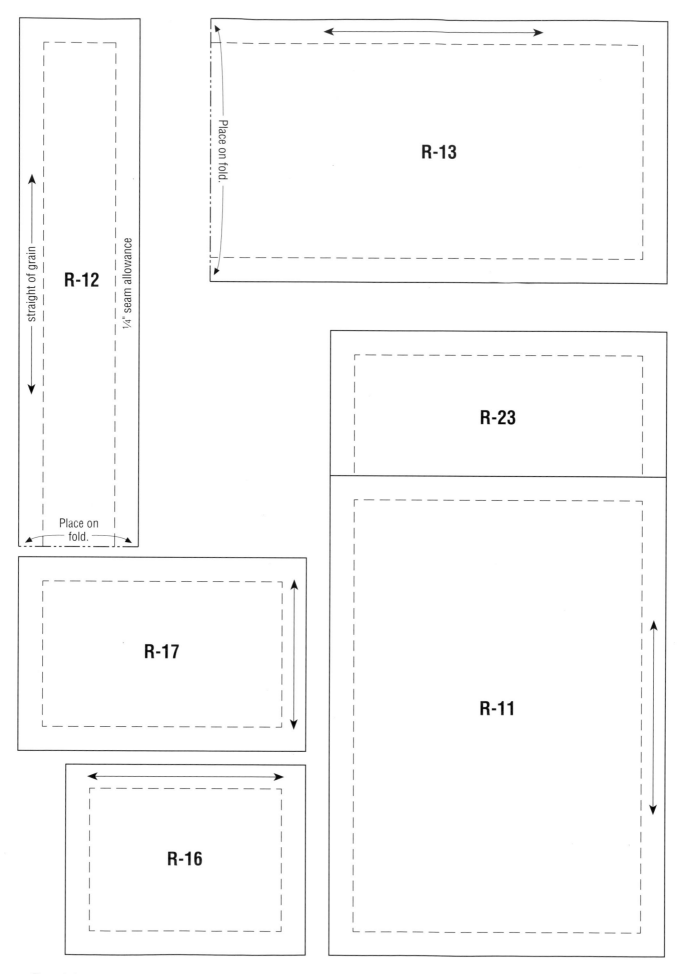

R-13

R-12

straight of grain

¼" seam allowance

Place on fold.

Place on fold.

R-23

R-17

R-11

R-16

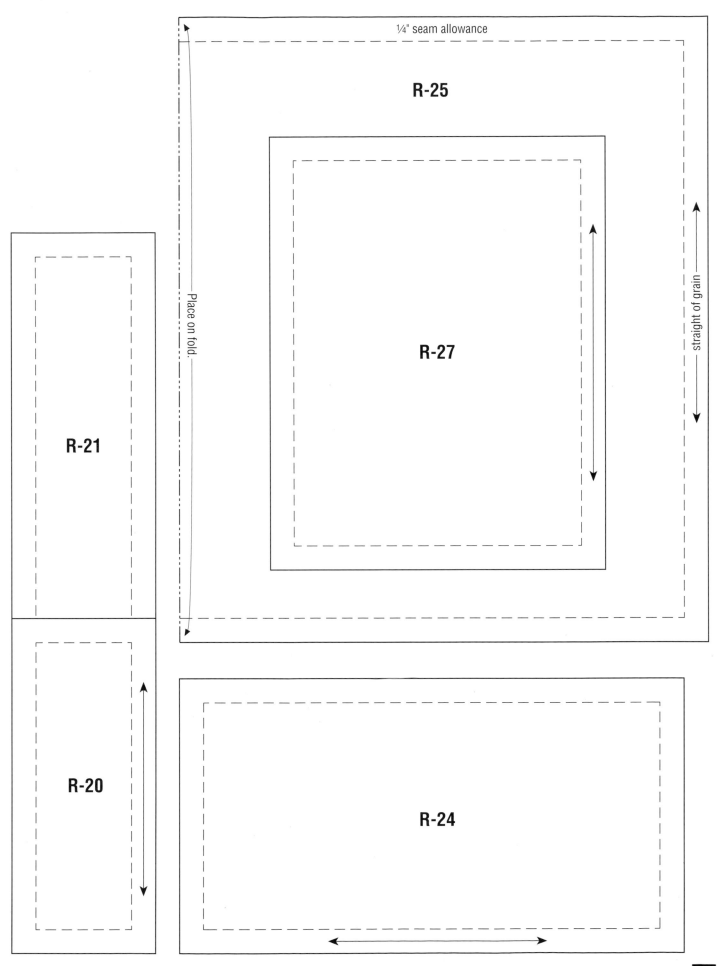

¼" seam allowance

R-25

R-27

Place on fold.

straight of grain

R-21

R-20

R-24

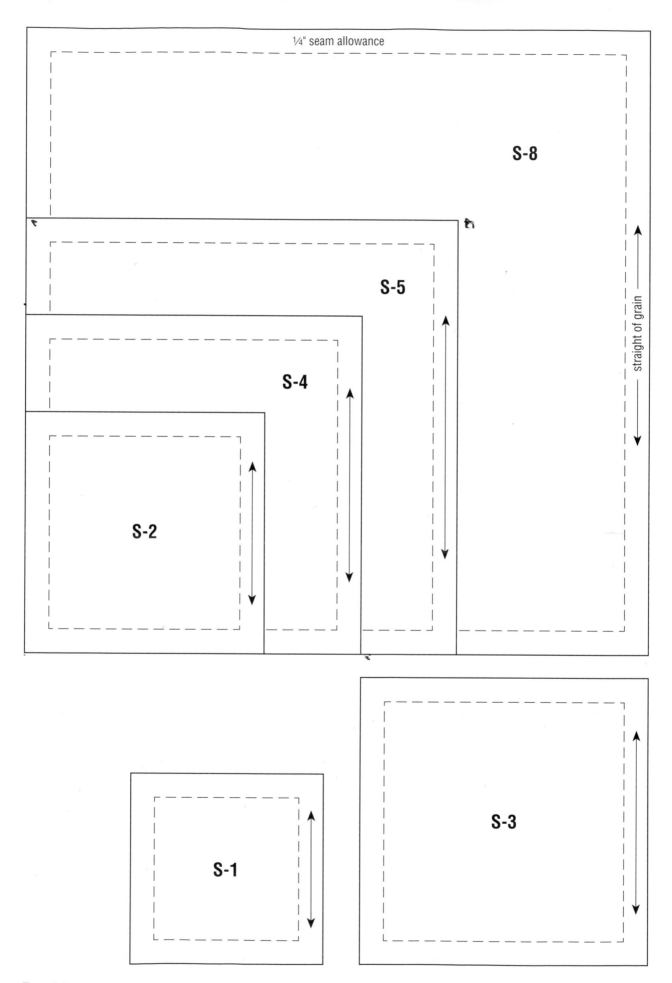

¼" seam allowance

S-8

S-5

S-4

S-2

straight of grain

S-1

S-3

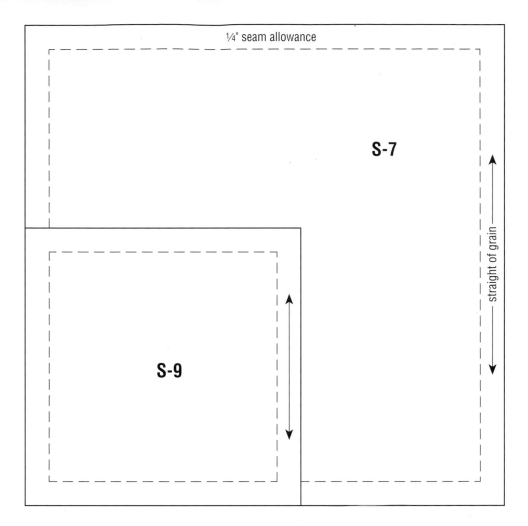

¼" seam allowance

S-7

straight of grain

S-9

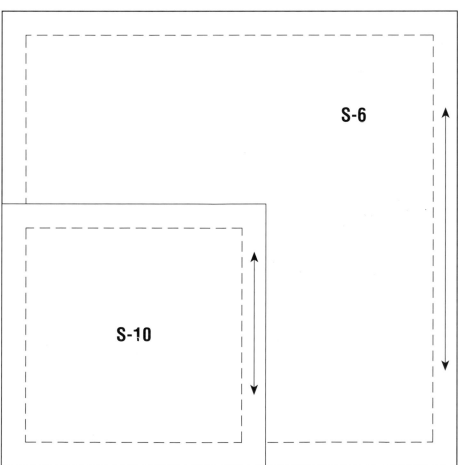

S-6

S-10

¼" seam allowance

Index

Numbers in **_bold italic_** indicate photos.

Books from
Martingale & Company

Appliqué

Appliquilt® Your ABCs
Appliquilt® to Go
Baltimore Bouquets
Basic Quiltmaking Techniques for Hand Appliqué
Coxcomb Quilt
The Easy Art of Appliqué
Folk Art Animals
From a Quilter's Garden
Stars in the Garden
Sunbonnet Sue All Through the Year
Traditional Blocks Meet Appliqué
Welcome to the North Pole

Borders and Bindings

Borders by Design
The Border Workbook
A Fine Finish
Happy Endings
Interlacing Borders
Traditional Quilts with Painless Borders

Design Reference

All New! Copy Art for Quilters
Blockbender Quilts
Color: The Quilter's Guide
Design Essentials: The Quilter's Guide
Design Your Own Quilts
Fine Art Quilts
Freedom in Design
The Log Cabin Design Workbook
Mirror Manipulations
The Nature of Design
QuiltSkills
Sensational Settings
Surprising Designs from Traditional Quilt Blocks
Whimsies & Whynots

Foundation/Paper Piecing

Classic Quilts with Precise Foundation Piecing
Crazy but Pieceable
Easy Machine Paper Piecing
Easy Mix & Match Machine Paper Piecing
Easy Paper-Pieced Keepsake Quilts
Easy Paper-Pieced Miniatures
Easy Reversible Vests
Go Wild with Quilts
Go Wild with Quilts—Again!
A Quilter's Ark
Show Me How to Paper Piece

Hand and Machine Quilting/Stitching

Loving Stitches
Machine Needlelace and Other
    Embellishment Techniques
Machine Quilting Made Easy
Machine Quilting with Decorative Threads
Quilting Design Sourcebook
Quilting Makes the Quilt
Thread Magic
Threadplay with Libby Lehman

Home Decorating

Decorate with Quilts & Collections
The Home Decorator's Stamping Book
Living with Little Quilts
Make Room for Quilts
Soft Furnishings for Your Home
Welcome Home: Debbie Mumm

Miniature/Small Quilts

Beyond Charm Quilts
Celebrate! with Little Quilts
Easy Paper-Pieced Miniatures
Fun with Miniature Log Cabin Blocks
Little Quilts All Through the House
Lively Little Logs
Living with Little Quilts
Miniature Baltimore Album Quilts
No Big Deal
A Silk-Ribbon Album
Small Talk

Needle Arts/Ribbonry

Christmas Ribbonry
Crazy Rags
Hand-Stitched Samplers from I Done My Best
Miniature Baltimore Album Quilts
A Passion for Ribbonry
A Silk-Ribbon Album
Victorian Elegance

Quiltmaking Basics

Basic Quiltmaking Techniques for Hand Appliqué
Basic Quiltmaking Techniques for Strip Piecing
The Joy of Quilting
A Perfect Match
Press for Success
The Ultimate Book of Quilt Labels
Your First Quilt Book (or it should be!)

Rotary Cutting/Speed Piecing

Around the Block with Judy Hopkins
All-Star Sampler
Bargello Quilts
Block by Block
Down the Rotary Road with Judy Hopkins
Easy Star Sampler
Magic Base Blocks for Unlimited Quilt Designs
A New Slant on Bargello Quilts
Quilting Up a Storm
Rotary Riot
Rotary Roundup
ScrapMania
Simply Scrappy Quilts
Square Dance
Start with Squares
Stripples
Stripples Strikes Again!
Strips that Sizzle
Two-Color Quilts

Seasonal Quilts

Appliquilt® for Christmas
Christmas Ribbonry
Easy Seasonal Wall Quilts
Folded Fabric Fun
Quilted for Christmas
Quilted for Christmas, Book II
Quilted for Christmas, Book III
Quilted for Christmas, Book IV
Welcome to the North Pole

Surface Design/Fabric Manipulation

15 Beads: A Guide to Creating One-of-a-Kind Beads
The Art of Handmade Paper and Collage
Complex Cloth: A Comprehensive Guide
    to Surface Design
Dyes & Paints: A Hands-On Guide to Coloring Fabric
Hand-Dyed Fabric Made Easy

Theme Quilts

The Cat's Meow
Celebrating the Quilt
Class-Act Quilts
The Heirloom Quilt
Honoring the Seasons
Kids Can Quilt
Life in the Country with Country Threads
Lora & Company
Making Memories
More Quilts for Baby
Once Upon a Quilt
Patchwork Pantry
Quick-Sew Celebrations
Quilted Landscapes
Quilted Legends of the West
Quilts: An American Legacy
Quilts for Baby
Quilts from Nature
Through the Window and Beyond
Tropical Punch

Watercolor Quilts

Awash with Colour
Colourwash Quilts
More Strip-Pieced Watercolor Magic
Strip-Pieced Watercolor Magic
Watercolor Impressions
Watercolor Quilts

Wearables

Crazy Rags
Dress Daze
Dressed by the Best
Easy Reversible Vests
Jacket Jazz
More Jazz from Judy Murrah
Quick-Sew Fleece
Sew a Work of Art Inside and Out
Variations in Chenille

Many of these books are available through your local quilt, fabric, craft-supply, or art-supply store. For more information, call, write, fax, or e-mail for our free full-color catalog.

Martingale & Company
PO Box 118
Bothell, WA 98041-0118 USA

1-800-426-3126
International: 1-425-483-3313
24-Hour Fax: 1-425-486-7596
Web site: www.patchwork.com
E-mail: info@patchwork.com